Multilingual Education

Volume 30

The book series Multilingual Education publishes top quality monographs and edited volumes containing empirical research on multilingual language acquisition, language contact and the respective roles of languages in contexts where the languages are not cognate and where the scripts are often different, in order to be able to better understand the processes and issues involved and to inform governments and language policy makers. The volumes in this series are aimed primarily at researchers in education, especially multilingual education and other related fields, and those who are involved in the education of (language) teachers. Others who will be interested include key stakeholders and policy makers in the field of language policy and education. The editors welcome proposals and ideas for books that fit the series. For more information on how you can submit a proposal, please contact the publishing editor, Jolanda Voogd. E-mail: jolanda.voogd@springer.com

More information about this series at http://www.springer.com/series/8836

Toni Dobinson • Katie Dunworth

Editors

Literacy Unbound: Multiliterate, Multilingual, Multimodal

 Springer

Editors
Toni Dobinson
School of Education
Curtin University
Bentley, WA, Australia

Katie Dunworth
Department of Education
University of Bath
Bath, UK

ISSN 2213-3208   ISSN 2213-3216   (electronic)
Multilingual Education
ISBN 978-3-030-01254-0   ISBN 978-3-030-01255-7   (eBook)
https://doi.org/10.1007/978-3-030-01255-7

Library of Congress Control Number: 2018962372

This Springer imprint is published by the registered company Springer Nature Switzerland AG
The registered company address is: Gewerbestrasse 11, 6330 Cham, Switzerland

Contents

Contributors

Faisal Al Saidi Department of Education, University of Bath, Bath, UK

Julian Chen School of Education, Curtin University, Perth, WA, Australia

Kenan Dikilitaş Department of English Language Teaching, Bahçeşehir University, Istanbul, Turkey

Toni Dobinson School of Education, Curtin University, Perth, WA, Australia

Alison Douthwaite Department of Education, University of Bath, Bath, UK

Katie Dunworth Department of Education, University of Bath, Bath, UK

Paul Gardner School of Education, Curtin University, Perth, WA, Australia

Qian Gong School of Education, Curtin University, Perth, WA, Australia

Jennifer Howell School of Education, Curtin University, Bentley, Australia

Kyoko Kawasaki School of Social Sciences, University of Western Australia, Perth, WA, Australia

Sarah Kent School of Education, Curtin University, Perth, WA, Australia

Helen CD McCarthy School of Education, Curtin University, Perth, WA, Australia

Jim McKinley UCL Institute of Education, University of London, London, UK

Paul Mercieca School of Education, Curtin University, Perth, WA, Australia

Rhonda Oliver School of Education, Curtin University, Perth, WA, Australia

Hugo Santiago Sanchez Department of Education, University of Bath, Bath, UK

Von Sawers School of Education, Curtin University, Bentley, Australia

Wai Ling Yeung Independent Researcher, Perth, WA, Australia

Grace Zhang School of Education, Curtin University, Perth, WA, Australia

Introduction

Toni Dobinson and Katie Dunworth

Abstract This first introductory chapter presents the rationale for the selection of chapters in this volume. It outlines how the protean construct that is literacy has been presented across time, domains and cultures and explains how the chapters were selected to embody, as far as possible, the multiplicity of research contexts in which literacy has been explored in education. The chapter summarises each of the contributions made by the authors in this book, whose different writing styles and approaches to their texts also reinforce the idea of literacy being multiple and unbound. This chapter concludes that across the differing conceptions of literacy, what unites them is a sense that literacy, however it is defined, can be a force for liberation.

Keywords Literacy as liberation · Multiliteracies · Multimodal literacy · Literacy as multilingual

If there is one thing on which all recent writers on literacy agree, it is that there is no such thing as an unbiased or objective approach either to conceptualisations of literacy or to pedagogical practices designed to promote literacy development. As a construct, literacy has over time and contexts been (re)-defined according to prevailing ideologies and attitudes (Miller 2015: Street 2013; Whitehead and Wilkinson 2008). As communities, beliefs, attitudes and practices change, so the term itself shifts to accommodate the environment within which it is being discussed. While the word is still frequently used within the popular media to allude in some way to the process of reading and writing, in particular, in many other social, educational and professional settings it is acknowledged that literacy is much broader than this,

T. Dobinson (✉)
School of Education, Curtin University, Perth, WA, Australia
e-mail: T.Dobinson@curtin.edu.au

K. Dunworth
Department of Education, University of Bath, Bath, UK
e-mail: c.m.dunworth@bath.ac.uk

© Springer Nature Switzerland AG 2019
T. Dobinson, K. Dunworth (eds.), *Literacy Unbound: Multiliterate, Multilingual, Multimodal*, Multilingual Education 30,
https://doi.org/10.1007/978-3-030-01255-7_1

and that it is multifaceted, far-reaching, complex and in flux. Current conceptions of literacy within the research literature embrace the multiple modes, symbols and forms by which humans communicate or learn. Literacy can be understood as a form of meaning-making, either interpersonal or intrapersonal, and is recognised as context or domain-specific and transcultural. These conceptions can be, and have been, scrutinised from multiple epistemological, axiological and political perspectives, so much so that it might well be argued that the term itself has become meaningless, an umbrella term for a multitude of different notions. The challenge that underpinned the development of this book, therefore, was to seek out and explore some of the many ways in which literacies have been investigated theoretically or empirically so that it might be possible to make connections, to identify those core features that draw together these different ways of thinking about literacy practices, or, conversely, to see how the field has dispersed and evolved to an extent that eschews commonality.

Given the current research environment in which these conceptions of literacy, or literacies, are explored, it was decided for this book that it would be important to include, as far as possible, material that as a collection reported on diverse educational environments, discussed literacy development across different age groups, examined different modalities and adopted different theoretical or conceptual perspectives. In addition, it was intended that the chapters should be based on original empirical research or original theory development so that they would in themselves help move forward our understandings of the particular issues identified within each chapter. Thus, the chapters in this volume include as their focus young learners, secondary school students and adults; discuss technology enhanced literacy education, face-to-face class learning and one-to-one supervision; explore the experiences of L1 and L2 students, student teachers and qualified educators; report on research in geographical contexts that include Australia, Japan, Turkey and the UK; and are underpinned by theoretical or conceptual frameworks that include sociocultural theory, reader response theory, critical pedagogy and communities of practice. They all draw on their authors' experiences as teacher educators, language and literacy teachers, and researchers on aspects of literacy; and promote a thought-provoking discussion on contemporary issues surrounding the teaching of language and literacy based on first hand experiences and research.

Given the deliberate intention to explore the diverse ways in which literacy is conceived, it is unsurprising that the collection incorporates vastly varying contexts, understandings and approaches to the issue. It is also evident that the contributors have markedly different writing styles and ways of engaging with their topics. This is the result of the editorial decision to place minimal constraints on the authors so that the chapters themselves embody the principle that underpins this volume – that ideas of what it means to be literate are dynamic and that we need to challenge our own preconceptions about the nature and form that literacy practices take. As a consequence of this openness, the process of arranging chapters in their final order has to some extent been somewhat arbitrary. Ultimately, it was decided that for our readers, it would be their professional contexts that would be likely to play a key role when deciding which of the chapters would be most personally relevant and resonant, and so the decision was made to group them broadly around the different educational environments in which literacy development takes place. The first four chapters following this introduction are located within higher education contexts in a range of countries (Australia, Turkey, the UK and Japan) and explore aspects of English L2 student literacy development. While the first three of these are clearly focused on academic writing, the last of this initial group examines contextual literacy and universality. The next two chapters are also sited within a higher education environment, but their concerns specifically revolve around issues of literacy and literacy development within pre-service teacher education programmes. Following these, there is a further chapter situated within a higher education environment; this uniquely in this book examines issues relating to the learning of an additional language: in this case Chinese and Japanese.

The first three of the four final chapters take us out of higher education as a specific context to consider literacy development at earlier stages of students' lives. What they all have in common, aside from their concern with the younger learner, is their interest in technology in relation to literacy development. Chapter Eight "Students' Perceptions of the Use of Video Recording in Additional Language Oral Assessments" stays within the context of education to examine multimodal literacy development as part of the secondary school English curriculum in the UK. The subsequent chapter more broadly examines the translanguaging experiences of Aboriginal youth in Australia with a particular focus on Facebook, and the penultimate chapter addresses pedagogical issues relating to young children and their early literacy development. The final chapter in this volume is a theoretical consideration of language, literacy and intercultural competence development across educational contexts, using the technology of blogs as its focus. Each of these chapters is described in more detail below.

In Chapter Two, *World Englishes in Academic Writing: Exploring Markers' Responses*, Toni Dobinson, Paul Mercieca and Sarah Kent show how action research can produce unexpected findings and how researchers need to be able to respond to this. The chapter explores the issues involved in assessing the tertiary academic writing of students whose first language is not English. Using a critical action research approach, the authors conduct a linguistic analysis of a sample of students' written work from one university setting, noting the use of World Englishes. Through textual analysis they investigate the feedback that these students receive from academics across disciplines on these same written samples, documenting the occurrence and type of feedback. The study was approached with the premise that 'non-standard' forms would be treated as errors rather than features of the students' WEs by markers and the authors were prepared to argue, therefore, that universities needed to be more tolerant and imaginative in the way they provide language feedback to students whose first language is not English, particularly in terms of student writing. However, the study takes a slightly different turn when authors discover that there are few occurrences of World English variety usage in the selected scripts and conversely little feedback from academics on WEs usage . Subsequently, attention is turned to type of feedback given to students' about their writing as a whole;

the extent to which linguistic feedback is provided and the nature of that feedback.

Hugo Santiago Sanchez and Kenan Dikilitaş, in the third chapter, *Developing Academic Writing Literacy While Responding to Tutor Written Feedback*, are also concerned with conceptions of literacy within the context of writing in a higher education environment. Adopting a perspective of literacy as incorporating cognitive, social and affective dimensions, they describe a study that sought, in particular, to uncover the internal factors that are at work as postgraduate research students undergo a process of academic writing literacy development through feedback. Focusing specifically on the experiences of two individuals, the study used introspective and retrospective research approaches rarely adopted in this area of applied linguistics research, in order to access the internal factors that mediated participants' progress with their academic writing. They found that the participants had extended their knowledge and understanding not only in those areas which have been widely documented in the research literature, such as genre awareness and technical writing skills, but also in heightened cognitions relating to, inter alia, self-efficacy, criticality and self-knowledge. In addition, participants perceived that they had enhanced their realisations of the social nature of knowledge since they saw themselves as engaging in collaborative learning within a professional community of practice. By focusing on the internal factors, Sanchez and Dikilitaş were able to show that literacy development is a complex and expansile but also idiosyncratic process, and they conclude by arguing that educational programmes focusing on academic writing need to become more aligned with the most recent research; in other words that practice should acknowledge the results of studies that continue to reveal a wide range of mediating factors, and which show literacy development to be multifaceted, complex, and impacted by differences between individuals.

In the following chapter, *Becoming a Member of a Community of Practice: Postgraduate Researcher Literacy Development in a UK University*, Katie Dunworth and Faisal Al Saidi explore the concept of literacy development in a postgraduate higher education context as the construction of a professional identity within an international community of practice. Drawing on Wenger's (1998) foundational dimensions of a community of practice: mutual engagement, involvement in a shared enterprise, and access to a shared communicative repertoire, Dunworth and Al Saidi illustrate through an empirical study how one PhD student struggled to recognise, internalise and produce the discourses of the community in order to facilitate his own membership of it, while at the same time uncovering a growing confidence in his capacity to portray a personalised identity. Within the community of practice model described in this chapter, literacy is therefore conceived of as a form of learnt performance, a particular way of presenting oneself, a chosen positioning within a specific professional context. The PhD thesis, as explained in this chapter, was constructed from the communicative repertoire that had been developed. It instantiates, and so is inseparable from, academic knowledge, thereby demonstrating to others that its author has access to that particular community of practice.

Chapter Five, *Developing Contextual Literacy English for Academic Purposes Through Content and Language Integrated Learning*, by Jim McKinley, adopts an approach derived from Freire's theory of critical pedagogy, with its emphasis on dialogue, knowledge as constructed rather than transmitted, and education as the posing and addressing of problems. The study described in the chapter took place in a Japanese university where English was the medium of instruction, with student participants from a mix of backgrounds who were registered in a compulsory public speaking course. In this environment, where English is an international language, McKinley suggests, conceptions of contextual appropriateness need to expand beyond the local to embrace universality, and literacy can be viewed as incorporating the critical, the cultural and the academic. The participants' engagement in a student-centred, problem-solving and compromise-based activity led, McKinley argues, not only to a more egalitarian classroom where opportunities for inclusion are more evenly distributed, but also, according to student data, was successful in resulting in increased contextual literacy.

Helen McCarthy's chapter, *Learning by Design: Crafting the Knowledge Processes to Enable Pre-service Secondary Teachers to Design Authentic Learning*, aims to give the reader insights into the transformative experience that took place when her first year Bachelor of Secondary pre-service Science, Technology, Engineering and Maths (STEM) students learned to use a pedagogical approach called Learning by Design and became acquainted with the four intrinsic structures there-in, namely Knowledge Processes, Experiencing, Conceptualising, Analysing and Applying as ways of becoming active designers of meaning. Using an ethnographic approach involving close observation and documentation of her students' journeys through the stages of Learning Design and detailed, reflective self-report from the students themselves in the assignments that were set, McCarthy witnessed a group of students who were initially resistant to the idea of having 'to do' literacy units as part of their teacher education degree become cognisant of the necessity to interweave skills which would develop children's multiliteracies into their subject teaching. An approach aimed at developing the different literacies embedded within content areas could also be multimodal in design. McCarthy has the satisfaction of seeing her students grow in their realisations of the benefits of adopting a *Learning by Design* approach to their teaching and becoming confident to design wide ranging and engaging plans of learning in their subject fields.

In Chapter Seven, *Pre-service Teachers' Literacy Abilities: An Exploration Amidst the Criticisms*, Jennifer Howell and Von Sawers explore the negative discourse surrounding pre-service teachers and the so-called 'literacy crisis' in schools and higher education that has grabbed the attention of the media and governments in Europe and Australia. The personal literacy of pre-service teachers and their ability to teach literacy to children effectively has been called into question in a deficit and highly critical discourse which the authors refer to as 'sketchy' and 'largely anecdotal'. Teachers' personal literacy, moreover, has been assessed by their ability to complete successfully a narrow set of literacy requirements of the highly political pre-registration tests. Through a qualitative ethnographical approach which uses an empirical case study design, Howell and Sawers investigate the literacy skills, abilities and expectations of 170 undergraduate, pre-service teacher education students. They also focus on the pre-service teachers conceptualisations of their own personal literacy skills and their perceptions of the impact that good literacy will have on their development as a teacher. Allowing the pre-service teachers to speak for themselves, the authors attempt a redefinition of what it means to be 'literate', questioning current traditional definitions that they believe may have constrained discourses and proposing that central to these discourses is a misunderstanding of the word literacy.

The final chapter located within a higher education context, *Students' Perceptions of the Use of Video Recording in Additional Language Oral Assessments*, by Qian Gong, Kyoko Kawasaki, Wai Ling Yeung, Grace Zhang and Toni Dobinson, also looks at literacy through the optic of learning an additional language in a tertiary setting; in this case Chinese and Japanese language. Using an action research approach the authors investigated 86 students' perceptions of the effectiveness of using recorded oral language assessments in their university units. Students in the study were encouraged to write and film a speech, a role-play or a documentary type project and then upload these audio-visual recordings to YouTube. This multimodal approach to the additional language literacy process allowed students to have agency in their script writing, the practising of the oral component of the task, filming experience (i.e. acting, directing, filming), disseminating and sharing of the end product online and writing feedback on other students' blog pages. Students' comments were collected from surveys and interviews and categorised into three main areas of response: mode of presentation, engagement, reflection and student-centred learning. On the whole, students appreciated the opportunity to use video recorded oral assessment and talked about greater engagement, reflection and student-centred language learning with this mode of evaluation. They talked about reduced anxiety and improved performance due to the rehearsal effect of using video. However, while beginner level students preferred video-recorded oral assessment to live performance in front of an audience, what is most interesting in this study are the responses of the more advanced language level students who could see the value of video recorded performances for reflection on performance but who were slightly less convinced about this mode as an evaluative summative tool. The authors speculate on the reasons for this discrepancy in their discussion and suggest a more cautionary approach when assessing more advanced language learners as a result.

Alison Douthwaite's chapter, *A Rich Mix: What Is English? Integrating Literature, Literacy, Language and Multimodal Dimensions of Meaning-Making in the UK Secondary School English Classroom*, is the only one in this volume to have as its central concern the development of literacy in the setting of UK secondary school English literature classes. By examining this context in association with the opportunities afforded by technology, the chapter presents a unique insight into how the multiple and complex elements of literacy development intersect and have the potential to be translated into a holistic and coherent approach to pedagogy within an educational system that is currently not conducive to such activity. Douthwaite's particular focus is on the development of criticality and a critical voice in the students she observed in her study; individuals who had been identified by the school as low achievers. She draws on a number of related or complementary theories to justify the choice in her research study of particular classroom tasks and activities: sociocultural theory, Rosenblatt's reader response theory and Langer's later work, and Kress's social semiotic perspective on meaning-making. She suggests that a synthesis of these theoretical perspectives in the 'critical voice' approach may help move literacy development practices in the secondary school system forward. Her findings resonate with those described in other chapters in this volume, as she portrays the growth of a critical voice as complex, multimodal, and social; mediated by a range of internal and external factors.

In a chapter which focuses on the current preferred communication modes of Australia's young indigenous population, Rhonda Oliver and Helen McCarthy discuss *Using Facebook as a Conduit to Communicate: Translanguaging Online*. They describe how the term 'translanguaging' has replaced 'codeswitching' because it is now recognised that bilingual speakers do not so much move between separate internal linguistic monoliths but rather draw on all the linguistic resources they have available to them. In their introspective, observational and longitudinal study the authors note how the use of Facebook gives Australian Aboriginal youth a platform for experimenting with multilingual expression and translanguaging as they draw on a wide range of linguistic resources and cement their identity as both an Aboriginal person with their own language and cultural understandings and a young person operating in a second parallel linguistic world. Such a dual approach to literacy can also have unexpected impacts. In the study described by Oliver and McCarthy, the use of Facebook also draws participants' attention to Standard Australian English. Indigenous youth post for a wider audience than their family and friends so they must also translanguage between Australian Standard English, Aboriginal English and their own Aboriginal language. The authors argue that the use of Facebook as a learning tool has the potential for making schooling and literacy more relevant to Australian indigenous children and may help to improve education outcomes for these children.

Paul Gardner, in Chapter Eleven, *Goldilocks and the Three Semiotic Bears: Young Children's Engagement with Early Literacy–A Vygotskian Approach*, describes what he calls 'an experimental approach to literacy acquisition'. Focusing on one West Australian school for early learning, Gardner approaches his study with the premise that young children are born semioticians with the ability to decode and encode signs and symbols in their textual context and that this ability precedes the capacity to use the alphabetic code. This premise tends to run counter to the current discourse gaining popularity in England, the USA and Australia that teachers should be focusing almost exclusively on the back to basics teaching of systematic synthetic phonics (SSP) in early reading with SSP being promoted over holistic approaches to teaching reading. The battle for the exclusive use of SSP in early learning environments is currently being fought by political diktat using selective research evidence rather than comprehensive research reviews of research, documented experience or theories of language acquisition, according to Gardner. Using a qualitative, participant approach to data collection which is minimally intrusive, he utilises field notes, video and photographs of children in lessons, reviews of documentary evidence and involvement in naturalistic discussion with parents, to answer questions about the nature of language and appropriate pedagogy for teaching language. He concludes that pedagogy, social relationships and recognition of children as active agents in their own learning are important components in developing literacy and, in particular, reading skills.

In the final chapter in this volume, which explores aspects of technology in relation to language and literacy development, Julian Chen in *"To Blog, Not To Block": Examining EFL Learners' Language Development and Intercultural Competence in the Blogosphere Through the Sociocultural Lens* has created a synthesis of recent studies into the mediating effect of blogs in second language acquisition, viewed through the prism of sociocultural theory. He initially reports how empirical studies have illustrated that blogs can be used in educational contexts to perform multiple functions associated with literacy development, such as drawing together language and literature studies; and how the capacity of certain software to create audio blogs has promoted multimodal educational input and enhanced learner output. Chen goes on to argue that sociocultural theory, as articulated by Vygotsky, incorporates two key concepts that that can be observed in blog use. The first of these is mediation, where online tools such as blogging can mediate a learner's language acquisition through collaborative engagement. The second is social learning, where it is theorised that learners operating within the zone of proximal development can develop through the assistance of more knowledgeable peers; in this case fellow blog writers and readers. Furthermore, Chen argues, since language and culture are indivisible, blogging serves an important function by bridging the learner's experience within and outside the classroom, thereby playing an important role from the perspective of languaculture. Through his review of the blogging research literature, Chen concludes that, from the perspective of sociocultural theory, blogs can be a valuable learning tool. In the chapter he identifies ten particular advantages that can accrue to users, including increased autonomy and agency, motivation, audience awareness and intercultural competence, as well as language knowledge and skills.

Within all these chapters is a clearly articulated sense that literacy development, however it is conceptualised, is important and valuable and has the capacity to enrich learners' lives. Although the theoretical frameworks differ between chapters and the researchers have adopted different methodologies within the empirical studies, with different contexts of learning and educational levels, each chapter is informed by an understanding of literacy as expansive, as an opening out and broadening of perspectives. Alongside such understandings the notion of agency, whether it is theoretically referenced through the work of Paulo Freire or identified through the description of independent and autonomous practices, shines through each chapter. Ultimately, for the contributors to this volume, and what unites the chapters, is that literacy is seen as a form of liberation.

The title of this volume was selected to reflect the eclectic nature of the contributions and the emancipatory nature of the concept. This is captured in the first part of the title, 'Literacy unbound'. The three adjectives that follow: 'multiliterate, multilingual, multimodal' draw together key themes that unite the contents. The first indicates the multidimensionality of the construct which is evident from the range of contexts and interpretations of literacy discussed across all the chapters, and is examined in detail in the chapter by Howell and Sawers. The term 'multilingual' reflects the focus in Dobinson, Mercieca and Kent's and Oliver and McCarthy's chapters, as well as drawing attention to the overlap between first language and additional language development that the term 'literacy' can be used to describe, as is shown in the chapters by Chen, Dunworth and Al Saidi, Gong et al., McKinley, and Sanchez and Dikilitaş. Finally, McCarthy, Gong et al., Douthwaite, Oliver and McCarthy, Gardner, and Chen all explicitly discuss and explore the multimodality inherent in current conceptions of literacy.

References

Miller, A. (2015). On paper, in person, and online: A multiliteracies framework for university teaching. *Journal of Academic Language and Learning, 9*(2), A19–A31.

Street, B. (2013). Literacy in theory and practice: Challenges and debates over 50 years. *Theory Into Practice, 52*(1), 52–62.

Wenger, E. (1998). *Communities of practice: Learning, meaning, and identity*. Cambridge: Cambridge University Press.

Whitehead, K., & Wilkinson, L. (2008). Teachers, policies and practices: A historical review of literacy teaching in Australia. *Journal of Early Childhood Literacy, 8*(1), 7–24.

World Englishes in Academic Writing: Exploring Markers' Responses

Toni Dobinson, Paul Mercieca, and Sarah Kent

Abstract Widening participation in higher education and inclusivity policies have meant more university students with different cultural schemas for writing and varying levels of proficiency in academic English. In particular, international and migrant students may bring with them their own legitimate varieties of English. The authors of this chapter draw on a small project conducted at one Australian university which sought to investigate the use of World Englishes (WEs) in the written work of students who speak English as an Additional Language or Dialect (EAL/D) and the feedback given to these students by lecturers across disciplines. Findings revealed limited occurrences of features that could definitely be linked with WEs, particularly in the area of lexis. Likewise, there were few examples of lecturer feedback on the students' use of WEs or WEs picked up as errors due to the use of standardised rubrics which did not have this capacity. Discussion points to the need for greater transcultural competence amongst academics in the tertiary sector against a backdrop of increased student numbers and shorter feedback turnaround times. It also suggests the need for students to be able to identify the boundary between dominant discourses in their disciplines and ways to negotiate standard forms to include their own language identities.

Keywords Academic writing literacy · Feedback on writing · Higher education, Language identity · World Englishes · EAL/D students

T. Dobinson (✉) · P. Mercieca · S. Kent
School of Education, Curtin University, Perth, WA, Australia
e-mail: T.Dobinson@curtin.edu.au; P.Mercieca@curtin.edu.au; Sarah.Kent@curtin.edu.au

© Springer Nature Switzerland AG 2019
T. Dobinson, K. Dunworth (eds.), *Literacy Unbound: Multiliterate, Multilingual, Multimodal*, Multilingual Education 30,
https://doi.org/10.1007/978-3-030-01255-7_2

1   Introduction

Increased internationalisation of education (Harman 2005) has resulted in greater numbers of transnationally mobile students (British Council 2013) and programs run by university providers overseas in conjunction with the host university. The global population of internationally mobile students more than doubled from 2.1 million in 2000 to nearly 4.5 million in 2011 (OECD 2011). The push for greater internationalisation of the student body has also coincided with efforts by governments and educational organisations to widen participation in higher education. Cohorts previously under-represented in student enrolments, such as students from diverse educational and social backgrounds, now constitute a more sizeable proportion of the university student population (Bradley et al. 2008; Browne 2010; Kim and Creighton 2000; Murray 2014; Osborne 2003; U.S. Government Office of Social Innovation and Civic Participation 2009). Ironically, however, increasing diversity in the tertiary sector coincides with greater standardisation of assessment practices. The drive to impose 'a standard' can mean that students from diverse linguistic backgrounds may be disadvantaged by some of the criteria by which academic writing is marked.

This chapter draws on a wider critical action research project (Creswell 2008) which sought to develop a resource to inform academics about the issues involved in assessing the academic writing of students whose first language was not English. The project was funded by an Australian university Teaching Excellence Development Fund in 2015. It was a response to the Tertiary Education Quality and Standards Authority (TEQSA 2013) which called for the assessment of student literacy and feedback on writing (both local students speaking English as their first language and English as an Additional Language or Dialect (EAL/D) students) to be embedded into discipline areas and all assessments across the university and for every lecturer to be competent in the assessment of language. This last requirement mirrors the Australian Curriculum's call for all teachers to be 'responsible for teaching the language and literacy demands of their learning areas' (ACARA 2014, p. 6). The initial stage of the project described in this chapter involved (1) an exploratory, descriptive linguistic analysis of EAL/D students' use of World Englishes (WEs) in a small sample of 20 academic assessments from the four different faculties in the university and (2) a descriptive textual analysis of the kind of feedback provided by academic staff to those students on their work.

The authors kept an open mind about the work of the EAL/D students and the kind of feedback lecturers might give, but the study was approached with the premise that 'non-standard' forms would be treated as errors rather than features of the students' WEs by markers. The authors were prepared to argue that universities needed to be more tolerant and imaginative in the way they provide language feedback to students whose first language is not English, particularly in terms of student writing. However, few examples of WEs emerged from the students' samples and there was little to no feedback from academics on the WEs that were used by students. Moreover, feedback on language use generally was limited.

Background to the project includes literature on standardisation, language and identity and the assessment of language proficiency as well as issues related to academics' transcultural awareness and an appreciation of contemporary tertiary teaching conditions. These are all discussed in the sections that follow.

2   Standardisation of Language

Across higher education worldwide, there have been efforts to improve the transferability of student qualifications. However, such higher education initiatives as the Lisbon Strategy and the Bologna Process in Europe, and the increased use of standardised international testing such as the International English Language Testing System (IELTS), have produced a very homogeneous outcome 'in a collusion of mediocrity based on immediacy, hedonism and financial return', according to Gibbs (2010, p. 251). Ironically, this comes at a time when campuses globally are becoming more diverse with the internationalisation of education, immigration, government policy initiatives designed to increase the numbers of school leavers entering higher education, reduced financial contributions from governments and pressures to extend higher education to a more socio-culturally and educationally diverse proportion of the population.

In Australia, the context in which the project described here took place, such developments have changed the profile of the students entering universities (Murray 2010) and their English language abilities, particularly in the area of academic literacy. This necessitates a cross disciplinary and embedded approach to English language assessment and provision (Murray 2014). Students entering the first year of their degree can clearly be faced with anxieties about their writing, as evidenced in the following comments by first year students who said they were worried about:

going on tangeants in writing
going off topic in essays
sentence organisation
writing for a certain audience
not sounding smart enough
literacy and grammar
swearing/inappropriate language

Note: The student who was worried about going 'on tangeants' [sic] was also the one who added *spell check is ruining my life*.

If students whose first language is English are often under confident when it comes to writing, EAL/D students carry an extra linguistic burden in terms of their accuracy in English and their ability to write in Standard Australian English, especially if they are used to writing in a different variety of English. The continued expectation that 'standard' academic English (or standard academic Australian English) should be used in assessments is in conflict with the significant role of local context and student use of WEs in programme provision, and tends to deny the connection between language and identity.

3   Language and Identity

Standard English is not merely a concept contested linguistically, but also ideologically (Pennycook 2000, 2008). The term is often used in the singular, where it is most often related to what McArthur (1987) referred to as 'World Standard English'. The term is also used plurally, where it may refer to the range of different varieties, such as, for example, Standard Australian English. This chapter will use the singular form for consistency.

Issues surrounding academic literacy and standards are obviously more pronounced when it comes to students whose first language is not English. In a world that is increasingly cognisant of the validity and complexity of WEs (Jenkins 2006, 2014; Kirkpatrick 2007, 2011), translanguaging (García 2009; García and Li 2014; Sussex and Kirkpatrick 2012; Young et al. 2013) and the importance of these for the retention of identity, variety in language can no longer be ignored or seen in a deficit light.

WEs have been described in numerous ways. The first thoughts on WEs were offered by Kachru (1985) who conceptualised English varieties within three concentric circles. The Inner Circle was regarded as the domain of native English speaking countries like the United Kingdom, USA and Australia. The Outer Circle contained those countries where English is recognised as an official language alongside other languages. Lastly, the Expanding Circle referred to countries in which English was a foreign language. While Kachru neatly demarcated English varieties according to geographical location, more recent research has argued that this is problematic. Varieties of English constantly evolve and combine with each other in our global context (Horner et al. 2011; Saraceni 2015). Use of English is dynamic, moving across regions, and complex, taking into account multilingualism, code switching, relationships and differing levels of competence (Modiano 2001). Jenkins (2009) argued against value distinction between speakers of English, suggesting that the term 'WEs' should be used for any form of English including varieties of Standard English. Mahboob (2014), with his Framework of Language Variation, talks about three intersecting continuums:

1. Users of English and the geographical distance between them e.g. local or global
2. The purpose of the language e.g. specialisation language at one end of continuum and casual conversation at the other
3. The mode e.g. spoken or written or combination of the two in virtual communication

Each continuum is independent of any other continuum, but at the same time they are not mutually exclusive. There are eight possible kinds of language variation including local written every day; local oral every day; local written specialised; local oral specialised; global written everyday etc.

Matsuda and Matsuda (2010) have argued that lecturers and researchers should challenge dominant views of language use in academic spheres. Similarly, Canagarajah (2006, p. 603) has viewed students' linguistic and cultural backgrounds 'as a resource, not a problem'. Writing can be marked by features no longer regarded in sociolinguistic fields or amongst informed assessment experts, as malformed interlanguages (Thuy 2009). Seidlhofer (2011) has reminded us that native–speaker English use is just one reality and this reality may be called into question in 'lingua-franca contexts' (p.19), as arguably, some of these may be university settings (Jenkins 2014).

Another group of researchers question the insistence on the use of Standard English in writing and stress the importance of retaining speaker identity, advocating a translanguaging approach. Young (2010) and Canagarajah (2013) have suggested that the less normative approach inherent in 'code-meshing' could help to re-invigorate much academic English writing. This approach to bilingualism is in line with that of García (2009), Sussex and Kirkpatrick (2012) who state that translanguaging:

- focuses not on languages as systems but as practices
- goes beyond code-switching to include hybrid language use – meshing languages together
- values bilingual students, their communities, language practices and language rights
- implies forms of assessment which account for the languaging of bilingual students
- raises concerns that students speaking varietal Englishes are stigmatised as needing remedial help

There has also been a call for a translingual approach to academic writing (Horner et al. 2011, p. 306) with writers encouraged to learn and understand the standard form as well as the non-standard form so that they are empowered to 'work with and against, not simply within, those expectations'. Using a translingual approach does not mean that errors in writing are ignored, or non-existent, but assumptions about correctness in spelling, punctuation use and sentence structure can be challenged when giving feedback on student writing. In this way learners' variety of English and identity can be respected.

A more cautious view has been put forward by Matsuda and Matsuda (2010), however, who point out that students may encounter criticism for non-standard usage, and need to be made aware of this when challenging dominant English language usage. In fact, students are often unaware of dominant discourses in the first place and so discipline-specific practices need to be explicitly taught (Hyland 2013). At the writing level, Matsuda and Matsuda (2010) further suggested that students be taught to develop their own credibility in their writing in the way they structure their arguments. Further, they suggested non-standard language forms should be used in an intentional way, highlighted perhaps with specific punctuation marks. Indeed, multilingual writers often make these deliberate linguistic choices to 'achieve their communicative purposes' (Canagarajah 2006, p. 602). Nevertheless, the use of WEs raises the question of which variety to teach and how to assess writing in an academic context. It can no longer be assumed that Standard English is *the* variety that students should acquire (Jindapitak 2013). With this in mind, Matsuda and Matsuda (2010, p.372) have recommended that students be taught the standard and non-standard forms of English as well as 'the boundary between what works and what does not'. In conjunction with this, it could be argued then that academics assessing students' written work should also be aware of the non-standard varieties in the form of WEs that they may encounter with their EAL/D students.

4 Assessing Language Proficiency

Contingent diversity and heterogeneity have created tensions between more normatively-inclined academic writing gatekeepers and those on the periphery. Critical approaches negotiate identity in writing (Wingate 2012) and acknowledge 'the social contexts that influence writing at any point' (Thuy 2009, p. 62).

As more WEs emerge, the question of which Englishes should be privileged in assessment looms larger. L1 and L2 English markers (defining L1 here as the language in which someone is most proficient), who may traditionally defer to the 'standard' form of English, need to decide how much cultural diversity to respect. In the area of writing Hamp-Lyons and Zhang (2001) pointed out that L2 English writers (defining L2 here as the second or additional language of the writer), who adopt different rhetorical patterns, may be disadvantaged unless marked by L2 English raters. However, L2 raters may feel they need to uphold 'the standards'. EAL/D students' writing may actually go unnoticed when they are enrolled in courses which are not linguistically demanding or which have short answer type assessments, but writing becomes a struggle when they commence language-rich courses, especially in the humanities or health sciences.

Broader arguments about the meaning of equivalence and comparability, standards and norms, relate directly to issues of language choice. One of the considerations in any program delivered in a second language is the question of whether student writing evidences interlingual error or the emergence of an endonormative WEs variety. Thuy (2009, p. 64) has suggested that 'grammatical errors should not be seriously judged if they do not affect the transformation of meaning in the writing'. However, the challenge is to keep a social realist perspective (Maton 2014), maintaining a non-deficit stance without lapsing into an overly relativistic perspective.

Academics who work within different discipline areas of a university will have different perceptions of relevant knowledge and skills for that area, including the English they are willing to accept from students. As Chapman (2002) suggested, subject study essentially entails the study of conventional discourses in the area and assessment is usually based on evaluating whether and how such discourse expectations are met. These are often entrenched in the university's statements about graduate attributes. Subject and language domains cannot be neatly separated. The university in question states that students should 'Communicate Effectively'. They need to exit the university able to 'communicate in ways appropriate to the discipline, audience and purpose'. Discipline area staff might also have different views on who controls the knowledge in their area i.e. the student or the academic. As well as this, opportunities for timely formative feedback are increasingly constrained by workload and time pressures (Winefield et al. 2008). These pressures are framed by the overall expansion of access to university education and transformations driven by technology in the way in which courses are delivered and accessed (Comeau and Cheng 2013).

The study described below was an attempt to look more closely at the writing of students for whom English was not a first language to discover if their non-standard language use could be attributed to use of WEs (Standard English is not treated as a WEs variety in this instance) or their developing interlanguage. It also investigated markers' responses to the students' use of WEs and the type of feedback that was given on students' written samples generally.

5 Method

The study drawn on in this chapter could be described as critical action research (Mills 2006) or critical emancipatory research (Burns 2005, 2011; Paltridge and Phakiti 2015). The first stage of the project was led by the authors (who are also academics involved in the marking of EAL/D students' written work) with the second stage being actioned later by a larger 'community of practice' (The Glossary of Education Reform 2015). Such research is focused on 'improving and empowering individuals in …systems of education' (Creswell 2008, p. 603) and has emerged from the work of Freire, Habermas, Kemmis and Stringer (Schmuck 1997). It addresses issues that may constrain or 'repress the lives of students and educators' (p. 603) and promotes egalitarian and democratic aims. Critical action research can be less formal, prescriptive, or theory-driven since the goal is to address practical problems in a specific educational context rather than to produce independently validated and reproducible findings for others outside of the context (The Glossary of Education Reform 2015). A number of different strategies were thus employed in order to achieve the aims of the project.

This chapter is only concerned with the first stage of the project in which the authors collected 20 samples of anonymised students' written assessments and lecturer feedback from the Science, Humanities, Health Sciences faculties and a private campus provider which provides tertiary pathways for students who do not meet direct entry requirements. The original intention was to collect far more than twenty scripts but it proved to be difficult for Unit and Course Coordinators to gain access to student work from their teachers and to track students down and gain their permission to use their work. It was decided, therefore, that this study could be used as a basis for further investigation on a larger sample of scripts at a later date.

Some of the samples were also taken from students who are taking the common first year communication skills units provided by each faculty as concurrent language and academic literacy support. Written permission to use the scripts was given by the students and lecturers. The intent behind this collection of students' written texts was to conduct a descriptive linguistic analysis and see first-hand the kinds of language 'errors' or 'non-standard uses' (varieties other than the standard variety and attributable to typical variety-specific features of different countries around the world) that lecturers encountered in EAL/D students' written assessments. The intent behind the collection of academic feedback on those scripts was to do a descriptive textual analysis of how assessments of EAL/D students are currently marked and where lecturers may need help in recognising the difference between errors and the students' use of WEs varieties. Once the students' texts and lecturer feedback had been collected and analysed project leaders would be in a better position to develop a resource which catered for the needs of lecturers in assessing EAL/D students' written work and continue to the stages of resource development and evaluation in the collaborative enquiry project.

Analysis of both the students' texts and the lecturers' feedback was qualitative in design and carried out by the authors. WEs were classified from Kirkpatrick's perspective (2007, 2013) as varieties other than the standard form and not from Jenkins's perspective (2009) where WEs include the standard form. The study was not designed to measure the quantity of non-standard use of English nor various types of feedback. Descriptive linguistic analysis focused on what could be called *features* (forms that could be attributed to the use of a WEs) and *errors* (forms which cannot be traced back to a variety of WEs and therefore may be deemed to be an interlanguage error). Students' scripts were analysed for 'errors' or 'features' reflecting the taxonomy developed by Groves (2010). Errors were defined as inaccurate grammar, syntax, cohesion/coherence or more idiosyncratic inaccuracies (according to the rules of Standard English). Features were seen as 'the result of a productive process which marks the typical variety-specific features' of a WEs variety (Kachru 1983, p. 120); a systematic aspect of a WEs variety and/or non-standard dialect, and innovative rather than deviant (Groves 2010, p.120). Features are more acceptable in their places of origin, but often become perceived as errors in other locations. An example of this is the use of the word 'prepone' in Indian English; an example of WEs which is not internationally intelligible but very commonly used and extremely logical when talking about the opposite of 'postpone' or an intention to do something before it is necessary to do it (Li 2010).

It is not easy to clearly delineate between errors and features because language usage is changing as part of a natural process and so, to a large extent, the difference between errors, features and instances of usage is a matter of judgement, with some flexibility needed when marking written assessments (Hamid and Baldauf 2013). Decisions about what could be deemed to be a WEs variant were informed by Kirkpatrick's *Asian Corpus of English* (2013) and those colleagues he drew upon to develop the corpus (Breiteneder 2005, 2009; Cogo and Dewy 2012; Mauranen and Ranta 2009; Seidlhofer 2011) on the theme of the pragmatics of English as a lingua franca as well as articles on pragmatics and writing styles for various cultures. The Asian corpus was used because the majority of EAL/D students encountered at the university in question are of Asian extraction, mostly coming from India, Bangladesh, Vietnam, Malaysia, Singapore, China and Indonesia. Kirkpatrick's (2013, p. 23) summary of the common syntactic characteristics of Asian WEs is reproduced below:

- non-marking of the third person singular with 's';
- interchanging of relative pronouns 'who' and 'which';
- flexible use of the definite and indefinite articles;

- extended use of common or 'general' verbs;
- uncountable nouns treated like plurals;
- use of one uniform question tag (e.g. isn't it?);
- use of the demonstrative 'this' with both singular and plural nouns;
- use of prepositions in different contexts.

Other variations found in the Asian Corpus of English (ACE) are the use of the base form of the verb for past tense, omission of the copula 'be' and omission of the plural 's' (Kirkpatrick 2013). The search for other distinctive forms of English that might be deemed non-standard and characteristic of English spoken in certain geographical regions was guided by Kirkpatrick's earlier comprehensive text, *World Englishes: Implications for international communication and English language teaching* (2007). An example that Kirkpatrick highlights is the use of the present continuous form in place of the present simple form in Indian English and other notable lexical differences between different geographical regions of the English-speaking world.

6 Findings

6.1 Examples of WEs in Students' Scripts

Excerpts 1 and 2 were selected from Sample 1 by the authors to highlight the difference between what was deemed an error and what was deemed a feature in work completed for an assessment in a unit offered by the School of Occupational Therapy and Social Work called Foundations for Professional Health Practice 100.

Excerpt 1 From Sample 1: Student Assessment Showing a Grammatical Inaccuracy or 'Error'

> the Australian health system and the roles of the health professional who collaborate together with parents and children.
>
> **2.0 Physical Abuse of Child and Neglect**
>
> The definition for physical abuse of child and neglect has a few explanations that lead to various statistics based on reports from families and friends. Physical abuse defined "maltreatment in which injury is inflicted on the child by a caregiver, including hitting with a hand, stick, strap, or other it object; stabbing; or choking to the extent that demonstrable harm results" (The Third National Incidence Study, 2011). There is also an interaction between the amounts of stress present in the family in response to caregivers (Straus and Kantor, 2011).

Excerpt 1 above has the word 'Child' highlighted because the student has neglected to add the irregular English plural form of this where it is needed and, therefore, this has been classified as a grammatical *error* in the interlanguage of the student.

Excerpt 2 From Sample 1: Student Assessment Showing a 'Feature' of a WEs Variety

---

5.0 Health Professionals

General Practitioners diagnose health assessments for patients and responsible to provide treatment according to the diagnosis of the patient. The roles of the General practitioners are challenging and need to be involved with the patients and community. The health system in Australia is constantly relying on the overseas trained doctors. There are general practitioners who practice in rural areas as there is a shortage.

In Excerpt 2 above, however, the highlighted language can be classified as a *feature* of a WEs variety rather than an error. The use of the present continuous form in 'constantly relying on' is a common feature of Indian English on the sub-continent and indeed can be spotted in other English language varieties.

Other expression that was considered to be a *feature* rather than an *error* was picked up in eight of the other nineteen samples of student writing and these examples are listed below in Table 1.

At a glance, it can be seen that very few obvious *features* were observed in the samples of writing analysed – no more than two in any sample. Because the list of Asian WEs common features compiled by Kirkpatrick (2013) can also be conflated with errors made in students' interlanguage, it was often difficult to decide when a non-standard form was a common WEs feature or just a slip/error on the student's part. As a result, only lexis and syntax that was distinctly varietal was chosen for comment as included in Table 1.

Another problem that presented itself was that many non-standard responses could not be classified as errors or features but simply language that at one time would have been judged to be inaccurate but which now is in common usage. Kirkpatrick (2013) talks about this and points to the simplification of the inflectional system of English over the years and the regularisation of regular past tense verbs (Kirkpatrick 2013). Examples of this are seen in the past tense 'worked' (which used to be 'wrought') and the past tense 'reached' (which was 'raught' until about 1650) (Lass 1999, p. 174). A list of some of the common usages found in students' work is given in Table 2.

Overall, the occurrence of features that could definitely be linked with WEs was enough to be of interest, but was not present to the extent that had been expected at the conceptualisation stage or outset of the project, particularly in the area of lexis found only in certain WEs. Although there were many non-standard forms, which fitted Kirkpatrick's description of common forms in WEs varieties, it was difficult to relegate these to a WEs category without knowing the background of the student or their level of English or their intentions in writing. The implications of this are discussed later on in the chapter.

Table 1 Some features of WEs and non-standard varieties found in student writing

Sample number, discipline and feature	Researchers' comments
S2 Media On *another* hand…	Idiomatic expressions are not always matched exactly, but can still be comprehensible and are used widely by EAL/D learners
S3 Communication and Cultural Studies If someone want to know others, *one of the good ways* to know each other is to learn their language	Idiomatic expressions are not always matched exactly, but can still be comprehensible and are used widely by EAL/D learners
S4 Communication and Cultural Studies … because it makes us think that rape caused by man's *behaviors*	Use of countable/uncountable nouns is different in many WEs
S6 Communication and Cultural Studies *Because* of the skin colors, people do not want to interact to other skin color people	Chinese varieties of English often put the reason first
S7 Tertiary Pathway Studies: a) I deleted some information that *aged* the story	a) Would normally be 'dated' – first language alternative not suitable in terms of accuracy but perfectly adequate to convey the right meaning
b) Finding *a* suitable accommodation to rent…	b) Uncountable treated as countable which is common in many WEs
S8 Media…the application of copyright over *the* recent years	Zero article normally required but this does not compromise the intended meaning and is used in many WEs varieties
S9 Media …this creates an *ominous-feeling setting*	Possibly first language influence…not 'accurate' English but creative and effective in conveying the right meaning
S15 Education. There is a contention in some circles whether those *yellow-complexion persons*, namely Asian learners, are in favor of rote learning memorization	Not quite right, but comprehensible, colourful and probably influenced by first language

6.2 Lecturers' Feedback on the Writing Which Contained Examples of WEs

Once the 20 scripts of the EAL/D students had been analysed for features or errors the authors commenced analysis of the feedback given by academics on the scripts found to contain examples of WEs (with Standard English not included in this definition). The summary of this analysis can be seen in Table 3.

As might have been expected, there was little evidence of attempts by markers to separate errors from features of different varieties of English in their feedback. The closest that comments came to addressing this was in a unit run as part of an MA Applied Linguistics course. Lecturers in this course are all English language teachers and therefore it is not surprising that feedback provided by them to S15 was more nuanced. Moreover, the students in this course are often international students who are upgrading their qualifications and already qualified English language teachers, so their understanding of linguistic feedback might be superior to that of students from other disciplines.

Table 2 Examples of language change and usage

Usage	Researchers' comments
S10 Communication and Cultural Studies *Due to* Joanne's American culture, her husband's family asked him to divorce her.	Now a feature of most varieties of English accepted at the beginning of a sentence
	Assessors often resort to ready-made comments which are based on outdated style suggestions from internet or print sources
S11 Communication and Cultural Studies When was the last time in The Unites States of America did we see security detail running alongside the cars? A very long time ago *in the twentieth century.*	The marker has ignored the rather uncomfortable use of 'did we see' in the first sentences and chosen to comment on the second, although many varieties have a sentence which does not have to have a verb (a fragment) in common usage
S14 Health Sciences In addition, data *is* mainly obtained from medical records, such as clinical and death registers	Most varieties of English accept in singular or plural, though APA still insists on plural
S18 Science and Engineering ...there are many disadvantages that are caused *from* the burning of fossil fuel...	Should really be 'by', but it could be argued that usage is changing
S22 Science and Engineering global warming leads to the *increasement* in hurricanes	In this case usage has moved on since the seventeenth century, or maybe not

Only one instance was found of a lecturer marking a WEs expression as 'incorrect' when, in fact, it was just an example of a WEs variety. This was in the work of Sample S7 (see Table 3) where a Spanish student wrote: 'I deleted some information that *aged* the story' and the lecturer corrected it to 'dated'. The marker went on to comment that the use of the word 'aged' was 'cumbersome or difficult to read' and that the student should 'consider rewriting' this sentence.

Of course, as stated earlier, the allocation of non-standard forms, such as non-marking of the third person singular 's' or flexible use of the definite article, to the WEs category was impossible to do, as these forms could be either WEs varieties or merely errors on the students' parts. Therefore, if lecturers corrected these it remained unclear whether they were correcting WEs varieties or errors.

In summary, surprisingly few distinct examples of WEs use by EAL/D students were found in the 20 writing samples that were gathered. Whether this was because the sample was fairly limited, or because students have taken on board the importance of using standard Australian English in an academic genre, is unclear. Regardless of this, the examples that were gathered are examples that are common practice amongst many EAL/D students and therefore worthy of noting by assessors in any resource that is developed to help them give feedback on writing in the future. Likewise, there were few examples of lecturer feedback on the students' use of WEs or WEs picked up as errors. This could be seen as a good sign. It might be interpreted as lecturers being tolerant of the use of WEs. However, the fact that lecturers' attention to students' use of language overall was limited would indicate that omission may not have been by design, but due to other factors including time pressures or lack of sufficient knowledge about language.

Table 3 Lecturers' feedback on the writing which contained examples of WEs

Sample number, discipline and feature	Lecturers' feedback
S1 Occupational Therapy The health system in Australia *is constantly relying on* the overseas trained doctors	No specific feedback on this language use and no feedback on language in the essay generally.
S2 Media On *another* hand…	No specific feedback on this language use and no feedback on language in the essay generally.
S3 Communication and Cultural Studies If someone want to know others, *one of the good ways* to know each other is to learn their language	No specific feedback on this language use but some limited feedback on language in the essay generally, particularly with regard to informality and formality
S4 Communication and Cultural Studies …because it makes us think that rape caused by man's *behaviors*	No specific feedback on this language use and no feedback on language in the essay generally.
S6 Communication and Cultural Studies *Because* of the skin colors, people do not want to interact to other skin color people	No specific feedback on this language use but some limited feedback on language in the essay using the comment: This was 'cumbersome or difficult to read'. Note: This phrase was a stock phrase lifted from a bank of feedback responses provided to all markers
S7 Tertiary Pathway Studies a) I deleted some information that *aged* the story	a) The lecturer corrected 'aged' to 'dated' then commented: The use of 'aged' was 'cumbersome or difficult to read'. Note: This phrase was a stock phrase lifted from a bank of feedback responses provided to all markers.
b) finding *a* suitable accommodation to rent…	b) The lecturer crossed out 'a'.
S8 Media…the application of copyright over *the* recent years	No specific feedback on this language use and no feedback on language in the essay generally.
S9 Media ...this creates an *ominous-feeling setting*	No specific feedback on this language use and no feedback on language in the essay generally except for one spelling mistake picked up.
S15 Education There is a contention in some circles whether those *yellow-complexion persons*, namely Asian learners, are in favor of rote learning memorization	You have a very idiosyncratic style of writing which makes use of 'colourful language and images' and which I find very attractive but which many in the field of education may find too 'social sciencey'. Be careful with expressions like 'yellow-complexion persons' when writing in educational academic contexts.

The study took a rather unexpected turn, as indicated earlier on in the introduction to this chapter, with so little data being generated from the EAL/D students' writing samples. It was not a lost opportunity, however. During the search for the use of WEs in student writing, lecturers' approaches to feedback were noticeable. The authors, therefore, decided to turn their attention to the types of feedback provided to EAL/D students on their written assessments irrespective of WEs. This line of investigation was still very relevant to the study, as providing assistance with feedback to EAL/D students was the main aim of the project.

6.3 Other Observations About Marker Feedback Generally

The feedback that lecturers did give to the EAL/D students represented in the samples ranged from holistic feedback on meaning, content and task performance to micro level feedback e.g. spelling mistakes, use of quotation marks, referencing conventions. This feedback was often dictated by the use of standardised rubrics which were mandated in certain units and schools. The feedback given to the student who had written Sample 2 in the unit Engaging Media, for example, is shown in Fig. 1.

Other feedback given to the student who wrote Samples 3, 5 and 6 was delivered via the online marking tool which annotates students' work with codes that can be selected from the Turnitin marking bank or comments boxes. In the case of Sample 3 the marker had provided comments on content as well as codes which indicated informal usage, in-text referencing errors and missing quotes. The informal usage code was explained by the phrase: This particular phrasing is informal and the meaning is unclear. This feedback is vague but was not directed at the use of a WEs form by the student. In Sample 5 the codes awk (awkward), del (delete) and improper citation had also been used to indicate where revision was needed. Sample 6 had more referencing codes applied and a code which indicated that a statement had been too general and went on to comment: This is a very general statement that contributes little to refining your topic or thesis. It also had comments which pointed out when a student had been too 'vague and sketchy'.

Samples 4 and 7 were marked in a similar way to Sample 2 with a standardised rubric which rated the student's writing according to the criteria 'needs attention', 'partially correct', 'good' or 'excellent' (Sample 3), or just gave a mark. The rubric for Sample 3 contained a comment box on language as follows:

> Presents ideas in a clear, coherent fashion; sentences and paragraphs are clear, well-structured, grammatically correct; writing shows evidence of being edited and proof-read.

Sample 7 had the same type of feedback rubric, but there was more detail provided on structure, style and writing skills, with up to two marks deducted for every spelling error. Throughout the samples, where comments were made about gram-

	Needs Attention	Partially Correct	Good	Excellent
Provides an informed, critica lanalysis	X			
Presents information in a clear, coherent manner		X		
Engages the reader and effectively communicates		X		
Correctly references sources used		X		
Submission conforms to presentation requirements	Yes			

Fig. 1 Feedback given to the student who had written Sample 2 in the unit engaging media

mar, they were often not specific and were part of a standardised marking rubric as seen in the comments taken from rubrics that were used:

- There are many sections of this essay which were grammatically ineffective
- Language and grammar problems need to be addressed
- The expression or construction is cumbersome or difficult to read. Consider rewriting

Occasionally, grammar was commented on more specifically using the Turnitin marking guide as seen below:

FRAG
Fragment: A sentence fragment is a phrase or clause that is in some way incomplete. Such fragments become problematic when they attempt to stand alone as a complete sentence. The most common version of this mistake occurs when a writer mistakes a gerund (a verb that acts like a noun) for a main verb, as in the following sentence: "In bed reading Shakespeare from dusk to dawn."

When scripts were annotated by markers themselves, comments were sometimes vague, e.g. 'the data is good but the sentence is lousy' and 'another very poorly worded sentence', and often did not provide guidance with writing, although there was some detailed comment made about specific language use at a micro level, with lecturers in the Health Sciences annotating scripts with comments such as, 'keep your sentences a bit shorter – they are too complicated'; or 'none of these words need to be capitalised as they are not proper nouns'. On the whole, a large amount of feedback was devoted to pointing out problems with the formatting of in-text referencing. There was also considerable comment on essay organisation and 'flow' with comments like:

Although paragraphs are separate, individual steps of your paper, it is important to clearly demonstrate a logical connection between them. A paragraph that begins with "also" or "in addition" offers a weak transition from the previous point, even though it may develop a highly interesting and related point.

On the whole, academics' feedback did not refer to the students' use of WEs forms distinct from Standard English forms. However, they were presented with little opportunity to do so, as there was minimal use of these forms in the twenty samples analysed. The authors observed that very little detailed feedback on language was provided at all to EAL/D students by academics, due to the use of standardised rubrics which did not have the capacity for this.

7   Discussion

As all writing samples were gathered anonymously, it was difficult to attribute aspects of the students' writing to the background of the student. Similarly, it was difficult to differentiate between learner errors and WEs features without knowing students' levels of English or their intentions in writing. Moreover, the common syntax formations mentioned by Kirkpatrick (2013) are difficult to separate from learner error. Nonetheless, the fact that relatively few examples of definitive WEs use (e.g. distinctive lexis, grammatical and syntactical formations) were procured from the writing samples in this case study took the researchers a little bit by surprise. However, in some ways this finding is more of a discussion point than the reverse finding, if we assume, as Young (2010), Sussex and Kirkpatrick (2012) and Wingate (2012) have done, that language practice is a marker of identity. Relatively few distinct markers of this identity appeared in students' writing and this may be more of a reason for concern than satisfaction. Moreover, the analyses of the feedback from lecturers on the twenty samples did not reveal their capacity to recognise WEs varieties and comment on them in the limited examples that were found. This could have been because the students' use of the WEs form did not interfere at all with meaning making or that lecturers could not differentiate WEs features from learner interlanguage error, just as the current researchers had been unable to do. The feedback that was provided by academics was generally focused on task fulfilment and content. Commentary which attempted to instruct students on language use was either very vague, standardised (so one size fits all) or at an extremely micro level e.g. spelling. A large amount of commentary was provided on referencing and, particularly, the formatting involved in this, but again this was via standardised rubrics. The implications of this are that academics across disciplines are not really ready to take on the job of being able to recognise WEs varieties in student writing, nor do they have the time to really develop EAL/D students' language at a close level throughout their course.

The Australian Department of Education, Employment and Workplace Relations (Australian Universities Quality Agency, 2009, p. 2) reported that 'with widening participation across tertiary education and the increasing numbers of international students, it can no longer be assumed that students enter their university study with the requisite academic language skills'. It was suggested that these skills needed to be developed whilst at university. From the examples reviewed here, it is difficult to see how language skills can be developed across disciplines and embedded within them, if academics are tied to standardised rubrics. The step towards being transculturally competent enough to recognise the difference between errors and features of WEs (Groves 2010) in students' written work would appear to be one step too far in such a scenario, even if a checklist of common WEs forms were provided. However, designed-in transcultural competence content in initial pre-service teacher education or professional development courses offered in-service in universities or schools might go some of the way towards raising awareness of the existence and legitimacy of WEs varieties and common WEs characteristics and their links with learner identity. This 'awareness' would not have to involve educators memorising long lists of possible WEs variations, which would be an impossible requirement on top of commitments to teaching and research involvement already sanctioned in many university and school settings. It does mean, however, understanding and recognising the need to be tolerant and inclusive when marking students' work and, at the very least, thinking 'Oh I remember something about this in my transcultural competence session … Indian English often makes use of …'.

8 Conclusion

The authors began their project journey with the conviction that checklists of WEs use (Englishes other than Standard English) could be an important resource for university academics across disciplines, but increasingly as they analysed the feedback given to students on their writing it became apparent that this was unrealistic due to constraints such as time, workloads and the growing necessity for standardised marking rubrics as a result of this. Moreover, students in this particular small study did not demonstrate a propensity to use WEs varieties in their work although it cannot be concluded from this that WEs varieties might not appear in the writing of a larger cohort of students or students in other different university contexts. Nevertheless, transcultural competence in universities should still be developed in order to provide academics with a deeper level of understanding of the language of their EAL/D students. This may help them to develop a more informed approach to the marking of EAL/D students' academic writing in the event that they are not tied to standardised rubrics.

Pragmatic, yet critical approaches can pay attention to wider literacy and identity issues, with all academics and educators being encouraged to challenge their own views on correctness in English writing given the diversity of university cohorts and disciplines. Students, likewise, could be taught to identify the boundary between dominant discourses in their disciplines and ways to negotiate standard forms effectively. Language policy at the government level could be derived from more than one standpoint and represent the diversity of stakeholders and views on what constitutes 'standards' and 'quality', particularly in the area of second language writing. Closer collegial contact between onshore academics, local counterparts (Dunn and Wallace 2006) operating in transnational settings and even local primary and secondary teachers, might facilitate a contingent development of more informed approaches to assessment of writing.

Acknowledgement of the need to reassess writing on its terms rather than against a 'standard' is already evident in journal publications such as the *Nordic Journal of English Studies* (see Ranta 2006). This journal does not involve itself in 'linguistic cleansing', but publishes articles with a minimal amount of stylistic and linguistic editing, keeping WEs intact and ensuring very wide dissemination of these articles across the world (Mauranen et al. 2010). The hope is that this is just the beginning of the recognition of the need for more inclusive, informed approaches to academic writing which are based on greater transcultural awareness of WEs (and the corpora that exist) and the legitimacy of different language varieties when they do not interfere with meaning and intelligibility (Hamid and Baldauf 2013). Reflection on this, in terms of students' written work, however, can only happen in academic contexts where academics are not tied to unrealistic feedback turnaround times with very large classes, necessitating the use of standardised rubrics which do not go any way towards developing the language of EAL/D students.

References

Australian Curriculum Assessment and Reporting Authority (ACARA). (2014). *English as an additional language or dialect teacher resource.* Retrieved from http://www.acara.edu.au/verve/_resources/EALD_Overview_and_Advice_revised_February_2014.pdf

Australian Universities Quality Agency (2009). Good practice principles for English language proficiency for international students in Australian universities. Retrieved from www.aall.org.au/sites/default/files/Final_Report-Good_Practice_Principles2009.pdf

Bradley, D., Noonan, P., Nugent, H., & Scales, B. (2008). *Review of Australian Higher education: Final report [Bradley review].*

Breiteneder, A. (2005). The naturalness of English as a european lingua franca: The case of the third person's. *Vienna English Working Papers, 14*(2), 3–26.

Breiteneder, A. (2009). English as a lingua franca in Europe: An empirical perspective. *World Englishes, 28*(2), 256–269.

British Council. (2013). *Going global.* Retrieved from http://www.britishcouncil.org/education/ihe/knowledge-centre/transnational-education/the-shape-of-things-to-come-2

Browne, J. (2010). *Securing a sustainable future for higher education.* Retrieved from www.independent.gov.uk/browne-report

Burns, A. (2005). Action research: An evolving paradigm? *Language Teaching, 38*(2), 57–74.

Burns, A. (2011). Action research in the field of second language teaching and learning. In E. Hinkel (Ed.), *Handbook of research in second language teaching and learning* (Vol. 2, pp. 237–253). New York: Routledge.

Canagarajah, S. (2006). TESOL at forty: What are the issues? *TESOL Quarterly, 40*(1), 9–34.

Canagarajah, S. (2013). *Translingual practice: Global Englishes and cosmopolitan relations.* New York: Routledge.

Chapman, A. (2002). *Language practices in school mathematics: A social semiotic approach.* Lewiston: Edward Mellen Press.

Cogo, A., & Dewy, M. (2012). *Analysing English as a lingua franca.* London: Continuum.

Comeau, J. D., & Cheng, L. T. (2013). Re-defining the concepts of generational labelling perspective form Malaysia. *ARPN Journal of Science and Technology, 3*(3), 259–276.

Creswell, J. W. (2008). *Educational research. Planning, conducting, and evaluating quantitative and qualitative research.* Upper Saddle River: Pearson Education Internationa.

Dunn, L., & Wallace, M. (2006). Promoting communities of practice in transnational higher education. In *Breaking Down Boundaries: International Experience in Open, Distance and Flexible Learning.* Selected papers, Charles Sturt University, Bathurst, Australia: ODLAA.

García, O. (2009). Education, multilingualism and translanguaging in the 21st century. In T. Skutnabb-Kangas, R. Phillipson, A. K. Mohanty, & M. Panda (Eds.), *Social justice through multilingual education* (pp. 140–158). Clevedon: Multilingual Matters.

García, O., & Li, W. (2014). *Translanguaging: Language, bilingualism and education.* London: Palgrave Macmillan.

Gibbs, P. (2010). The commoditization and standardization of higher education. In F. Maringe & N. Foskett (Eds.), *Globalization and internationalization in higher education* (pp. 241–254). London: Continuum.

Groves, J. (2010). Error or feature? The issue of interlanguage deviations in non-native varieties of English. *HKBU Papers in Applied Language Studies, 14*(1), 108–129.

Hamid, M. O., & Baldauf, R. B. (2013). Second language errors and features of World Englishes. *World Englishes, 32*(4), 476–494.

Hamp-Lyons, L., & Zhang, B. W. (2001). WEs: Issues in and from academic writing assessment. In J. Flowerdew & M. Peacock (Eds.), *Research perspectives on English for academic purposes* (pp. 101–116). New York: Cambridge University Press.

Harman, G. (2005). Internationalization of Australian higher education: A critical review of literature and research. In P. Ninnes & M. Hellsten (Eds.), *Internationalizing higher education* (pp. 119–140). Dordrecht: Springer.

Horner, B., Lu, M. Z., Royster, J. J., & Trimbur, J. (2011). Language difference in writing: Toward a translingual approach. *College English, 73*(3), 303–321.

Hyland, K. (2013). Writing in the university: education, knowledge and reputation. *Language Teaching, 46*(1), 53–70.

Jenkins, J. (2006). Current perspectives on teaching WEs and English as a Lingua Franca. *TESOL Quarterly, 40*(1), 157–181.

Jenkins, J. (2009). English as a lingua franca: Interpretations and attitudes. *World Englishes, 28*(2), 200–207.

Jenkins, J. (2014). *English as a Lingua Franca in the international university: The politics of academic English language policy*. Abingdon: Routledge.

Jindapitak, N. (2013). The politics of standard English: An exploration of Thai tertiary English learners' perceptions of the notion of standard English. *Asian Social Science, 9*(5), 118.

Kachru, B. B. (1983). *The indianization of English: The English language in India*. Delhi: Oxford University Press.

Kachru, B. (1985). Institutionalized second language varieties. In *The English language today* (pp. 211–226). Oxford: Pergamon Press.

Kim, K., & Creighton, S. (2000). *Participation in adult education in the United States: 1998–1999*. (NCES 2000–027). U.S. Department of Education. Washington, DC: National Center for Education Statistics.

Kirkpatrick, A. (2007). *World Englishes: Implications for international communication and English language teaching*. Cambridge: Cambridge University Press.

Kirkpatrick, A. (2011). English as an Asian lingua franca and the multilingual model of ELT. *Language Teaching, 44*(2), 212–224.

Kirkpatrick, A. (2013). The Asian corpus of English: Motivation and aims. *Learner Corpus Studies in Asia and the World, 1*, 17–30.

Lass, R. (1999). Phonology and morphology. In R. Lass (Ed.), *The Cambridge history of the English language* (Vol. 111, pp. 1476–1776). Cambridge: Cambridge University Press.

Li, C. S. D. (2010). When does an unconventional form become an innovation? In A. Kirkpatrick (Ed.), *The Routledge handbook of world Englishes* (pp. 617–633). London: Routledge.

Mahboob, A. (2014). Language variation and education: A focus on Pakistan. In S. Buschfeld, T. Hoffmann, M. Huber, & A. Kautzsch (Eds.), *The evolution of Englishes: The dynamic model and beyond* (pp. 267–281). Amsterdam: John Benjamins Publishing Company.

Maton, K. (2014). A TALL order? Legitimation Code Theory for academic language and learning. *Journal of Academic Language and Learning, 8*(3), A34–A48.

Matsuda, A., & Matsuda, P. K. (2010). World Englishes and the teaching of writing. *TESOL Quarterly, 44*(2), 369–374.

Mauranen, A., & Ranta, E. (2009). *English as a lingua franca: Studies and findings*. Newcastle: Cambridge Scholars Publishing.

Mauranen, A., Pérez-Llantada, C., & Swales, J. M. (2010). Academic Englishes: A standardized knowledge. In A. Kirkpatrick (Ed.), *The Routledge handbook of World Englishes* (pp. 634–652). London: Routledge.

McArthur, T. (1987). The English languages? *English Today, 33*, 9–13.

Mills, G. E. (2006). *Guide for the teacher researcher*. Upper Saddle River: Prentice Hall.

Modiano, M. (2001). Linguistic imperialism, cultural integrity, and EIL. *ELT Journal, 55*(4), 339–347.

Murray, N. (2010). Considerations in the post-enrolment assessment of English language proficiency: Reflections form the Australian context. *Language Assessment Quarterly, 7*(4), 343–358.

Murray, N. (2014). Reflections on the implementation of post-enrol English language assessment. *Language Assessment Quarterly, 11*(3), 325–337.

OECD. (2011). How many students study abroad? In *OECD Factbook 2011–2012: Economic, environmental and social statistics*. Paris: OECD publishing.

Osborne, R. D. (2003). Higher education in further education: Northern Ireland. *Higher Education Quarterly, 57*(4), 376–395.

Paltridge, B., & Phakiti, A. (Eds.). (2015). *Research methods in applied linguistics: A practical resource*. London: Bloomsbury Publishing.

Pennycook, A. (2000). English, politics, ideology: From colonial celebration to postcolonial performativity. In T. Ricento (Ed.), *Ideology, politics & language policies* (pp. 107–120). Amsterdam: John Benjamins.

Pennycook, A. (2008). Translingual English. *Australian Review of Applied Linguistics, 31*(3), 1–30.

Ranta, E. (2006). The attractive "progressive" – Why use the *–ing* form in English as a Lingua Franca? *Nordic Journal of English Studies, 5*(2), 95–116.

Saraceni, M. (2015). *World Englishes: A critical analysis*. London: Bloomsbury.

Schmuck, R. A. (1997). *Practical action research for change*. Arlington Heights: IRI Skylight Training and Publishing.

Seidlhofer, B. (2011). *Understanding English as a lingua franca*. Oxford: Oxford University Press.

Sussex, R., & Kirkpatrick, A. (2012). A postscript and a prolegomenon. In *English as an international language in Asia: Implications for language education* (pp. 223–231). Dordrecht: Springer.

TEQSA. (2013). Tertiary Education Quality and Standards Agency (TEQSA) *Quality assessment of English Language Proficiency (ELP) Terms of Reference*. April 2013. Retrieved from http://www.teqsa.gov.au/sites/default/files/EnglishLanguageProficiencyQATerms.pdf

The Glossary of Education Reform. (2015). Retrieved from http://edglossary.org/action-research/

Thuy, N. H. H. (2009). Teaching EFL writing in Vietnam: Problems and solutions – a discussion from the outlook of applied linguistics. *VNU Journal of Science, Foreign Languages, 25*, 61–66.

U.S. Government Office of Social Innovation and Civic Participation (2009). *Investing in education: The American graduation initiative*. Retrieved from http://www.whitehouse.gov/blog/Investing-in-Education-The-American-Graduation-Initiative/

Winefield, A. H., Boyd, C., & Saebel, J. (2008). *Job stress in university staff: An Australian research study*. Bowen Hills: Australian Academic Press.

Wingate, U. (2012). Using academic literacies and genre-based models for academic writing instruction: A 'literacy' journey. *Journal of English for Academic Purposes, 11*, 26–37.

Young, V. A. (2010). Nah, we straight: An argument against code-switching. *JAC, 29*(1–2), 49–76.

Young, V. A., Barrett, R., Young-Rivera, Y., & Lovejoy, K. B. (2013). *Other people's English: Code-meshing, code-switching, and African American literacy*. New York: Teachers College Press.

Developing Academic Writing Literacy While Responding to Tutor Written Feedback

Hugo Santiago Sanchez and Kenan Dikilitaş

Abstract This chapter reports on research that investigated the learning experiences of doctoral students for whom English was an additional language in terms of the ways in which these students developed academic writing literacy as they read, reflected on and responded to tutor-written feedback. The project took the form of a within-site, multiple-case study of individual PhD students conducted at a higher education institution in northwest Turkey. Data were collected through preliminary background interviews, think-aloud protocols and retrospective accounts. Our analysis generated evidence of both a wide variety of forms of perceived academic writing literacy development as well as the internal student factors mediating this process. The study shows that academic writing literacy development is a holistic, complex, interconnected, expansile and idiosyncratic process that is unique to students depending on what they bring to the academic writing learning experience and how these internal factors impact on their academic writing development.

Keywords Academic literacy development · Tutor written feedback · EAL research students · Turkey

1 Introduction

Academic literacy has for decades been an established field of research, providing insights into a number of aspects that range from the conceptualisation of academic literacy (e.g., Henderson and Hirst 2007; Leki 2000); through literacy variations across contexts, cultures, languages, disciplines and genres (e.g., Barton and Hamilton 1998; Carter 2007; Golebiowski and Liddicoat 2002); to academic literacy instruction (e.g., Roberge et al. 2009; Tribble and Wingate 2013) and

H. S. Sanchez (✉)
Department of Education, University of Bath, Bath, UK
e-mail: H.S.Sanchez@bath.ac.uk

K. Dikilitaş
Department of English Language Teaching, Bahçeşehir University, Istanbul, Turkey

© Springer Nature Switzerland AG 2019
T. Dobinson, K. Dunworth (eds.), *Literacy Unbound: Multiliterate,*
Multilingual, Multimodal, Multilingual Education 30,
https://doi.org/10.1007/978-3-030-01255-7_3

31

development (e.g., Lea and Street 1998, 2006). Within this body of work, however, limited attention has been given to the investigation of academic writing literacy development, particularly in relation to second-language students (Braine 2002) undertaking postgraduate research studies (Maher et al. 2008). The study reported here contributes to this tradition of research by examining the learning experiences of doctoral students for whom English is an additional language in terms of the ways in which these students developed academic writing literacy as they read, reflected on and responded to tutor written feedback.

Academic literacy development has been conceptualised in the recent literature as multidimensional, including more than the acquisition of a set of discrete skills or competences (Gilliver-Brown and Johnson 2009). It has been interpreted as a holistic process that may entail linguistic, cognitive, social and affective improvements (Kathpalia and Heah 2008) and, therefore, various forms of development such as increased linguistic and metacognitive knowledge, improvements in critical thinking and problem-solving skills, a higher sense of self-efficacy and confidence, and a deeper sense of personal and social identity. This is the interpretation of academic literacy that was adopted for this study. Evidence from the literature suggests, however, that the skills agenda still dominates approaches to academic literacy instruction and research. Recent empirical studies, for example, while grounded in an understanding of academic literacy as social practice and its development as multifaceted, have either aimed to investigate or emphasised in their findings the acquisition of specific academic writing skills. Therefore, it is not uncommon to read programme evaluation reports or research findings that document forms of academic literacy development in such skills as self-editing and reorganisation of academic texts (Romova and Andrew 2011); referencing, idea generation, planning, editing and revising (Rafik Galea et al. 2012); field-specific lexis, reframing, textual structure and organisation, and writing conclusions (Hoadley-Maidment 1997); and syntax, paraphrasing and structuring of ideas (Orsini-Jones 2009). This seems unsurprising given the arguably measurable and transferable nature of skills and their potential to provide visible manifestations of writing literacy that can be used to assess students' literacy deficits. This fits in well with the prevailing deficiency approaches to academic writing instruction adopted by many higher education institutions, which focus on the transmission of knowledge and the learning of discrete, transferable language skills (Badenhorst et al. 2015; Crème and Lea 1999).

Despite this emphasis on knowledge transmission and the transfer of skills, academic literacy development is mediated and profoundly shaped by student factors that are not always readily observable. Some of these have occasionally been documented in the literature and have been shown to relate to linguistic factors such as target language proficiency (Magyar et al. 2011) and individual literacy history (Barton 2007), pragmatic factors such as knowledge of L2 writing conventions (Cotterall 2011) and institutional academic writing expectations (Paltridge 2004), physical factors such as disability (Orsini-Jones 2009), and psychological factors such as fear of failure (Fernsten and Reda 2011) and lack of confidence (Hoadley-Maidment 1997). Notwithstanding their relevance to the learning process, these factors, especially internal ones, have not been systematically explored in the literature.

In line with current conceptualisations of academic literacy development and acknowledging the key role that students' internal factors play in the learning process, our study aimed to examine, adopting a holistic perspective, the forms of academic writing literacy that the participating research students developed and the internal factors that mediated this development. To this end, it addressed two main research questions:

- How do research students develop academic writing literacy as they respond to tutor written feedback?
- What aspects of their academic writing literacy do they develop and what internal factors influence such development?

2   Methodology

The context for the study was a 6-month course in a postgraduate research programme in English language teaching at a foundational (private) university in the northwest of Turkey. This course aimed to develop an understanding of theories of learning and their implications for initial and in-service teacher education. It was conducted through an exploratory, interactive and staged approach that involved students in ongoing theoretical and practice-based class discussions that informed the design and delivery of their individual research projects and the writing up of an assessed single-authored research paper. The students received tutor written and oral formative feedback on each section of their papers, such as literature review, methodology, findings and discussion. Two doctoral students taking this class (Melis and Pınar, pseudonyms) agreed to participate in this study (three other students had originally accepted to take part, but they either discontinued their participation or did not engage systematically with the introspective method described below). Both were female and Turkish, spoke Turkish as a first language and English as an additional language, and had an educational background in English language and literature. Further information is provided in the next section.

The study was exploratory-interpretive in nature (Grotjahn 1987), drawing on verbal commentaries and reflective writing for data collection (Borg 2006). The first method was a background interview conducted at the start of the course in order to establish a profile of the participants' educational and professional background, previous academic writing experience and conceptualisations of academic writing literacy. The second method was think-aloud protocols, an introspective oral elicitation instrument that was used to elicit and then examine the thoughts the students verbalised while they read, reflected on and responded to their course tutor's written feedback (Charters 2003). Both participants recorded three think-aloud protocols, each based on a different draft section of their paper and its corresponding written feedback from the tutor. Finally, the students wrote, after they had completed the course, a retrospective account that elicited their perceptions of improvements in their academic writing literacy and the factors, including tutor written feedback, that may have supported this development. Both participants chose to speak or write in English during the study and all verbal data were recorded and then transcribed for analysis. In addition, the use of multiple methods and participants over a period of 6 months facilitated methodological and data triangulation respectively, and thus enhanced the trustworthiness of the study.

Previous studies on academic literacy development have relied heavily on examining student written assignments and the accompanying tutor written feedback, occasionally complementing these with individual or focus group interviews with students and/or tutors. The present study, on the other hand, adopted a combination of retrospective and introspective methods, which offered a different perspective on student learning experiences and provided evidence of developmental processes and perceived impact. The use of think-aloud protocols, in particular, constitutes an innovation in academic literacy research, as it enabled us to access students' mental landscapes and collect evidence of a wider range of forms of development.

The data collected were analysed inductively in relation to each participant adopting content analysis procedures (Boyatzis 1998). Codes were first produced using key words, phrases and text chunks (codification). Themes were then identified (thematic analysis) and eventually grouped into categories (categorisation). The data were analysed by the two researchers independently and the emerging codes, themes and categories were then compared through a series of discussions. The study also followed the ethical guidelines published by the British Educational Research Association, which involved obtaining voluntary informed consent from all participants, explaining their right to withdraw from the project at any time, and protecting their anonymity and the confidentiality of the data.

3   Findings

The present study generated a database of 17,058 words across the two cases and three data collection instruments. This constituted a meaningful amount of data considering that the purpose of the study was to obtain depth rather than breadth of responses.

The presentation of the findings is organised by research student participant and, within each case, around themes and sub-themes that illustrate the aspects of academic writing literacy that the students developed as they read, reflected on and responded to their tutor's written feedback. Students' commentaries are provided to support the analysis, and the following conventions are used to locate these quotes within the data corpus: 'BI' for background interviews, 'TAP' for think-aloud protocols and 'RI' for round-up interviews.

3.1 Melis

Melis held bachelor's and master's degrees in English literature and had an interest in fiction writing both in English and Turkish. Her postgraduate coursework included process-based writing of literary papers, on which she received feedback from tutors mainly in relation to 'mistakes', 'integrating information' and 'interpreting [texts]' (BI). At a professional level, Melis had been involved in English language teaching for 7 years, a discipline that she had learned, she argued, 'while working as a teacher' and through short teacher training workshops (BI).

Influenced by her academic background in literature and personal interest in fiction writing, Melis perceived academic language as 'dull', which motivated her to use structures which looked more literary (BI):

> I kind of try to make it [my academic writing] look less dull and boring. I tend to start sentences with such expressions like 'after coming back to Turkey', 'having done that'. I don't know why but I do this a lot, and I'm not sure if it's ok in an academic context… I like inverted and shortened sentences; they look poetic to me, and artistic. (TAP4)

In addition, though Melis believed that she was 'good at writing' and liked 'to play with words' (BI), she experienced difficulty in writing academically, as she found the process of producing academic papers different from that involved in writing literary essays; in her words, 'right now I'm having difficulty because this time I'm not free as I used to be. I'm not writing literature; I'm not producing or interpreting [literary texts] anymore; now I'm analyzing and thinking' (BI). Reflecting on this range of cross-disciplinary issues thus supported the development of Melis's awareness of discipline-specific writing processes, genres and styles.

Receiving input from tutors in the form of written feedback also served, Melis felt, to induct her into the academic course she was studying: 'I should … get more [tutor] input. I'm like in the baby-face of some big thing which is PhD, which is a very big process and I'm a bit foreign to this field still' (BI). This academic socialisation, in turn, contributed to heightening her sense of professional identity and to raising an awareness of her own motivations:

> I always thought myself as an academician, as a person who reads and writes all the time and shares it with other people. I'm not actually doing it for the purpose of having a better job or for some other external instruments and I'm doing it for my own knowledge and learning forever. (BI)

In addition, this process-based approach to writing afforded opportunities for Melis to develop a number of life skills that constituted an inherent part of her academic writing literacy. For example, Melis perceived divergences in the quality of writing between her quotes from the literature and her own paraphrased sentences:

> There is a huge difference between the sentences I quoted and the sentences I wrote myself. When I look at these two sentence structures, I see that mine are not as academic as they are supposed to be, so this is really very difficult for me… So I'm really trying to understand what kind of words we can use in research papers. (TAP1)

Reflecting on this issue enabled Melis not only to become aware of her own improvement areas and, therefore, develop an ability to assess her academic writing needs, but also to adopt self-study strategies, which, while often motivated by tutor feedback, facilitated learning beyond the support provided by the tutor:

> The feedback that I have received led me to pay attention to my weaknesses and read other research like sources to improve my writing skills. As I read more, I noticed that researchers wrote in a formal way, and refrained from frequent direct quotations. While reading, I paid special attention to how others paraphrased and moreover combined several quotations in one sentence. (RI)

Melis' initiative of comparing her work with published materials also promoted the development of autonomy, noticing skills and criticality.

A further life and professional skill Melis at times displayed while responding to feedback was agency, as evidenced in the following comment she made during the last interview:

> When I receive written feedback, I do not usually correct my mistakes immediately. I rather visit and revisit them and review my writing in blocks. I mean I do not solely pay attention to the points that were given feedback on but also the whole piece of writing. (RI)

Melis addressed areas for improvement at her own pace ('not … immediately') and in her preferred way (e.g., 'in blocks'). She thus exercised agency by formulating her individual choice of actions that would support her in improving her academic writing.

The aspect that featured more strongly in Melis' data was, however, an increased understanding of specific academic writing skills. One of the most recurrent concerns this research student expressed involved writing introductions and conclusions to paragraphs, sections and papers. The challenge posed by introductions in particular was rooted in Melis' perceived inability to write something with more impact:

> Writing an introduction has always been a difficult job for me… The beginning sentences, the beginning paragraphs, the preliminary things are always challenging for me because I don't think that I can make a good start. (TAP1)

Similarly, Melis experienced difficulty in writing conclusions, as they involved summarising content without sounding repetitive: 'I'm not very fond of writing conclusions. I'm not good at summarizing things, and maybe my conclusions are very repetitive' (TAP1). As a result, she always postponed writing these parts: 'like the beginnings and introductions, I also postpone writing conclusions, I do them after some time' (TAP1). Evidence from think-aloud protocols shows, however, that Melis made gradual improvements as she responded to tutor written feedback. Initially, she became cognizant of the issue, but did not address it, as noted above. She then decided to make some changes, but displayed little confidence in them:

> I'm writing a conclusion for literature review although I'm not very happy about it because it's still short. At least I'm closing the literature review now, because I have a tendency to finish everything very abruptly while I'm writing. At least this time, I'm mentioning, rementioning my aim for doing this research. (TAP2)

Eventually Melis identified the specific issues in her introductions and conclusions, addressed them, and felt satisfied about the modifications made, as evidenced below:

> I am aware of the fact that I really have much trouble writing introduction part, and my first draft's introduction is very short. So I have to now expand this part and give the relevant information… Now I will explain the factors which led to the interest in theorizing language teacher identity… So I had to meticulously pick these factors and kind of paraphrase them. And I believe now the paragraph looks better. (TAP3)

Another area of difficulty, Melis argued, was quoting and paraphrasing. This included knowing when to quote or paraphrase ('I'm experiencing a similar problem which is whether I should give direct references, quotations, or paraphrase the sentences', TAP1) and how to quote ('sometimes I tend to … copy and paste very long paragraphs… I should learn how to use the quotation effectively, not copy everything from a quotation', TAP4). However, Melis' most serious concern was, she believed, producing writing which she perceived as academic and of quality:

> I have to rephrase what other sources say… In these sources there are so good sentences, and I really have trouble paraphrasing these beautiful sentences, because they don't look good anymore after I change them. This requires more academic skills, I think. (TAP4)

The reason behind Melis' tendency to use frequent and long quotes seemed to relate, therefore, to her low sense of self-efficacy when paraphrasing ('I finished the research with a quotation again… Why can't I use my own sentence after doing all this analysis, examination, reading, researching? ' TAP4), especially as she compared her writing with that in published papers, as illustrated above. While she responded to feedback, however, Melis felt that she had made improvements since she developed specific techniques for paraphrasing: 'I had difficulties in paraphrasing quotations and I tended to insert quotations directly. After feedback, I worked more on paraphrasing and especially studied which words could be used to make arguments such as argues, suggest, claim, etc.' (RI).

These self-efficacy issues and perceived difficulties in producing quality academic writing accounted, too, for the challenge she faced when synthesising the literature ('I still don't trust my own sentences. And I can't combine other people's thoughts in a nice-looking sentence; I'm not capable of doing that', TAP1). This was also connected with her ability, Melis thought, to reduce material ('I really had a lot of hesitations … [when] synthesizing the ideas because the topic is so wide, and to narrow it down, that was really difficult for me', TAP1), which she also experienced when she handled a large amount of qualitative data ('in the interviews they give you so much information that really writing those things concisely is very difficult' TAP4). Actually, being concise in general was, Melis argued, a challenge which she consistently faced when writing academic papers:

> I want to be very concise and I want to give a lot of things in a very simple but varied way. But I can't do this because it really requires a style, good knowledge and command of English. But as I look at my paper I see that I don't see this talent in me. I don't have it yet. (TAP1)

At the end of the course she appeared satisfied as she had 'learned more about ... avoiding redundancy, especially being more to the point' (RI).

In relation to her perception of the quality of her writing, Melis made reference to a wide range of specific language-related issues that she believed she had developed more awareness of and improved as she responded to tutor written feedback. For example, she reported coherence and cohesion issues, which she attributed to limitations in her English language proficiency:

> I don't see a very good connection between the paragraphs. I don't think that the topic sentences are very well connected, some of the paragraphs don't have a topic, they just start something very new abruptly ... . I don't see a flow ... This stems from many facts, the language, the background knowledge of mine. (TAP1)

Specifically, Melis often expressed concerns in her knowledge of cohesive devices ('whenever I'm trying to sequence my sentences, I don't know which words I have to use', TAP2) and their use ('now I'm using "besides", but I don't know if it really looks good or not', TAP2). Nevertheless, she sometimes addressed issues of connectedness by working on the organisation of information ('I had to relocate a sentence from ... the literature review ... Now I believe it makes sense, and it looks like more connected than before', TAP3).

Additionally, difficulties with grammar, lexis and register were extensively voiced by Melis as she reflected on and responded to the feedback she received. The most recurrent grammar issue concerned her use of tenses in general ('since they [the participants] mention flashbacks and also talk about the present, again I have a problem with the tenses', TAP4) or specifically when integrating in-text references:

> I'm still not very sure about which tense to use when I say 'argues', 'suggests', 'imply' ... I'm not very consistent in the use of tense. Should I use present tense or should I use past tense? When I use present tense, should I continue the quotation part with the present tense? In short I'm not sure about the consistency of tenses when I'm referencing to an author. (TAP1)

Lexical choice was problematic, Melis thought, particularly when she wanted either to avoid repetition ('sometimes I couldn't find alternative words ... Instead of "think" ... I said "she further explains", "he believes", "she asserts"', TAP4) or use more academic language ('Here I fell short of vocabulary; I wanted to use the word "abstain" ... instead of "avoid" ... to make my research look a little bit more sophisticated ... Sometimes I don't feel I know enough academic words', TAP4). Lexical use appeared to be influenced by a perceived limited knowledge of vocabulary, especially academic lexical items. This had an impact, in turn, on Melis' use of register, which was shaped not only by the said lexical knowledge restrictions but also by her perception of deixis and the level of formality that different person deictic terms convey: 'I noticed that I used "the researcher" instead of "I" ... I don't know why ... Maybe, to make it look more formal, I didn't want to mention myself and used the subject her or she, not I' (TAP4). Evidence of improvement in these areas can be noted in Melis' increased awareness of specific language-related issues and the informed changes made to her writing, as documented in this comment she made at the end of the course:

> I believe that I have improved my writing skills especially in terms of syntax, word choice, and punctuation. What I conceive in my mind is usually very different from what I write. Having received feedback, I have managed to make more appropriate sentences and thus expressed my thoughts in a more elaborate way. (RI)

Further individual academic writing skills that Melis developed while engaging with tutor written feedback included referencing and formatting. Referencing issues related to Melis' efforts to adhere to appropriate referencing conventions concerning the citation of page numbers ('Another problem I encountered is whether to put page numbers. Should I use them in journal references or book references? I noticed that I'm not aware of this … I'm just in case putting all the page numbers', TAP1), the use of quotation marks ('I have problem with the quotation marks; I always put them in the wrong place. So now I'm looking at Google to see how it is done in APA style and changing all the mistakes related to this', TAP2) and italics ('in the references part I have some confusion of knowing when to do italics or when not do them', TAP2), and the order when citing multiple sources ('I didn't know that I had to write them alphabetically. So I have learned it very recently', TAP1). Related to this are Melis' difficulties in adapting to a new formatting style:

> I'm not sure about the subtitles. Should I insert them? Should I write them with lower keys or with capitals? Should I put a period at the end? Should I write them in italics? … I feel I know APA style, but the fact that I'm never sure about what I'm doing definitely shows that I'm missing some points … The reason is that, during my undergraduate years before PhD, I always used … MLA style. So I'm not very good at the APA style. And to me, this style does not look good as good as the other style'. (TAP1)

Melis' familiarity with one formatting style (MLA) influenced her perception, learning and use of another style (APA).

3.2 Pınar

Pınar had bachelor's and master's degrees in English language and literature. Her academic background was, like Melis's, mostly literature-based, though she had also attended undergraduate classes in linguistics, such as academic writing, text analysis and English language teaching methodology. Her previous coursework experience included take-home reading assignments, class discussions and presentations and literary analysis papers. At postgraduate level she had learned to write, she argued, by practising and receiving tutor feedback and through self-discovery. Professionally, Pınar was a university English language teacher with 16 years of teaching experience. Her main responsibilities involved teaching 'reading, writing and speaking … at different levels', 'testing, [teacher] training, and material[s] development' (BI). She had an academic interest in 'teacher training, quality assurance systems, … learner autonomy, lifelong learning, learning to learn' (BI).

Pınar's previous writing experience and knowledge, she believed, had an impact on how she adapted to a new writing genre:

> The basic problem that I had at the beginning was that all too often my mind slipped into thinking the way I wrote my MA papers on literary criticism. My prior knowledge kept interfering with what I was actually doing. All through the writing process, this has been hard for me to overcome. I think it is really hard to unlearn a habit. So I have had to work hard to free my mind from what I thought was correct before. (RI)

The development of academic writing literacy thus entailed a process of cognitive dissonance that Pınar conceptualised as unlearning old habits and acquiring new ones. Though requiring hard work, this process appeared to have enabled her to develop an awareness of discipline-specific writing processes and genres.

On the other hand, Pınar encountered difficulty in applying previous knowledge derived from her professional experience teaching writing:

> Even though I had been teaching a writing class at prep school, I found it ever so hard applying them myself because I felt the content I was trying to write about was lofty, containing some serious stuff and so it was pushing my limits. I think the content difficulty … affects the way you use your skills at this point. Or maybe the prejudice that I had in mind about the difficulty of writing an academic text may also have affected how efficiently I used my skills. (RI)

The process of transferring her professional skills to support the development of academic writing literacy was, therefore, not straightforward and was hindered by Pınar's perception of the complexity of both the subject matter and academic writing. Reflecting on these experiences while engaging with tutor feedback promoted this student's self-awareness of prior cognitions brought to the course and an increased understanding of academic writing development as a constructivist learning process involving the interaction between prior cognitions on the one hand and new material and experience on the other.

Not surprisingly, given her relevant and extensive academic and professional experience and her reflective disposition, the aspects which featured more strongly in Pınar's data concerned the acquisition of life skills. For example, Pınar developed autonomy as she did self-initiated, independent reading ('I did a lot of reading at home. This was very helpful to gain general understanding about the style, conventions and steps of academic writing', RI) and analysed written samples ('seeing examples of good and bad academic writing in comparison also helps me gain understanding over what and how I am supposed to write', BI). Pınar believed that 'these examples should not be seen as the absolute guide by students because then we would be shifted away from originality', BI). This illustrates her sense of criticality, which was further developed as she received tutor feedback: 'Every time I received feedback, I was prompted to question the things I wrote. So that taught me to be critical about what I was doing' (RI). Pınar's criticality was additionally evidenced in her response to her tutor's suggestions, which indicates a sense of this student's ownership of the learning writing process and, therefore, of agency. For instance, her comments in think-aloud protocols consistently show that she decided 'whether' to make the suggested change ('I thought only this part should be included, but I think you want me to give the basic concepts involved in socio-constructivist approaches. Ok, I'll think about it', TAP1) and 'when' to do so ('I think I need to make some serious changes. But I want to make the changes after I finish all the coding process then because it affects the content a lot', TAP2). Furthermore, in line with her previous educational experiences, class discussions, Pınar argued, supported the development of her academic writing skills ('A class discussion over such examples might be very effective, and can help me develop my writing skills', BI; 'The in-class discussion … was also very useful. It clarified several ambiguities … related to concepts and terms', RI), which helped reinforce her belief in collaborative learning. Finally, Pınar thought that revising her work based on tutor feedback had made her aware of her own strengths and improvement areas as well as her academic writing needs ('I think I have started to question myself more… I have been able to discover several strengths of mine and become aware of my weaknesses as well', RI).

In addition, reading, reflecting on and responding to tutor written feedback had facilitated, Pınar believed, several forms of personal development, particularly regarding her 'personality traits and social skills' (RI). To Pınar, this process had aroused a number of emotions and enabled her to develop an ability to regulate her emotions:

> At first, I was a bit stressed and had lack of confidence about the data collection and analysis phases and how to report the data in written form, because I didn't know truly how they are done. I was highly motivated to do something new [but] writing a research paper looked such a big challenge; it was like a ladder to climb up or, better to say, a jungle gym, … To be honest I wouldn't dare to take the initial step myself if I hadn't been encouraged at the beginning, thinking I am not ready for it academically. (RI)

Engaging with oral and written tutor feedback had also increased her self-efficacy ('I have become more confident about my skills and knowledge', RI) and nurtured a sense of belonging to a community of practice ('it helped me see that I could indeed join in the academic world, that at least I can have a small spot on which I can stand on in this field, and that it is achievable', RI).

Additionally, Pınar displayed, though perhaps not as markedly as Melis, an increased understanding of specific academic writing skills. For example, she expressed concerns about writing an abstract and an introduction, in terms of making sense of both their purpose ('I was not sure about what an abstract stands for, what an intro stands for. I was confused a bit', TAP1) and the process of producing them:

> You said that this [abstract/introduction] can be written towards the final stage, which I actually thought that I should write at the beginning just to frame my study, … like starting a journey, so a journey starts at a point, and this introduction is a starting point. Probably I'm wrong… Please correct me if I am. (TAP1)

Pınar thus developed not only knowledge of the content and purpose of specific paper sections but also an awareness of individual writing processes and styles. Similarly, she addressed issues relating to the length ('you said … context is a bit too long… How should I decide on the length of this? For example, they say introduction should be 10 percent of the whole text… What is the length for context? TAP3) and level of specificity of sections ('I just wrote the method in two sentences because I really didn't know how I could handle this… So, I'm going to explain … these things in detail', TAP3).

Another recurrent issue that Pınar examined concerned citing. In the early stages of writing a paper she seemed to prioritise the development and flow of ideas over referencing, citing sparingly only when she felt confident:

> I need a reference. Ok, I will provide a reference. I was just trying to find my way through text. So, I did not bother for citation over here. I've just used the ones that I'm a hundred percent sure where I've got them from. But the other ones were a bunch of ideas that I've collected through reading. I just sit down and summarize what I have in my mind, thinking later on I can just put parenthesis and connect them. I don't know if this is the right procedure to follow. (TAP1)

Reflecting on citation issues then served not only to raise awareness of individual writing processes and of the value of providing supportive evidence ('I need to support it with more references … so that I can strengthen what I say and it looks more plausible, more academic', TAP4), but also, with the support of tutor feedback, to promote the development of academic integrity ('the development of ethical perspectives … necessitates cultivation, guidance and support… Reading about citation rules may not always be enough; … you may need to hear the know-how from an expert', RI).

Finally, Pınar explored a few language-related issues while engaging with tutor-written feedback. One of them concerned the acquisition of specific terminology, as illustrated in this comment:

> 'Do you mean semi-structured interviews?' Yes, actually, I was not sure about the word 'reflective interview', because we were saying that we should ask open-ended questions which allows them to reflect on the topic, so I think I made it up … Ok, that's the wording that I actually was looking for, thank you. (TAP1)

Worth noting here is the student's 'coinage' of the term 'reflective interview'. This might suggest that the process of learning specialised language might involve not only the input from external sources, such as the tutor or materials, but also some self-initiated, strategic behaviour on the part of the learner to compensate for the perceived lack of technical language. A further language aspect that Pınar examined was cohesion, particularly to establish a connection between paragraphs:

> I don't know if this [using rhetorical questions as bridges between paragraphs] stands against the rules of writing a research. If that is so, why? … Can we use rhetorical questions just as a hook to arouse curiosity? Is it not possible? (TAP1)

This response provides evidence of Pınar's agency, criticality and efforts to understand how her own writing style, heavily influenced by her previous academic background in literature, as noted above, fit in with the new writing genre which she was learning.

4   Discussion

The present study generated, through verbal commentaries and reflective writing, substantive qualitative data not only about academic literacy development but also about the factors that mediated this development.

The forms of perceived academic writing literacy development identified in this study provide evidence of the multifaceted nature of this process. The participating students noted, for example, knowledge enhancement of specific academic writing skills, including writing paper sections (increased understanding of the content, purpose, length and specificity level of paper sections), quoting, paraphrasing, citing, referencing, formatting, synthesising, conciseness, coherence, cohesion, grammar, lexis and register. These forms of development have been widely documented in the literature (e.g., Hoadley-Maidment 1997; Orsini-Jones 2009; Rafik Galea et al. 2012). In addition, the participants in this study perceived improvements in a wider range of features that can be associated with academic literacy. These were linguistic (awareness of discipline-specific writing processes and genres, awareness of individual writing processes and styles), cognitive (self-awareness of prior cognitions, ability to regulate emotions, self-efficacy, autonomy, noticing skills, criticality, agency, awareness of own strengths and improvement areas, ownership of the learning writing process, ability to assess own academic writing needs), social (a sense of professional identity, understanding of academic writing development as a constructivist learning process, sense of belonging to a community of practice, collaborative learning, academic integrity) and affective (awareness of their own motivations to pursue an academic career; see learning dimensions in Kathpalia and Heah 2008). These findings thus support current conceptualisations of academic literacy development as holistic (Gilliver-Brown and Johnson 2009; Henderson and Hirst 2007; Leki 2000).

In addition to being holistic, the findings of this study suggest that academic writing literacy development is a complex, interconnected, expansile and idiosyncratic process. It is complex not only because of its multifaceted nature, but also because of the intricate way in which these aspects are developed, particularly given the variety of facilitating and inhibiting factors that often interact to motivate individual or combined forms of development. For example, Melis' personal interest in fiction writing and her literature-based background influenced both her perception of academic language as dull and her inappropriate cross-disciplinary transfer of language structures. Reflecting on these issues while responding to tutor written feedback enabled her to develop an awareness of discipline-specific writing processes and genres. Similarly, Pınar's perception of the subject matter and academic writing as complex accounted for her perceived difficulty to transfer relevant professional skills. Reflecting on this helped her increase her self-awareness of prior cognitions and her understanding of academic writing development as a constructivist learning process.

Moreover, the process of acquiring academic writing literacy is interconnected in the sense that forms of improvement may be linked to others. For example, Pınar's increased knowledge of the content, purpose, length and specificity level of paper sections was related to her heightened awareness of her individual writing processes and writing styles. This is closely related to the expansile nature, or ripple effect, of academic writing literacy development. Thus, the development of one aspect seemed to encourage the acquisition of others. As noted above, for instance, Melis' awareness of her own areas for improvement, which was heightened while comparing the quality of her writing with that of published materials, appeared in turn to support her development of noticing skills, criticality, the ability to assess her own writing needs, and learning autonomy. This indicates, in turn, that academic writing literacy development is idiosyncratic. Within each individual student, forms of development may vary in kind and degree and interact in unique ways depending on the factors, both internal and external, that motivate them.

Another theme drawn from the data concerns the student factors that facilitated or hindered the process of developing academic writing literacy. Although external influences, such as tutor feedback, might influence the improvements in academic writing that students make, it is students' internal factors, we believe, that will play a major role in defining what aspects they develop and how. For example, Melis' perceived limitations in her own English language knowledge and low sense of self-efficacy may account for the emphasis she placed on the development of specific language-related issues. Pınar, on the other hand, had a high sense of self-efficacy in her English language and writing skills, possibly partly as a result of her academic and professional background. Her concerns and developed areas, unlike Melis', focused more on personal and life skills rather than on specific academic writing skills. Overall, the mediators, usually overlapping, that influenced Melis' and Pınar's development of academic writing literacy included: individual literacy history, discipline-specific background, relevant professional experience, perception of academic language, conceptualisation of academic writing literacy, perception of the academic writing process, target language proficiency, self-efficacy, knowledge of academic language, familiarity with academic writing conventions, perception of different genres, perception of the subject matter, beliefs about learning, learning styles, perception of self, motivation, autonomy, agency, criticality, emotions, personality and perceived relevance of tutor written feedback support. These findings reinforce and, most importantly, add to the mediating factors documented in previous studies (e.g., Barton 2007; Cotterall 2011; Fernsten and Reda 2011; Hoadley-Maidment 1997; Magyar et al. 2011; Orsini-Jones 2009).

5 Conclusion

Our analysis of how research students develop academic writing literacy as they respond to tutor written feedback generated evidence of both a wide variety of forms of perceived development as well as–and we feel this is a particularly valuable outcome here–the internal student factors mediating this process. The study shows that academic writing literacy development is a holistic, complex, interconnected, expansile and idiosyncratic process which is unique to students depending on what they bring to the academic writing learning experience and how this has an impact on their academic writing development. This study thus contributes to our understanding of academic writing literacy development by providing insights not only into its multifaceted and intricate nature but also into its unobservable dimension.

It can therefore be argued that there is a need for academic literacy programmes and research to move beyond skills-based deficiency approaches to academic writing and rather align with current conceptualisations of the process which highlight notions of multidimensionality, complexity, interconnectedness, expansion and idiosyncrasy. This will facilitate the creation of appropriate pedagogies and learning environments that promote meaningful and sustainable forms of academic writing literacy development.

References

Badenhorst, C., Moloney, C., Rosales, J., Dyer, J., & Ru, L. (2015). Beyond deficit: Graduate student research-writing pedagogies. *Teaching in Higher Education, 20*(1), 1–11.

Barton, D. (2007). *Literacy: An introduction to the ecology of written language* (2nd ed.). Oxford: Wiley-Blackwell.

Barton, D., & Hamilton, M. (1998). *Local literacies*. London: Routledge.

Borg, S. (2006). *Teacher cognition and language education: Research and practice*. London: Continuum.

Boyatzis, R. E. (1998). *Transforming qualitative information: Thematic analysis and code development*. Thousand Oaks: Sage.

Braine, G. (2002). Academic literacy and the non-native speaker graduate student. *Journal of English for Academic Purposes, 1*(1), 59–68.

Carter, M. (2007). Ways of knowing, doing, and writing in the disciplines. *College Composition and Communication, 58*(3), 385–418.

Charters, E. (2003). The use of think-aloud methods in qualitative research an introduction to think-aloud methods. *Brock Education Journal, 12*(2), 68–82.

Cotterall, S. (2011). Doctoral students writing: Where's the pedagogy? *Teaching in Higher Education, 16*(4), 413–425.

Crème, P., & Lea, M. R. (1999). Student writing: Challenging the myths. In P. Thompson (Ed.), *Academic writing development in higher education: Perspectives, explorations and approaches* (pp. 1–13). Reading: Centre for Applied Language Studies/University of Reading.

Fernsten, L. A., & Reda, M. (2011). Helping students meet the challenges of academic writing. *Teaching in Higher Education, 16*(2), 171–182.

Gilliver-Brown, K. E., & Johnson, E. M. (2009). *Academic literacy development: A multiple perspectives approach to blended learning*. Same places, different spaces. Proceedings ascilite Auckland 2009.

Golebiowski, Z., & Liddicoat, A. (2002). The interaction of discipline and culture in academic writing, literacy in academic contexts. *Australian Review of Applied Linguistics, 25*(2), 59–72.

Grotjahn, R. (1987). On the methodological basis of introspective methods. In C. Faerch & G. Kasper (Eds.), *Introspection in second language research* (pp. 54–81). Clevedon: Multilingual Matters.

Henderson, R., & Hirst, E. (2007). Reframing academic literacy: Re-examining a short course for "disadvantaged" tertiary students. *English Teaching Practice and Critique, 6*(2), 25–38.

Hoadley-Maidment, E. (1997). From 'story' to argument: The acquisition of academic writing skills in an open-learning context. *Language and Education, 11*(1), 55–68.

Kathpalia, S., & Heah, C. (2008). Reflective writing: Insights into what lies beneath. *RELC Journal, 39*(3), 300–317.

Lea, M. R., & Street, B. V. (1998). Student writing in higher education: An academic literacies approach. *Studies in Higher Education, 23*(2), 157–172.

Lea, M. R., & Street, B. V. (2006). The "Academic Literacies" model: Theory and applications. *Theory Into Practice, 45*(4), 368–377.

Leki, I. (2000). Writing, literacy, and applied linguistics. *Annual Review of Applied Linguistics, 20*, 99–115.

Magyar, A., McAvoy, D., & Forstner, K. (2011). 'If only we knew what they wanted': Bridging the gap between student uncertainty and lecturers' expectations. *Journal of Learning Development in Higher Education, 3*, 1–18.

Maher, D., Seaton, L., McMullen, C., Fitzgerald, T., Otsuji, E., & Lee, A. (2008). 'Becoming and being writers': The experiences of doctoral students in writing groups. *Studies in Continuing Education, 30*(3), 263–275.

Orsini-Jones, M. (2009). Measures for inclusion: Coping with the challenge of visual impairment and blindness in university undergraduate level language learning. *Support for Learning, 24*(1), 27–34.

Paltridge, B. (2004). Academic writing. *Language Teaching, 37*(2), 87–105.

Rafik Galea, S., Arumugam, N., & De Mello, G. (2012). Enhancing ESL students' academic writing skills through the term-paper. *Pertanika Journal of Social Sciences & Humanities, 20*(4), 1229–1248.

Roberge, M., Siegal, M., & Harklau, L. (2009). *Generation 1.5 in college composition – Teaching academic writing to U.S.-Educated learners of ESL*. Abingdon: Routledge.

Romova, Z., & Andrew, M. (2011). Teaching and assessing academic writing via the portfolio: Benefits for learners of English as an additional language. *Assessing Writing, 16*, 111–122.

Tribble, C., & Wingate, U. (2013). From text to corpus – A genre-based approach to academic literacy instruction. *System, 41*, 307–321.

Becoming a Member of a Community of Practice: Postgraduate Researcher Literacy Development in a UK University

Katie Dunworth and Faisal Al Saidi

Abstract This chapter draws on the concept of communities of practice as described by Wenger (Communities of practice: learning, meaning, and identity. Cambridge University Press, Cambridge, 1998; Communities of practice and social learning systems: the career of a concept. In: C Blackmore (ed) Social learning systems and communities of practice. The Open University, Milton Keynes, pp 179–198, 2010) to examine a doctoral researcher's written literacy development through interaction with his supervisor. The term community of practice is used here to describe a group of individuals who are mutually engaged in a joint enterprise who share a repertoire of knowledge, activities and discourses. Membership comes into being through participation, interaction, and negotiated meaning: a situated process of identity construction (Ewing Discourse and the construction of identity in a community of learning and a community of practice. In: T Stehlik, P Carden (eds), Beyond communities of practice: theory as experience. Post Pressed, Upper Mount Gravatt, pp 149–170, 2005). Two key elements of a community of practice are participation and reification; these two elements are explored in detail in this chapter through the concept of feedback, where feedback is understood not as a form of output produced by a provider and transmitted to a receiver but as a social, situated process which is not complete until an initial input is engaged with and transformed (Dunworth, K., & Sanchez, H. H. (2016). Perceptions of quality in staff-student written feedback in higher education: A case study. *Teaching in Higher Education, 21*(5), 576–589). The chapter explores this process of contestation and negotiation which is part of the development of a member-as-writer within a community of practice.

Keywords Community of practice · Postgraduate researcher · Higher education · Literacy development · Writing a thesis · Postgraduate supervision

K. Dunworth (✉) · F. Al Saidi
Department of Education, University of Bath, Bath, UK
e-mail: c.m.dunworth@bath.ac.uk; F.S.A.Al.Saidi@bath.ac.uk

© Springer Nature Switzerland AG 2019
T. Dobinson, K. Dunworth (eds.), *Literacy Unbound: Multiliterate, Multilingual, Multimodal*, Multilingual Education 30,
https://doi.org/10.1007/978-3-030-01255-7_4

1 Introduction

Over the last two decades, there has been a growing international body of research and scholarship in the field of doctoral study. However, much of this work, as Bastalich (2017) and Petersen (2007) point out, has been conducted from the perspective, ubiquitous in higher education today and prioritised by governments, of efficiency and effectiveness, as measured, for example, by doctoral completions or student withdrawals. There has been rather less research into the experience of supervision, and very little that includes the shared experience of both supervisor and student, which is the topic of this chapter. Indeed, some of the more recent literature consciously distances this relationship by acknowledging the changing nature of doctoral education, in particular pointing out that 'contemporary candidates not only interact with a diverse range of individuals from within and beyond the academy, but also engage in creative mixes of education, training, research, work and career development' (Cumming 2010, p. 26). Nevertheless, student-supervisor interaction still lies at the heart of doctoral programmes within the disciplinary field of education at the institution where the study described in this chapter took place, and it is regarding this that the chapter seeks to add to our understanding and knowledge. The framework from which the experience was interpreted is that of the community of practice; this is described in more detail below.

2 Communities of Practice

The concept of a community of practice is one that has for some time been in wide use within the field of education, both as a means of portraying the construction and practices of groups of professionals within academic organisations and as a way of explaining the teaching and learning that takes place between teachers and students. While over time the term itself has remained constant, interpretations of how it is theorised or actualised have diverged, resulting in sometimes incommensurable perspectives on how a community of practice may be formed, maintained and transformed (Cox 2005). In this chapter, 'community of practice' is used specifically to describe a group of people who are brought together through a common enterprise: the undertaking of institutionally-recognised academic research that is intended to move forward society's knowledge and understandings within a particular discipline – in this case that of applied linguistics. These individuals are bound together by 'shared values, expertise and standards' (Kogan 2000, p. 210) within the discipline. The community of practice conceptualised in this chapter is therefore seen as a broad grouping functioning at a trans-institutional level rather than as, for example, a specific collection of people mutually engaged in a particular collection of tasks that link them to the work of their department or organisation. It is important to clarify that it is a macro understanding of the term that will be used within this chapter because the use of the term to capture all aspects of any specific context for analysis is bound to reveal lacunae within the model.

Academics conducting teaching and research within any given discipline have, alternatively, been described as belonging to 'knowledge-building communities' (Hoadley 2012) since their primary purpose is knowledge generation and education, but their activities are nevertheless governed by particular understandings of that which constitutes relevant knowledge, the ways in which their work is undertaken, and the forms of discourse that are appropriate for expressing their shared enterprise. This repertoire, which is dynamic and interactive (Annala and Mäkinen 2016), enables mutual recognition of fellow members at a global level, and supports the use of the term, preferred for this chapter, 'community of practice'.

Within communities, doctoral students potentially have a unique position as members, depending on a range of contextual factors specific to a particular individual's circumstances. For example, doctoral students may be teacher-researchers themselves, and if they have a particular expertise might even engage in a certain amount of supervision of other doctoral students. They may come to doctoral study after many years of practice within a particular field of activity and bring to their projects high levels of existing expertise; or they may undertake their doctoral research immediately after completing an undergraduate degree, prior to undertaking any professional experience. At the commencement of their doctoral degree the status of their membership within a community of practice is therefore contingent on their previous participation, interaction with members and the way in which their identity is constructed (Ewing 2005). As Wenger has argued: 'participation in social systems is not a context or an abstraction, but the constitutive texture of an experience of the self' (Wenger 2010, p. 186).

As a dynamic entity, an academic community of practice is in a constant state of flux as participants engage in a process of contestation and appropriation over time. For the neophyte doctoral student who is not already an 'insider' within the academy, involvement in research activity and interaction with faculty staff, supervisors and fellow students represents 'legitimate peripheral participation' in that community of practice (Lave and Wenger 1991) and a process of identity construction. Through this, doctoral students not only learn to adopt the practices and discourses of the community, but also have the capacity to contribute to and change them: 'the legitimate peripheral participation of newcomers thus includes both their orientation to the community, and the recognition and inclusion of their potential contribution to the field' (Daniel et al. 2013, p. 161). The importance of the legitimate peripheral participant is also emphasised by Lunenberg et al. (2010), who argue that it can be an important feature that 'novices and experienced researchers work together in one community...[as this leads to] stimulating forms of exchange' (p. 1282).

Although understandings of the nature of a community of practice have splintered over the years (Ryan 2015), there are three key associated dimensions, originally identified by Wenger (1998), which have endured: *mutual engagement* of its members in a *joint enterprise*, drawing on a *shared repertoire* or discourse. These dimensions help illustrate the distinction which can be made between the doctoral student, even if the latter is a member of the academy, and the supervisor: while the difference between them may be smaller or greater on a case by case basis in terms of their 'acquired knowledge and capacity to handle it' (Kogan 2000, p. 210), and while they are mutually engaged in the joint enterprise of research within the discipline, there is at the same time a clear distinction in terms of their roles and obligations to each other within the broader educational context. In this study, therefore, the supervisor was considered to be an expert or 'full' member of the community of practice, while the doctoral student was, at least initially, a legitimate peripheral participant.

The means by which members communicate and the artefacts they produce in doing so are inextricably embedded within the community of practice model. This chapter focuses in particular on this dimension, the shared repertoire, as embodied within the production of the doctoral thesis, an artefact unique to doctoral study. Literacy development, in this chapter, is understood as the doctoral scholar's progress towards an understanding of this shared repertoire as experienced through undertaking the completion of the doctoral thesis, a process of situated learning, which is the theoretical perspective that underpins the community of practice model. From the situated learning perspective, learning is a social activity that takes place in authentic contexts within and through the social medium. It is achieved through engagement and acculturation, which result in the gradual development of expertise in terms of knowledge, skills, capacities and attributes, leading to the formation of an ongoing professional identity (Lave and Wenger 1991). Above all, it is context driven. While meaning making is undertaken by individuals, 'one's individual perspectives and understandings are shaped not only by participation, but also by reification, the process by which a person gives form to her [sic] experience' (Priest et al. 2016, p. 362), as embodied in this chapter by the production of a doctoral thesis. This is one key means by which the legitimate peripheral participant moves towards full membership.

3 The Project

As research that can broadly be classified as self-study, the project reported here is situated within a long tradition of practitioner inquiry that includes action research (McNiff and Whitehead 2010) and reflective practitioner studies (Lunenberg et al. 2010). Self-study has gained a status as an accepted genre particularly in educational settings, although this has expanded in recent times to include a range of other professional contexts. Associated research methods tend to draw primarily on qualitative approaches that foreground interpretation and the making of meaning, while 'generally transform[ing] those methods by taking them into a new context and using them in ways that often depart from the traditional' (Tidwell et al. 2009, p. xiii). For example, methods may be derived in self-study research from the context rather than from an initial specific research question, and practices that are the subject of the study may be changed as a consequence of initial data analysis conducted while the study is under way.

As many commentators have pointed out, a central characteristic of self-study research that distinguishes it from most other kinds of research on practice is the emphasis on the 'I', a feature that also appears in a few other qualitative approaches such as auto-ethnography. The eponymous self in self-study uses his or her own problematised experience as the source of data with a view to 'reframing and reconceptualizing' his or her role (Samaras and Freese 2009, p. 4). This inwardly-directed focus has led to criticism of the approach as vulnerable to narcissism and self-delusion, but, on the other hand, it has been suggested that concerns about the self are a distraction (Pinnegar and Hamilton 2009). This is because the self of this kind of research may indeed be the researcher but is not the sole or central object of study: 'it is not the self but the *self and the other in practice* that is of most interest' (Pinnegar and Hamilton 2009, p. 12, italics in the original). Indeed, as these scholars go on to argue, the ethical obligation to produce research that is trustworthy and credible may even be strengthened in such studies, given that this type of research is often conducted for a dual purpose – both making an original contribution to the public body of knowledge and also improving one's own practice. Trustworthiness in self-study projects, as for other qualitative research, involves a rigorous research approach, and elaboration and transparency in reporting that makes the study accessible to others for critical review and evaluation. Ultimately, therefore, assessment of trustworthiness of a self-study project is in the hands of the report's readers (Craig 2009).

For our study, as described above, literacy development was conceived as a process of becoming an expert member of a community of practice, specifically in gaining access to the community's 'shared repertoire'. The project took the form of a self-study investigation of the experiences of one supervisor/PhD student dyad, and focused particularly on the production of the main research outputs associated with doctoral study: the PhD thesis and other examined material associated with obtaining a PhD. Particularly important, as part of this area of focus, was the role of feedback, which is understood here not as a form of output produced by a provider and transmitted to a receiver but as a social, situated process which is not complete until an initial input is engaged with and transformed (Dunworth and Sanchez 2016). The feedback process is one of the primary ways in which supervisors and students interact, and, when that interaction is in written form, a record is created that documents the process in action. The primary source of data for the study was therefore the written output of both student (Faisal) and supervisor (Katie), which had been produced and retained on file over a period of 30 months. Documents included:

- A series of drafts of thesis chapters which incorporated Katie's written feedback input
- Summaries of supervision meeting outcomes produced by Faisal
- Meeting agendas produced by Faisal
- Reports produced by Faisal at the interim examination stage.

At the time the documents were produced, we had no plans to conduct a research study. This means that the data were 'authentic' in the sense that there was no possibility that concern over publication and therefore public exposure would cause the content to be sanitised or diluted even at a subconscious level. These data were augmented by written reflections produced by each of us separately, created after the decision to conduct the study had been taken. These documents served to clarify, enrich and triangulate the documentary data and so were classified as an additional data set, but they also helped contribute to the initial process of data analysis, given their retrospective and introspective nature.

The data were analysed through thematic analysis, data-driven within the over-arching community of practice framework and the concomitant understanding of literacy that informs this chapter. In essence, the process that was undertaken can be described as a search for patterns of meaning that involved initial generation of codes, which were then collated into potential themes that underwent a process of refinement and review until the eventual named themes were identified (Braun and Clarke 2006).

Identifying the study as one which would examine the process of 'becoming' a member of the community of practice as literacy development required certain initial understandings of the nature of participation and movement within it, particularly in terms of how we conceptualised roles, relationships and actions. As has already been explained, there was a clear initial understanding of the distinction between the positioning of Katie as 'full' member of the community of practice, and Faisal as legitimate peripheral member. In addition to this basic categorisation, however, there were other considerations to take into account where the project would need careful management. In particular, there were two associated issues that are implicit in any PhD supervisory relationship but which do not usually require explicit examination by the individuals involved unless the relationship itself is under scrutiny: contestation and power. With regard to the first, Kogan (2000, p. 210) has drawn attention to the 'danger of cosy ascriptions of community that eschew differentiation' and the tendency to connote community with consensus. This is an unfortunate side-effect of the use of that particular word, and one that Wenger (2010) is at pains to reject. Contestation, argument, disagreement or rejection are prerequisites to change in human activity, and can be seen as part of a process of 'critical transformative dialogue' (Daniel et al. 2013) that moves practice forward. Within academic discourse, however, disagreement can be cushioned through the use of a range of commonly-recognised discourse tools such as hedging or the use of questions, thereby minimising the affective impact that would result from direct confrontation. Yet a project that demanded honest reflection and commentary involved not only making the implicit explicit, but also could potentially involve difficult revelations that could threaten the equilibrium of the ongoing supervisory relationship.

With regard to the question of power, the community of practice model has often been criticised for failing to take into account power differentials within a workplace or community space (Hodkinson and Hodkinson 2004; Smit 2010), both in relation to positional authority and also from within the community where a newcomer's attempts at transformation may be resisted by the vested interests of those who are already participants and who might therefore deny the newcomer full participation (Handley et al. 2006). The expression of this power is starkly evident in the formal process by which a PhD student gains full participation through the conferring of a doctoral degree, obtained following examination of an individual's thesis by acknowledged experts in the field of study. However, the existence of a power differential between full participants and legitimate peripheral participants is not limited to these two groups. There are other external manifestations of relations of power, such as the culture of the university, institutional policies and regulatory regimes and government control. In this study, these were viewed as the background context within which the community of practice was situated, and so played only an indirect, albeit foundational, role in the analysis. The focus for this chapter is, rather, on another perspective of power: the legitimation of the academic researcher who 'comes into being by being appropriated by, and by appropriating, available enactments and desires that are recognisable as "academic"' (Petersen 2007, p. 478) within the particular community of practice.

Moreover, every research activity undertaken by a full member of the community of practice within academia involves the implementation of power and control by one's peers, for example with regard to reviewing peers' research output for publication, awarding of research funds, selecting research team associates, granting a professorial chair or other academic promotion, or selecting keynote speakers for a conference. This list is just a small sample of activities that involve primary decision-making that can impact on the career and professional standing of an individual in a substantial way, and there are many other, more or less indirect, ways in which power and influence are exerted from within an academic community of practice. An individual may therefore be simultaneously the evaluator and the evaluated at any given point in his or her career. This peer activity of management of the other is a core component of the academic enterprise, and, it could be argued, it is this process of mutual evaluation that helps maintain the boundaries of a context-specific, disciplinary, methodological and discourse-specific community of practice. Thus, developing an understanding of how to gain the acceptance of full members, and how to evaluate the work of others in a way considered to be appropriate, is an essential process for those who intend to participate in the joint enterprise of this particular community of practice.

When it comes to the ultimate decision about whether or not a student is able to obtain that key marker of community membership, the award of a doctoral degree, the supervisor has little influence other than involvement in the selection of examiners. Indeed, the supervisor's own professional reputation is to some extent also bound up with the outcome, since a very weak thesis, or a student's failure to obtain his or her doctorate, inevitably raises questions about the quality of supervision experienced by the student. Thus, the supervisor's own standing is linked to the success or otherwise of his or her student. While it cannot be denied that the imposition of subordination is one facet of the manifestation of power, it can therefore be seen that, when considering the student-supervisor relationship, conceptions of power need to be more complex and nuanced than its association with external suppression and control would allow.

Nevertheless, these two issues of contestation and power had to be taken into consideration if the study was to yield any useful insights, and were addressed in two ways. First, ethics approval to conduct the study was obtained through the university's standard approval procedures. This ensured that others had the opportunity to scrutinise the proposed project, ensure that it met with national and institutional ethical standards and confirm that any necessary protections were in place. In addition, as part of the ethics approval process, the researchers proposed that a 'critical friend' should be appointed, who would be able to provide impartial advice in the event of any difficulty arising. Most importantly, though, the project would not have taken place if there had not been a tacit acknowledgement from the beginning that each participant respected and trusted the other. Trust, in this case, related to certain shared but initially implicit understandings: that any data generated would avoid blame or personal censure; that the data obtained through reflection and analysis should be dislocated from personal feelings; and that the project had the goal of genuine discovery that would go beyond the individual concerns or sensitivities of the participants themselves.

4   Project Findings

It is important to emphasise in presenting the findings that, within the theory of situated learning that governed this study, it is both participation and reification that contribute to the progress of a legitimate peripheral member to full membership of a community of practice. Thus, it is not possible to divorce knowledge from its expression; language is not a conduit for ideas but instantiates the creation of meaning and the production of knowledge. Writing about research is as much a social practice as the conduct of research, and is just as constrained by local and discipline-based conditions (Kamler and Thomson 2006). In relation to the doctoral thesis, the study drew on an understanding of genre as a way 'of coordinating joint activity and regulating thought' (Russell et al. 2009, p. 408). Thus, the production of a thesis involves more than a set of writing skills; it is intricately involved in the research activity that is doctoral study and the thesis is an example of genres as 'recurring patterns of discursive action that arise in human collectives… [which] accomplish the goals of these collectives and allow participants to act together by tacitly inscribing expectations, proscriptions, values, and norms for who can write what, when, how, and with what impact' (Starke-Meyerring et al. 2014, p. A14).

In this section, the findings are reported in the third person even though we, the authors, were the participants. This is because some elements within this chapter may refer to one or other of us while we are joint authors of the chapter. Use of the third person avoids any confusion about which of us was the subject of the specific commentary provided in the analysis which follows.

Given that the study concerned a developmental process over a period of more than 2 years, it was unsurprising that the analysis involved progressive and fluctuating points of emphasis, with certain themes strongly apparent in the data obtained during particular temporal phases, which then lost their vigour or vanished entirely as other issues were identified in the data from subsequent phases. The changes in focus over time were not uniform; some issues gained prominence over a longer period, while others were observed only briefly. What this demonstrated at a holistic level was a process of ongoing growth, but it also indicated that Faisal's concerns as a doctoral researcher and Katie's as supervisor shifted as the study progressed through its various stages and areas of focus. At an overarching level, the major categories of interest could be placed very broadly along a chronological scale. The data from Faisal's initial period of enrolment referred to issues that could be categorised as epistemological – ways of understanding knowledge from the perspective of a researcher. As Faisal commenced the production of drafts and Katie commented on them, the data began to show a growing concern with issues of voice as Faisal sought to find a suitable communicative style and develop confidence in himself as a researcher. At this time, too, the concept of the thesis as a specific genre became a category of interest. By the end of the second year, once Faisal had completed the data collection for his project and was working on the analysis, an issue of increasing interest became the minutiae of language to express precision and accuracy: the presentation within the thesis of a researcher concerned with rigour and depth. These four overarching concerns became the main themes.

The table below summarises these themes, which are presented together with examples of the categories that contributed to the themes that were identified during the data analysis. They are discussed in more detail in the paragraphs that follow. While these themes are described within particular categories for purposes of clarity of presentation, it is emphasised that the processes which took place were interlocked, mutually-dependent and sinuous, even if there was an overall sense of movement and progression over time towards the ultimate goal.

4.1 Epistemology

The process of PhD recruitment within the Department where the study took place involves the submission by an applicant of a draft written proposal, on the basis of which, in conjunction with other evidence of the suitability of the applicant for doctoral study as determined by the institution, an offer of supervision is made. At the point where a PhD student commences their study, therefore, there has usually been little interaction between student and supervisor on the nature or details of the proposed study. The proposal is therefore just a starting point for discussion on all aspects of the study, including fundamental questions of ontology and epistemology. For Faisal and Katie the process began with the Departmental induction, which, as the then Director of Studies for the PhD programme, Katie was running. At one point in the induction, each participant was invited to briefly describe his or her intended study. Faisal noted in a reflection on that event:

> When it was my turn, I remember that I said something along the lines that despite the potential technology has to improve language learning and teaching, some language teachers still don't see the point of using it in the language classroom. So the aim of my PhD was to convince them to embrace the use of technology in their classes (Faisal Reflections)

Katie's generic comments following the students' brief descriptions included a statement that the function of a PhD was to find something out rather than to persuade, which Faisal immediately (and as Katie later confirmed, correctly) interpreted as applying to his own presentation. As he continued in his reflections: 'That piece of feedback made me rethink the purpose of my PhD which opened up the way for more changes that came after'. The experience, which Faisal also described as 'alarming right from the beginning' (Faisal Reflections), can be seen as the first of a number of what have been identified in education research as 'critical incidents' (Tripp 2012) that led Faisal to the position that would ultimately guide his study in terms of his approach to the purpose of research, his theoretical framework and selection of methodology.

As he produced chapters and participated in the feedback process, Faisal's perspective on the nature of the enterprise in which he was engaged shifted from a focus on himself as the producer of the thesis to a focus on the work that he was creating. In doing so, he became increasingly open to critique, thereby embracing a position in his own work aligned with that of philosophers of science such as Karl Popper, who argued that 'science could be distinguished from myth by its openness to critique and modification in the light of criticism' (Beecher-Monas 2007, p. 45). In his reflections, Faisal explained the process, which linked strongly to the idea of becoming a member of the community of practice:

> For some reason, I used to send what I write with high expectations, really high. I used to send a draft expecting comments along the lines 'this is outstanding, Faisal' on certain parts of it. However, that never happened. I used to feel disappointed because of that but now I am very happy that it did not happen... The disadvantage of that expectation was that it made me look for what was not in the feedback, what was absent according to me. Only when I stopped expecting anything did I start focussing on what was in the feedback. That made a huge difference in understanding my supervisor's feedback and in finding ways to improve... That is, I moved from 'expecting praise' on certain parts of my drafts to 'expecting and preparing for critique'. Now, I see that the latter is what can be called academic (Faisal Reflections)

As Faisal's conception of research as a particular way of thinking and knowing transformed his approach to his study, he also began to grapple with the development of a consistent and coherent paradigm within which to locate his research. His choice of complexity theory as his theoretical framework and an inductive approach at an early stage was decisive in determining this; once this was clear the issue of coherence of position nevertheless continued as a topic of student-supervisor discussion with regard to the way in which the position was evidenced through language. For example, when at one point Faisal wrote in a draft methodology chapter: 'that is, if language learning activities are characterized by collaborative meaning negotiation in which the computer(s) is used as a facilitative tool, there might be an effect (positive or/and negative) on the flow and structure of the linguistic mental representations', Katie responded with the question 'So you are working with a hypothesis?' In his meeting summaries, Faisal identified this issue on two occasions, stating 'some sentences seem to offer **hypotheses,** which is not what I intend to do. Therefore, I need to rephrase those sentences so that the focus is on **questioning** rather than hypothesising' (Meeting summary 12, emphasis in the original); and

Table 1 Summary of themes

Key theme/issue	Example categories
Epistemology	The goal of doctoral study
	Consistency of research paradigm
	Alignment of vocabulary with paradigm
	Choice and description of theoretical framework
	Selection and understanding of methodology
Voice	Meta-commentary on the text
	Style of argumentation and logical development
	Personal/impersonal voice
Genre	Audience, purpose and function
	Organisational structure
	Technical characteristics
Specific language choices	Use of syntax
	Use of metaphor
	Vague language
	Use of hedging
	Level of detail

'being an inductive study, I should focus on my RQs [research questions] and on understanding and making sense of the CBLA [computer based language activity] activities with all the social and cognitive aspects involved; i.e. no pre-assumptions and no hypothesising' (Meeting summary 15).

The focus on these issues of epistemology and the use of language to reflect a particular epistemological position appears primarily in the documents relating to the methodology chapter, literature review and associated notes. In the subsequent chapters, written after the data had been collected, engagement between student and supervisor tended to shift towards the other key themes listed in Table 1.

4.2   Voice

The struggle for voice within the doctoral thesis writing experience concerned both participants in different ways. For Faisal the ultimate concern was to develop an authentic and individually satisfying identity as a professional and member of the community of practice; this involved in the early stages some exploration and later abandonment of different approaches. Katie's focus, on the other hand, lay in attempting to encourage Faisal to conform to the conventions and expectations of doctoral research and writing, as she perceived them. One way in which Faisal's experimenting was instantiated was through his early use of meta-commentary included within the texts he submitted, particularly when it came to the literature review, which was the first thesis chapter he drafted. For example, in writing about a conflict of positions between two scholars, Faisal wrote in the chapter 'At this point, it might be palpable that this argument may go on endlessly', to which Katie's written response was 'avoid authorial comment on the process of argumentation that you are engaged with'. In another draft, Faisal included the statements 'I try to argue…' and 'I re-use it here [an extract from a scholarly work] to look at how…'. Again, Katie's response was to suggest avoiding authorial commentary, adding 'it is probably better to take yourself out of it and explain the theory behind what you are doing rather than discuss your own processes'.

By communicating in this style, Faisal appeared to Katie to be drawing on his previous readings, in particular of academic textbooks written by 'experts' who tend to adopt the tone of an omniscient and objective commentator, removed from the arguments that are being described. Thus, she interpreted his style as indicating that Faisal had conceptualised and internalised a particular image of the nature of an academic identity and was trying to reconcile his own writing to that viewpoint. On the other hand, this early exploration, it may be argued, captures a developmental process where Faisal, through writing, was familiarising himself with the arguments relating to any proposition put forward, and that this served as a necessary prerequisite for ultimately developing his own voice. Two other examples illustrate this struggle. In an early draft of the literature review, Faisal wrote:

It is UG's [universal grammar's] extensive focus on grammar that makes some linguists and psycholinguists skeptical about its fundamentals […]. This kind of focus, MacWhinney rationalizes, has led UG to assign essential areas of language structure to the 'periphery' (Faisal Literature review draft)

Katie's written comment on this extract was:

Again, this is an example of how you are presenting arguments between scholars, rather than presenting an argument and supporting it with evidence from the literature. Your topic isn't whether these people agree or disagree with each other, your topic should be the argument that you are making (Katie Comments in Literature review draft)

In the second example, taken from a draft of the methodology chapter, Faisal wrote:

Yin, however, does not provide a reason as why single case is useful for theory-based research. This might be because it seems to be straightforward. That is, a single case study has the least variables compared to the other three, so this probably makes it less distracting and much easier to relate the case behaviour/activities to the background theory (Faisal Methodology chapter draft)

Katie's written response to this was: 'You need to present your own methodology, not the views of others. Why do YOU think that a single case study is preferable?'

The meeting summaries that Faisal produced reflect both this early struggle towards an authentic academic identity and a corresponding voice, and his appropriation of Katie's feedback. For example, his meeting summaries included comments such as 'It [the literature review] should be more of "I'm telling you this because"; rather than, "I'm telling you this and this and that"' (Meeting summary 4); and 'Remember that the literature review presents "arguments" not "debates"… avoid the meta-comment style – don't discuss the discussion!' (Meeting summary 6).

Faisal's concerns about the presenting of himself within the study initially included a lack of certainty when it came to describing himself as an actor in it. A response from Katie within one draft of the methodology chapter illustrates this. In commenting on Faisal's use of the phrase 'the researcher' she stated 'You veer in this section between "the researcher" and "I". I'd recommend you pick one and stay with it'. There were other examples where Faisal explored ways of presenting his own voice such as 'This brings us to…' (Faisal Literature Review draft) where Katie questioned the pronoun by asking 'who?'; and 'to explain the non-linearity nature of CT, we will have to stop at each of these concepts as they come up' (Faisal Literature Review draft) which Katie responded to with 'Who will? And why? I'm not sure what you are imagining here' (Comment on literature review draft). It is notable at this point that Katie provided no guidance in the written feedback on what alternatives might be preferable, leaving Faisal to interpret and consider these comments by himself, prior to face-to-face meetings. With progressive drafts, however, Faisal indicated a growing confidence and an increasingly authentic voice that eschewed meta-discourse, as shown in an extract from a later draft of the methodology chapter:

> Although the main topic of these studies is creativity in music, they very much relate to the current study as they stress the importance of "questioning and challenging; making connections and seeing relationships…" (Rojas-Drummond et al 2008, p. 8) which reflect the same concept of collaboration presented in this section (Faisal Literature Review chapter draft)

Over time, data from within the documents on issues related to voice receded and disappeared entirely by the time the thesis chapter on the results of the study were presented in writing.

From the 'reflections' documents, it can be seen that Katie was ambivalent about her role as supervisor in this process of voice development. In particular, she had concerns about how to strike a balance between the potentially diminishing activity of 'moulding' Faisal within the boundaries, as she perceived them, of the community of practice and the enhancing activity of supporting creativity and individual expression. This was particularly associated with her awareness of the Anglocentricity of doctoral thesis production in the UK, and the likelihood of 'reifying the power structures in which genres are embedded' (Tardy 2006, p. 88), particularly in relation to the potential clash with Faisal's identity as a first language user of Arabic and his own literary and cultural heritage. While his English was highly proficient, Katie was worried that her

> '…insistence on a particular way of constructing argument was an attack on his identity as an Arabic user. I felt there was/is a conflict for me in helping someone to produce a written text in English according to a particular genre, when the production of the style associated with that genre is something like a colonial imposition and denies creativity (Katie Reflections)

Ultimately, however, she stated in her reflections that she adopted a conservative position because of the potential consequences, as she saw them, of doing otherwise: 'my obligation is to give Faisal information that is I believe most likely to result in a successful PhD, so I continue to comment on [such] matters even though I feel uncomfortable doing it'.

4.3 Genre

Unlike other academic genres, such as conference papers, journal articles or research proposals, the doctoral thesis is unique as a one-off artefact produced by an individual who has gone through the process of doctoral study. In recent years, universities have begun to acknowledge this, and have sought to maintain the relevance of the thesis to professional environments by permitting alternative formats, such as the production of a portfolio of articles. This option was not available to Faisal at the time he commenced his doctorate, which meant that he was expected to produce a 'traditional' thesis. In the Department where he was enrolled, this meant a volume of several chapters that together located the research within its research context through a review of the relevant literature, described the research methodology and associated ethics, analysed the data and discussed the contribution of the study to the current body of knowledge. In her reflections, Katie commented on the genre of the doctoral thesis:

> Writing a doctoral thesis is something that an individual does only once – at least at the point of writing it. An experienced supervisor, however, has witnessed and participated in the construction of multiple research projects and the writing of multiple theses and therefore has a certain level of knowledge based on experience that the doctoral student simply can't have. It's this kind of expertise that I feel as a supervisor I can pass on to my students (Katie)

Here, Katie's comments appear to echo the apprenticeship learning system from which the community of practice concept was originally derived, where in this case doctoral students have 'master' supervisors 'who give them entry into academic communities' (Wenger 1998, p. 101), the thesis being a type of artefact with which supervisors engage on an ongoing basis in the course of their practice.

When it came to the thesis, in this study the focus of the data obtained was on three areas in particular: the broad characteristics of a thesis, the organisational structure of a thesis and the function of its component parts. There is a rich body of literature on genres and genre development within an academic context which emphasises their importance for maintaining status and recognition within the field of practice (see, for example, Flowerdew 2000) and records the ways in which genre knowledge is acquired. One of these ways is through drawing on previous experience of and exposure to other genres, particularly those in related fields (Tardy 2006). Faisal's experience of academic genres at the commencement of his doctoral study, as either a reader or a writer, lay in scholarly articles, textbooks and master's dissertations, and it was these that he had recourse to and therefore had in mind as he sought to familiarise himself with the genre that he was expected to produce. For example, at one point early in the process of producing a thesis chapter he referred to how a certain idea was 'important to this paper', which attracted the written comment from Katie: 'You're not writing a paper, you're writing a thesis'. Later, Faisal was to write in his reflections: 'I used to think of my PhD as a journal article that is just bigger size-wise'. Similarly, at an early stage he had difficulty reconciling his technical knowledge that a thesis at his institution was expected to comprise around 90,000 words with his conceptual understanding of previous academic outputs he had produced and the nature of the genre that required such a lengthy document. As Faisal commented in his reflections:

> My basic knowledge of what a PhD is and what it is for, that I had in the beginning, limited the scope through which I was working on my PhD. This clashed with my awareness that I was writing the largest document I would ever produce.... For instance, I wrote about how Chaos Theory [CT] started in climatology and physics to the extent that I even included diagrams of pendulums and graphs of mathematical data. Despite being pointed out to me by my supervisor that that did not seem to be relevant, and how would I justify including it... because I was required to write a lot, it appeared fine to have written over 10,000 words introducing CT (Faisal Reflections document)

Shortly after writing the draft to which those reflections refer, Faisal experienced a critical incident that helped him begin to recognise how important genre knowledge and reproduction was from a social and disciplinary perspective. His co-supervisor was not, by agreement, much involved in the ongoing process of supervision as it was intended that he should provide overarching and holistic input at key points over Faisal's enrolment. This he first did shortly before an important progression point (a panel assessment which led to the confirmation of candidature) by reading and providing feedback on the chapters as they had been drafted to that point. He submitted his feedback to Faisal electronically, noting in the covering email:

> I hope you do not feel discouraged and see my comments as constructive criticism which is meant to help you revise your work and produce a new version which is more aligned with what we might expect of a literature review" (Co-supervisor email, reproduced with permission)

Faisal reported in his reflections that he was concerned about the expression 'new version' in that email, which he initially interpreted as meaning a complete re-write. However, as he stated: 'the most intimidating part of it was the phrase "what we might expect". This immediately made me feel... somewhere far from where I should be. It showed me that there was a 'we' and there was 'my work'. It said that the 'we' was somewhere and my work was somewhere else; that was scary' (Faisal Reflections). This was the first time that Faisal had been so baldly confronted with evidence of a community of practice that had certain discourse expectations, and led him to consult a number of PhD theses, 'so that I could understand the place of that 'we', and how I could bring my work closer to that' (Faisal Reflections).

From an organisational structure perspective, the management of a document larger than any he had previously worked with was also challenging in itself, as Faisal drew on his previous academic writing experience of writing sections of text under individual headings. For example, as the drafts expanded and become correspondingly ideationally more complex, Katie's feedback included advice on the hierarchical organisation of ideas:

> … you need to create levels of headings. That is, main heading, sub-heading level 1, sub-heading level 2, and so on. At the moment, it's rather difficult to work through the organisational structure of the chapter. Also if you do that, you can quickly create a table of contents that shows at a glance how your ideas are organised (Katie feedback on thesis draft)

Associated with this concern over organisation was a process of refinement of understanding how the content would be distributed within and across chapters. For example, when Faisal wrote in a first draft of his literature review that 'both of these cases… suggest that reports and diary studies may well produce sources of information that may help in capturing what has been noticed', Katie responded that this was a topic for the methodology chapter, and when Faisal wrote in an early draft of his discussion chapter 'Mediation in CBLA is the use of contextual tools from the (CBLA) environment in order to achieve goals', Katie commented: 'By the time you get to your discussion you should have identified and defined your terms' (Feedback on thesis draft). Thus, Faisal's knowledge and understanding of the thesis as a genre developed simultaneously from multiple perspectives: social and disciplinary alongside the functional, rhetorical and procedural.

4.4   Language Use

The final key theme, in practice of course impossible to dislocate from any of the other themes discussed above, related to the use of language at a micro-level, for example within sentences or paragraphs. There were many different instances of feedback interactions regarding specific language use, but to illustrate the theme two examples are presented in this category. Predominant among student-supervisor exchanges, from a frequency perspective, was the first of these, the use of metaphors. Faisal's early drafts were rich with imagery which he had, in part, extracted from the metaphor-dense research literature on dynamic systems but which, in Katie's eyes, did not sit well within his literature review, particularly when metaphors were used to explain metaphors. For example, when Faisal wrote that '[second language] fossilization might be a deep and steep hole in the trajectory of language use', Katie commented: 'This explains nothing, really. Fossilisation is a hole? It's just another image, just as fossilisation is an image' (Comment on literature review draft).

In response to a discussion on this use of metaphors, Faisal humorously includes in his meeting notes 'Avoid flowery language- the drier the better!' This was an area of contestation, not only between Faisal and Katie but as something that they struggled with in their reflections on their own practice. Although she criticised Faisal's use of metaphors, Katie noted in her reflections that she 'was rather worried [about] my frequent criticism of Faisal's use of metaphors (which I felt fell apart under analysis)' because she was concerned that it stymied his personal expression as a bilingual Arabic-English user. Although she had no knowledge of Arabic herself, she noted in one of her reflections that from her interactions with Arabic-speaking students in the past she had understood that the rich use of imagery was associated with professionally prestigious forms of Arabic. Faisal, on his part, reflected that he had been using metaphors, along with complex terminology, in order to 'sound sophisticated' (Faisal Reflections), perhaps here providing another example of his experimentation with performativity. He went on to add:

> I can say that every time we discuss my use of such metaphoric or the seemingly more sophisticated terms, we end up agreeing to replace them with more direct, clearer and less metaphoric terms. To be honest, I was not convinced about avoiding metaphoric terms. I believe the reason for my disagreement was my initial idea of the writing style of a PhD thesis... It is not that I eliminated the use of metaphors, but I did indeed put it to the minimum I could (Faisal Reflections)

A subsequent note in a meeting summary indicates that this issue had been resolved, or that a compromise position had been reached between student and supervisor: 'I need to be conscious about my use of metaphors – they should be carefully used and only when necessary' (Meeting Summary 9).

One other notable area where there was considerable student-supervisor interaction was with the use of language that could be broadly classified as 'vague', for example, where it lacked specificity of context or clarity of meaning. While it has been argued that vagueness in academic writing can be strategic and achieve particular objectives within a given context (Myers 1996), detail and specificity are often taken as the hallmark of rigour, in both quantitative and qualitative research. This may explain why feedback comments from Katie on vague language were particularly concentrated in Faisal's 'findings' chapter, although they did occasionally appear elsewhere. For example, in a draft of that chapter, Faisal noted that an observed class 'started with the teacher refreshing students' knowledge of Google Docs' which Katie described as 'a bit generic' in a written comment. In another example, Faisal had written 'language development affordances occur when cues available in the CBLA environment match the individual', to which Katie had responded 'Match the individual's what? What aspect of the individual? What do you mean by "match"?' (Comments on theoretical framework draft). Faisal noted in one of the meeting summaries that this was something that needed to be addressed: 'Some statements need to be reworded... to clarify meaning and avoid ambiguity' (Meeting summary 35).

5   Concluding Comments

The study described in this chapter explored the idea of literacy development for the doctoral researcher as a process of moving from legitimate peripheral participant towards full membership of a community of practice. With each of the key themes identified from the data: epistemology, voice, genre and language use, it can be seen that Faisal as doctoral student brought to his studies certain preconceptions and expectations from the periphery – about what it meant to be a researcher, and about the nature and language of a doctoral thesis. As his studies progressed, Faisal's understandings and practices changed and he shifted from embracing discourse and research behaviours which he had imagined an academic should produce, to performing discourse practices, developed through the appropriation of supervisor feedback, that he felt would be successful for communicating within the community in which he was participating. That is not to argue that within the community of practice model, as understood within this chapter, there is a binary state between engaging at the periphery and acting from the centre of a community of practice, and that there is a moment at which an individual shifts from one position to the other. Rather, for Faisal, movement towards understanding and adopting the 'shared repertoire' of this particular community of practice, these data indicated, took place on a multi-layered continuum, with change occurring for different aspects of that repertoire at different times, over different durations, through different trigger events as well as repeated interactions between himself and his supervisor. Katie, too, experienced a struggle as she engaged in the process of supervision. Her conflict lay between the responsibility she felt to assume a conservative position on the constraints as she perceived them of the discourse practices of the community in order to promote Faisal's likelihood of success with his doctorate, and her acknowledgement that the discourse practices within a community of practice are fluid and dynamic, open to and desirous of change, particularly with regard to the predominance in their field of a particular variety of Standard English.

These processes reflect what has been described as the development of a 'discursive identity', where discourse describes 'certain ways of using language, acting, interacting, behaving, believing, using tools, sign systems, and so forth, which characterise a particular community' (Allie et al. 2009, p. 361), and identity is envisaged as a way of presenting oneself and of being recognised as a fellow community member. Doctoral study has also been described as 'a process of subjectification – as coming to mastery through initial submission to discourses you never chose – and as a production of culturally intelligible and relevant academicity' (Petersen 2007, p. 485). These descriptions illustrate what the study found: that if literacy is conceived as becoming a member of a community of practice, it is not so much a process of becoming (in other words, the focus is not on psychological development) but of learning through participation how to 'perform' within a specific context to achieve recognition and acceptance within that community.

References

Allie, S., Armien, M., Burgoyne, N., Case, J., Collier-Reed, B., Craig, T., et al. (2009). Learning as acquiring a discursive identity through participation in a community: Improving student learning in engineering education. *European Journal of Engineering Education, 34*(4), 359–367.

Annala, J., & Mäkinen, M. (2016). Communities of practice in higher education: Contradictory narratives of a university-wide curriculum reform. *Studies in Higher Education, 42*, 1941–1957. https://doi.org/10.1080/03075079.2015.1125877.

Bastalich, W. (2017). Content and context in knowledge production: A critical review of doctoral supervision literature. *Studies in Higher Education, 42*(7), 1145–1157.

Beecher-Monas, E. (2007). *Evaluating scientific evidence. An interdisciplinary framework for intellectual due process*. Cambridge: Cambridge University Press.

Braun, V., & Clarke, V. (2006). Using thematic analysis in psychology. *Qualitative Research in Psychology, 3*(2), 77–10.

Cox, A. M. (2005). What are communities of practice? A comparative review of four seminal works. *Journal of Information Science, 31*(6), 527–540.

Craig, C. (2009). Trustworthiness in self-study research. In C. Lassonde, S. Galman, & C. Kosnik (Eds.), *Self-study research methodologies for teacher educators* (pp. 21–34). Rotterdam: Sense Publishers.

Cumming, J. (2010). Doctoral enterprise: A holistic conception of evolving practices and arrangements. *Studies in Higher Education, 35*(1), 25–39.

Daniel, G. R., Auhl, G., & Hastings, W. (2013). Collaborative feedback and reflection for professional growth: Preparing first-year pre-service teachers for participation in the community of practice. *Asia-Pacific Journal of Teacher Education, 41*(2), 159–172.

Dunworth, K., & Sanchez, H. H. (2016). Perceptions of quality in staff-student written feedback in higher education: A case study. *Teaching in Higher Education, 21*(5), 576–589.

Ewing, B. (2005). Discourse and the construction of identity in a community of learning and a community of practice. In T. Stehlik & P. Carden (Eds.), *Beyond communities of practice: Theory as experience* (pp. 149–170). Upper Mount Gravatt: Post Pressed.

Flowerdew, J. (2000). Discourse community, legitimate peripheral participation, and the nonnative-English-speaking scholar. *TESOL Quarterly, 34*(1), 127–150.

Handley, K., Sturdy, A., Fincham, R., & Clark, T. (2006). Within and beyond communities of practice: Making sense of learning through participation, identity and practice. *Journal of Management Studies, 43*(3), 641–653.

Hoadley, C. (2012). What is a community of practice and how can we support it? In D. Jonassen & S. Lund (Eds.), *Theoretical foundations of learning environments* (2nd ed., pp. 286–300). New York: Routledge.

Hodkinson, H., & Hodkinson, P. (2004). Rethinking the concept of community of practice in relation to schoolteachers' workplace learning. *International Journal of Training and Development, 8*(1), 21–31.

Kamler, B., & Thomson, P. (2006). *Helping doctoral students write*. Abingdon: Routledge.

Kogan, M. (2000). Higher education communities and academic identity. *Higher Education Quarterly, 54*(3), 207–216.

Lave, J., & Wenger, E. (1991). *Situated learning. Legitimate peripheral participation*. Cambridge: University of Cambridge Press.

Lunenberg, M., Zwart, R., & Korthagen, F. (2010). Critical issues in supporting self-study. *Teaching and Teacher Education, 26*, 1280–1289.

McNiff, J., & Whitehead, J. (2010). *You and your action research project* (3rd ed.). Abingdon: Routledge.

Myers, G. (1996). Strategic vagueness in academic writing. In E. Ventola & A. Mauranen (Eds.), *Academic writing* (pp. 3–18). Amsterdam: John Benjamins.

Petersen, E. (2007). Negotiating academicity: Postgraduate research supervision as category boundary work. *Studies in Higher Education, 32*(4), 475–487.

Pinnegar, S., & Hamilton, M. L. (2009). *Self-study of practice as a genre of qualitative research*. Dordrecht: Springer.

Priest, K., Saucier, D., & Eiselein, G. (2016). Exploring students' experiences in first-year learning communities from a situated learning perspective. *International Journal of Teaching and Learning in Higher Education, 28*(3), 361–371.

Russell, D., Lea, M., Parker, J., Street, B., & Donahue, T. (2009). Exploring notions of genre in "Academic Literacies" and "Writing Across the Curriculum": Approaches across countries and contexts. In C. Bazerman, D. Figueiredo, & A. Bonini (Eds.), *Genre in a changing world* (pp. 395–423). West Lafayette: Parlor Press and WAC Clearinghouse. Available from http://wac.colostate.edu/

Ryan, J. (2015). It ain't just what you do and the way that you do it: Why discourse matters in higher education communities of practice. *Higher Education Research and Development, 34*(5), 1001–1013.

Samaras, A., & Freese, A. (2009). Looking back and looking forward. In C. Lassonde, S. Galman, & C. Kosnik (Eds.), *Self-study research methodologies for teacher educators* (pp. 3–19). Rotterdam: Sense Publishers.

Smit, R. (2010). Doctoral supervision: Facilitating access to a community of research practice? *African Journal of Research in Mathematics, Science and Technology Education, 14*(2), 96–109.

Starke-Meyerring, D., Paré, A., Sun, K. Y., & El-Bezre, N. (2014). Probing normalized institutional discourses about writing: The case of the doctoral thesis. *Journal of Academic Language & Learning, 8*(2), A13–A27.

Tardy, C. M. (2006). Researching first and second language genre learning: A comparative review and a look ahead. *Journal of Second Language Writing, 15*, 79–101.

Tidwell, D., Heston, M., & Fitzgerald, L. (2009). *Research methods for the self-study of practice.* Dordrecht: Springer.

Tripp, D. (2012). *Critical incidents in teaching.* Abingdon: Routledge.

Wenger, E. (2010). Communities of practice and social learning systems: The career of a concept. In C. Blackmore (Ed.), *Social learning systems and communities of practice* (pp. 179–198). Milton Keynes: The Open University.

Wenger, E. (1998). *Communities of practice: Learning, meaning, and identity.* Cambridge: Cambridge University Press.

Developing Contextual Literacy English for Academic Purposes Through Content and Language Integrated Learning

Jim McKinley

Abstract Contextual literacy English for academic purposes (EAP) provides a valuable perspective on the increasing focus on the social and contextual aspects of academic and critical English literacy education. The focus on these aspects is in response to the perceived need to develop students' literacies to keep up with changing global trends in education and language use. This is especially evident in countries where English has a foreign-language status but where English is being used by bi- and multilingual speakers. In this chapter, a study examining an English-language public speaking course in a Japanese university using a content and language integrated learning (CLIL) pedagogy is used to illustrate the potential benefit of a novel, socio-historically contextualised approach, known as Reacting to the Past, to teaching English language skills. The use of CLIL pedagogies allows for contextual literacy EAP to develop through resourcing other languages, i.e., translanguaging, in the study of content that requires practicing the use of English for persuasive purposes. The chapter provides a further discussion to clarify that while academic literacy and critical literacy cover these concepts, it is significant to explore contextual literacy development as a way of understanding the learning and critical thinking that occurs in English language studies in an evolving, global context.

Keywords Contextual literacy · EAP · CLIL · Socio-historic language teaching · Translanguaging · Japanese university · Argumentation · Public speaking

J. McKinley (✉)
UCL Institute of Education, University of London, London, UK
e-mail: j.mckinley@ucl.ac.uk

© Springer Nature Switzerland AG 2019   67
T. Dobinson, K. Dunworth (eds.), *Literacy Unbound: Multiliterate, Multilingual, Multimodal*, Multilingual Education 30,
https://doi.org/10.1007/978-3-030-01255-7_5

1   Introduction

The definition of *contextual literacy* used in this chapter is taken from Paulo Freire's highly contextualized perspective of critical literacy. I define contextual literacy as an understanding of the complex ways historical change and perspective allow us to recognize and challenge the shaping of context through historical, socio-cultural and socio-political circumstances of human experience. Freire's theory of critical pedagogy is built on the idea of social movement, borrowing from critical theory and cultural studies. It provided an ideal foundation on which to build contemporary concepts of contextual literacy.

Scribner (1986) highlights Freire's work in her discussion of a socially contextual literacy, stating.

> Paulo Freire (1970) bases his influential theory of literacy education on the need to make literacy a resource for fundamental social transformation. Effective literacy education, in his view, creates a critical consciousness through which a community can analyse its conditions of social existence and engage in effective action for a just society. (p. 12).

Scribner offered three metaphors for a socially contextual literacy: literacy as adaptation, as power and as a state of grace. Scribner's focus on social change is key here, as the changes in recognition of the status of English, moving away from issues of linguicism and language imperialism, are having a profound effect on our understanding of what it means to teach and learn English. In 'norm-dependent' higher education especially, the development of contextual literacy is not a new movement, but instead an ongoing phenomenon that is finally being recognized and targeted as the expectations of students move increasingly toward building critical literacy in tandem with cultural and academic literacy in English.

Students' development of contextual literacy in an English medium-instructed university program occurs in learning through content and language integrated learning (CLIL). Students focusing on both content and language are in a better position to advance beyond their own values and belief systems toward a cultural and contextual literacy that is more expansive. This chapter proposes 'contextual literacy English for academic purposes' (EAP) as a conceptual theory targeting the changing literacy development practices in English-medium higher education in Japan.

Taking a contextual literacy approach to teaching EAP through CLIL in an English as a foreign language (EFL) context has not yet been widely explored. However, with developments in English as an international language in English-medium instruction (EMI) in Kachru's outer circle, or 'norm-developing' countries (i.e., have their own institutionalized variety of English; these include British colonial countries such as India and Singapore) and expanding circle, or 'norm-dependent' countries (i.e., do not have their own institutionalized variety of English of their own; these include academic EMI strongholds such as Denmark and Sweden, as well as East and Southeast Asia and the country of focus in this study, Japan), taking a contextual literacy approach to teaching EAP seems a significant area of inquiry, given the expectations of students to build both critical literacy and cultural and academic literacy in English. Taking the definition of contextual literacy from Freire's perspective of critical literacy, this chapter seeks to establish clarity on what it means to develop contextual literacy in EAP studies at the university level.

This chapter sees contextualizing academic literacy in terms of EFL and English as a second language (ESL) as increasingly irrelevant with the growth of English as an international language (EIL), and recognition that English no longer 'belongs' to Kachru's inner circle (i.e., 'norm-providing' countries). Haberland (2011), in a special issue of the *Journal of Pragmatics* focused on English as a lingua franca, distinguishes between an ownership discourse ('belonging to') and a maintenance discourse ('cultivated by') to make the argument that these discourses should no longer be left to the old norm providers. He points out that due to increased transnational student mobility, the use of English as a lingua franca in university teaching is the focus, rather than the use of English that reflects native norms. Haberland admits that a language in some sense does 'belong' to its first or native speakers, but argues that the concept of belonging should not be one that excludes others. As for language maintenance, Haberland claims that generally it is first-language speakers of a language who attempt to maintain or cultivate the language, but regarding the English language, this is not especially clear. The only argument in support of English ownership seems to be in the discussion of written English, in that the norms 'are not any direct result of informal language socialization, but have to be acquired through schooling' (Haberland 2011, p. 940). Indeed, written academic English has been described as a foreign language for everyone (Siegel 2007). With the understanding that academic English is a foreign language for everyone, it is significant now to take a more universal approach to contextual literacy, especially in higher education EMI in norm-dependent countries, such as Japan.

This chapter provides a conceptual framework for contextual literacy as it is understood for the purposes of the study in order to establish the argument that contextual literacy is the most effective focus in CLIL practices, as it allows us to appropriately value the development of critical engagement in English language education, with a specific focus on the strength of developing argument and debate skills.

2   Literature Review

In a review of relevant literature, the idea of contextual literacy is supported by theory related to critical literacy and critical pedagogy. From Freire's work on critical pedagogy, scholars have expanded the theory to consider the implications regarding context. This section will first provide an analysis of the conceptual framework for contextual literacy used for the study, followed by the role of CLIL in developing contextual literacy with a description of the specific contextual pedagogy used in the study.

2.1 Conceptual Framework for Contextual Literacy

In university-level EAP studies, contextual literacy development, or 'contextual literacy EAP', involves the study of English through an understanding of its historical, cultural and social implications, which includes rhetorical aspects of English as they concern the ability to use the English language persuasively in academic settings. As we can understand contextual literacy to be 'premised upon the importance of meaningful *content*' (Demetrion 2001, p. 106) and can understand a contextual approach to literacy to mean that 'literacy is developed while it is being applied' (Sticht 1997, p. 2), the linking of CLIL to contextual literacy is significant.

It is important to note that contextual literacy exists beyond language, and thus the development of contextual literacy is not only bound to the first language (L1) or second language (L2) but can be achieved via translanguaging practices. Translanguaging refers to communication involving the integrated, unconscious, meaning-making resourcing of multiple languages. Translanguaging in the language classroom therefore provides opportunities for teaching, as a variety of teaching approaches can be used drawing on language awareness from different languages, a concept supported by the literature on Global Englishes (e.g., Galloway and Rose 2015).

2.2 The Role of CLIL in Developing Contextual Literacy

In this section, CLIL will be discussed regarding its role in developing contextual literacy. The main argument here is that students focusing on both content and language are in a better position to advance beyond their own values and belief systems toward a cultural and contextual literacy that is more expansive (Brown et al. 2013). I also challenge the rejections of transferring notions of literacy from L1 literacy to EFL contexts (McKinley 2013a, 2017), while maintaining the view that we are moving toward a substantial acceptance of the contextualized nature of the reciprocated impact between L1 and L2 literacy behaviours (Rinnert and Kobayashi 2009).

First, the effectiveness of CLIL has been argued to depend on the L2 proficiency of students, teachers and management (e.g., Bruton 2013). However, with a view of CLIL in developing contextual literacy, there are a great many advantages regardless of proficiency levels if a translanguaging approach is taken. Studies have indicated that the role of students' L1 in knowledge co-construction and academic language learning in CLIL classrooms is significant (e.g., Lin and Lo 2017; Nikula and Moore 2016). These studies present traditional teacher-led models in which the success of CLIL relied on the teachers' bi- or multilingual understanding of the content and ability to teach it by resourcing perspectives from multiple languages. No studies on contextual literacy development have explored the student-led CLIL classroom, such as the one in the present study.

Brown et al. (2013), drawing on issues of globalization in education and evidence of the increasingly diverse student cohorts in higher education, highlight the need to clarify the meaning of 'context' and acknowledge students' varying interpretations of it and their own contexts. They point out that this diversity demands a contextualized pedagogy, one that moves beyond both outdated stereotypes of wise instructors imparting knowledge to students (see discussions of 'sage on the stage') and contemporary university teaching that ignores students' contexts. They clarify that contextual pedagogy is more than just recognition of cultural influences and diversity, emphasizing the value of experiential learning that draws on students' backgrounds while engaging in the study of content in which they can reflect on their experiences.

Such reflective learning is at the heart of integrating content with language learning, in that language is contextualized by each student in consideration of the social, cultural and historical aspects of the content (Thompson and McKinley 2018). Developing contextual literacy in this way closes gaps between local and international students, which is of increasing importance in globalized higher education (Singh and Shrestha 2008). This is a clear example of an appropriate transfer of a notion of literacy to an EFL setting, such as Japan, made possible through a CLIL approach.

2.3   EMI and CLIL in Japanese Higher Education

Although I used Kachru's model earlier to describe Japan's English-learning context as EFL, as Japan is in Kachru's list of norm-dependent countries, it is important here to emphasize that using national boundaries as the qualifying factor regarding the use of English is increasingly irrelevant, and newer models are needed to clarify Japan's position in the discussion of EIL. Alternatively, Modiano's (1999) emphasis on EIL language proficiency, where different varieties of English overlap, puts international usage and intelligibility at the core. With this understanding, the goal is not to move toward a particular variety of English, but instead toward the ability to use English proficiently among users of different Englishes. EMI in Japanese higher education has been around since the earlier part of last century, but traditionally it was focused on American models of English and education. With more current understanding of English as an international language, EMI in Japan has begun to reflect Modiano's model (e.g., Hino 2018; McKinley 2018).

Today, EMI in Japanese higher education has been expanded widely with the support of globalization initiatives set out by Japan's education ministry (Rose and McKinley 2018). There are now EMI programs in many Japanese universities, and EMI classes in most Japanese universities. While there are several issues faced by universities across Japan implementing new EMI programs, including teacher training, English language proficiency concerns of teachers and students, and increasingly international student cohorts, there have been some important examples of successful EMI implementation (e.g., McKinley 2018). The focus in this study that uses data collected in an EMI program at a Japanese university is on the development of English public speaking skills, specifically argument and debate skills, as these address the education ministry's push for increased critical engagement and critical thinking skills development in English language education.

CLIL in Japanese higher education has been explored in response to encouragement from Japan's education ministry to develop English language education for critical engagement. Coyle (2007) explains that such engagement is made possible through teacher-student questioning that is open for discussion, rather than teachers confirming students' understanding. In CLIL classrooms, situating language in social, cultural and historical contexts through content studies, questioning is more open than in traditional EFL classrooms, where students are asked questions to which instructors already know the answers. CLIL is promoted as 'effective' in this vein in Japanese higher education (e.g., Brown 2014; Pinner 2013) but is also difficult to implement depending on the content (e.g., Brown 2015 and Lockley 2014 on using Japanese history as the content).

The specific CLIL pedagogy I am exploring in this study was originally designed as a critical pedagogy for the teaching of history to students at Barnard College of Columbia University in New York City. The pedagogy is called Reacting to the Past (RTTP) and, through some careful adaptation for CLIL purposes, is now in use in a required public speaking course for students in an EMI program at a university in Japan. RTTP is an educational approach that uses content in the form of a roleplaying game to get students to engage in debates and research and to prepare papers and speeches in a way that allows them to develop skills in critical thinking, problem solving and teamwork. These skills match up with the three core skills for working adults promoted by the Ministry of Economy, Trade and Industry that are considered desirable from university graduates (McKinley 2013b):

- Action: The ability to move forward and stay engaged, to get up when you fall down. This includes taking initiative, motivating others and achieving goals.
- Thinking: The ability to question and think problems through. This includes identifying problems, planning and creative thinking.
- Teamwork: The ability to work with other people in pursuit of a common goal. This includes communication, listening, flexibility, awareness, cooperation and stress control (Reed 2010).

In the RTTP pedagogy, students participate in roleplay with detailed character descriptions based on real historical figures. Through the game format, they give speeches and participate in debates based on actual historical events. It is an engaging approach that is student centred and highly motivating. In an EFL context such as Japan, this pedagogy is essentially a CLIL approach that language teachers can use to incorporate a focus on content while developing students' ability to function academically through a second language.

Significant here is the operationalization of a critical pedagogy developed in the US for CLIL purposes in Japan, which, according to its status as a norm-dependent country, involves the teaching of English as a *foreign* language. This study examined a phenomenon that involved the transfer of a notion of literacy (in this case a critical literacy, developed through RTTP pedagogy) to an EFL context. This operationalization serves as an example of transferring notions of literacy to EFL contexts along the lines of Rinnert and Kobayashi (2009), who assert that the contextualized nature of the shared impact between L1 and L2 literacy behaviours is being increasingly accepted. Examples of this acceptance can be found in arguments in the areas of contrastive rhetoric (e.g., McKinley 2013a), writer identity (e.g., McKinley 2017) and translanguaging practices (Lin and Lo 2017; Nikula and Moore 2016). These arguments form a single challenge to the notion that literacy practices cannot be transferred from English L1 contexts to EFL contexts, as it is a matter of viewing English language education in EFL settings as informed and supported by the L1 of the context in forming more global conceptualizations of literacy.

The assertion that critical literacy practices of argumentation and rhetoric are not transferable to EFL contexts, specifically the Japanese EFL context, came commonly from examples of English L2 writing practices that indicated Japanese students were 'unable' to argue with qualification and certainty. The voice of Japanese students was often considered too indirect or too passive (Davidson 1995). However, such stereotypes are increasingly irrelevant in our globalized world, where argumentation and rhetorical moves in English output by Japanese EFL students is characteristically neither specific to Japanese nor English, but instead a balanced, compromised and resolute approach to argument and debate that borrows from both Japanese and English rhetoric (McKinley 2017).

3 Methods

The methods I used in this study included semi-structured classroom observations while preparing and giving of speeches and engaging in the debates using RTTP materials, specifically the game *The Threshold of Democracy: Athens in 403 B.C.* (Ober et al. 2015). Additionally, structured observations were made in the review of video recordings of the speeches and debates. This covered a period of 5 weeks, with 90-minute classes held twice each week. Additional data collected included students' written reflections at the end of the period.

3.1 The Setting and Participants

The university where the study took place is typical of Japanese universities in that the role of English varies in its different EMI offerings and atypical in that the level of English in the EMI program studied is much higher than most across Japan. This is due to the reputation of the program and the regular enrolment of students graduating from international schools, as well as international students, of whom some are native English speakers. Classes also include Japanese nationals who achieved high scores on standardized English language tests (mostly the Test of English as a Foreign Language, or TOEFL) or were recommended for the program by a selection of schools in Japan. The result is a mix of backgrounds and English proficiency levels, where, according to faculty policy goals, program and curriculum designers need to aim for an egalitarian classroom, not advantaging or disadvantaging any students according to proficiency. Pedagogical approaches in the faculty are meant to be inclusive and considerate of varying student needs. Aiming to develop contextual literacy in content and assessment was considered the best way to create more egalitarian environments in the required English courses, which involved completion of one to three writing courses before doing the public speaking course, depending on the students' needs.

The public speaking course was required for all undergraduate students in the EMI program at the university where the data were collected. The course was 15 weeks in length, the final 4 weeks of which were dedicated to using the Reacting to the Past materials in what was set as the 'debate module'. Leading up to this point, students were trained in researching and giving speeches focused on persuading their audience. So, by this stage, students had gained a certain level of comfort in speaking in front of the same group of students. There were 12 students in the class selected for the study, which is smaller than the average class size of about 16 for the public speaking course at this university. All students consented to participation in the study and use of data collected for both study and assessment purposes. The students, all in their second or third years, covered a typical range in the EMI program, as follows:

- Three Japanese nationals with Japanese schooling background
- Three Japanese nationals with international schooling background
- Three Japanese nationals with overseas schooling background (US)
- Two international students with international schooling background (South American, Southeast Asian)
- One international student with native English speaking background (US)

While these different backgrounds suggest varying levels of language ability to participate in an open group debate, it was understood that personality and character would play more of a role in their willingness to participate actively with the group in the preparation stage. In the assessed debates, as students played roles and were assessed not only on their displays of contextual knowledge but also the ability to get others to speak (scoring points for challenging others); participation was designed to be fairly balanced between students.

3.2   The Materials and Assessment

The debate 'game' used in the course was *The Threshold of Democracy: Athens in 403 B.C.* This game's premise is the historical event that was the rebuilding of Athens after its defeat in the Peloponnesian Wars, including the fate of Socrates, as the foundations of Western civilization and democracy were being established. In preparation, students were given several reading materials, most from the RTTP *Athens* textbook, including character role descriptions and game strategies, but additional readings were provided from Plato's *The Republic* and other sources. Students were also encouraged to check materials published in their first language in order to provide potential differences of perspective on the materials, thus breaking down language borders. Such practices are in line with current trends to incorporate translanguaging into language pedagogical practice. The preparation tasks involved checking comprehension of the content readings through discussions, group quizzes and debating skills practices, including a roleplayed interrupting activity (discussed later), pointing out opponents' errors and making rhetorical moves to develop an argument. In the third lesson in the preparation period, students were given their 'character sheets', which included a description of their character, their goals in the debate, some strategies for winning the debates in line with their characters and some ideas for additional readings. Therefore, a great deal of time was spent outside class researching character information so students could better understand their goals in the debates.

While the structure of the debates was originally designed to be entirely student led, in this environment in Japan, it was decided, in agreement with all instructors of the public speaking course, that the structure would be much more guided. This was due to the mix of proficiency levels and varying cultural backgrounds of the students in a single classroom, which amounted to those with international experience dominating classroom participation and discussions, often silencing those with Japan-only experience. The more guided version involved assigning students the specific topics of the debates, and scheduling them so students could prepare and submit outlines of their speeches beforehand to be checked by the instructor. In the lessons when debates were scheduled, students who were assigned speeches gave in-character speeches each limited to a maximum of 3 min using their outlines and/ or other notes. Once the assigned students finished their speeches, the debate was then held, timed by the instructor for anywhere from 8 to 18 min, depending on the number of topics covered in the debate. Students were assessed on the content and delivery of the speeches and debate. Further assessment was made based on students' submission of a 1000-word written reflection of each speech and debate in which they participated.

3.3   Data Collection

The observation data were collected through semi-structured observation in the form of brief note-taking as well as after-lesson written reflections, as I was an instructor on the course. Having taught in Japanese higher education for many years with a wide variety of students, I was in a good position to understand the students' different backgrounds and perspectives on their learning. Structured observation notes were made in reviewing videos of the speech and debate sessions, which made up the final 3 weeks of the four-week module.

The approaches to the observations were taken from the literature on action research (e.g., Leedy and Ormrod 2005; Mertler 2008). Semi-structured observations (sometimes referred to as unstructured observations) allow flexibility for the teacher to facilitate classroom activities, while taking occasional notes when possible. Mertler (2008) explains that 'unstructured observations are more typical of qualitative data collection, since they are "free flowing", allowing the teacher-researcher to shift focus from one event to another as new, and perhaps more interesting, events arise' (p. 107). Structured observations, requiring my full attention to students' actions and interactions, were made with the use of video recordings. The video recordings were made only of the speeches and debates, with a total of approximately 8 h of recordings.

An additional source of data collected for the study was the students' approximately 1000-word written reflections at the end of the module. This collection of this additional source of data provided reliability for the findings through triangulation, as my observation notes could be mapped onto the students' reflections.

3.4 Method of Analysis

Observation data were kept carefully as reflective notes after each lesson and further notes made using the video recordings of the debate sessions. Notations were made of students' individual development through the process for the purposes of assessment and this study. To systematize the notes, it is important here to point out that a subjective, etic analysis was avoided as much as possible by using an emic analysis that was based on the conceptual framework of 'contextual literacy EAP'. As explained earlier, contextual literacy EAP is the study of English through an understanding of its historical, cultural and social implications, with a focus on rhetorical aspects of English in use in academic settings. Therefore, this framework was used to develop the following criteria for which evidence from observation data were identified:

- Students engaging with rhetorical moves (based on Swales 1990)
- Students using structured argumentation

The rhetorical moves were identified using Swales' (1990) four standard rhetorical moves, as these were explicitly taught in the public speaking course. The moves are: demonstration of interest in the topic, selective review of what is known, establishment of a problem or gap to address, and focus on the currency of evidence. The use of structured argumentation was identified according to a typical internal structure, including one or more premises; a method of reasoning; and a conclusion.

The students' written reflections were analysed using thematic analysis for evidence of development of contextual literacy. This evidence was identified according to the themes of references to culture, references to history and references to society.

4   Findings

The historical nature of the materials in this CLIL pedagogy is ideal for the development of contextual literacy for students in an EIL context. The focus on history, society and culture in the content materials directed students toward reflecting on the use of English in persuading others, beyond lexical and syntactic forms, into critical thinking in English as an international language. From the preparations to the speeches and debates to the final reflection paper, students showed recognition of the roles that history, society and culture play in the shaping of persuasive interactions in English.

4.1   Semi–structured Observations

Field notes from the semi-structured observations were generally limited, as they were handwritten in the classroom while students were engaged in various activities. I was selective with what I wrote down, paying specific attention to students' engagement in activities designed to develop their persuasive skills. Many notes were recorded during the 'interrupting' activity, in which students were given short texts and roles to play in interacting with each other. I made notes according to individual students' ability to successfully complete the activity, but as four groups were doing the task simultaneously, I could focus only on one group at a time. In this activity, I found that students did not generally utilize the rhetorical move strategies they had read about for homework, but instead relied more on stereotypical ideas about aggressive approaches to interrupting and challenging others while speaking (which was led by the three Japanese students who had done most of their schooling in the US, perhaps embodying what they believed to be effective styles of arguing in English). Common approaches included actions such as shouting that resulted in laughter or awkward silence (most notably these responses were often from the three Japanese students who had done their schooling in Japan) as a form of interruption.

   The other activity for which there were more notes recorded was the strategizing time in the two lessons before the debates started. At this point all students had their character role sheets and moved around the room negotiating with other characters to prepare to achieve their prescribed goals. Again, I took notes on individual students' efforts in negotiation, but as this was happening in multiple pairings simultaneously, I was only able to focus on one pair or group at a time. Here I noted that as students now had their role sheets, they were changing some of their stereotypical behaviour noted in the interrupting activity, and instead seemed to be getting into character, which created a more egalitarian atmosphere, with more balanced participation and mutual support. They seemed to be very conscious of the game aspect of the debates and wanted to achieve their goals to win the game. Several students attempted to make deals with others, offering mutual support.

4.2 Structured Observations

The video recordings of the speeches and debates were clear and complete, allowing for comprehensive field notes to be taken in the structured observations. Notes were taken for each speech and debate that each student participated in, and were kept as a 'case file' for each student, which was shared with the students. Following are summarized notes for the four days of debates given by several students, with the roles they played:

Role: Thrasybulus

- Assembly Day 1: Good emphasis on the value of tributes from a military expedition, which certainly paid off! It would have helped to explain why Athens lost the Peloponnesian Wars and to emphasize the defeats caused by a divided Athens.
- Assembly Day 2: Well done drawing people's attention to individuals and the bigger issues from the past—the consistent reference to history helped make your arguments solid. You provided good, important support for Lysias for citizenship and maintained a strong focus on the importance of social welfare.
- Assembly Day 3: The supporting points were less clear and your participation was limited, but you somewhat made up for these deficiencies through appropriately challenging others. Your question to Aristocles was good and important, as was your challenge to Aristides. These challenges were consistent with your character, and very effective in moving toward your goals.
- Assembly Day 4: Your message that Socrates should be silenced and your emphasis on the importance of democracy to stabilize Athens were clear and seemingly well received by the audience, but some of your challenges to others fell flat (e.g., that Socrates ridiculed people) and needed more strength to support them.

Role: Hippocleides

- Assembly Day 1: Your speech emphasized the pride and glory of Athens—lovely hyperbole, but it lacked substance. It wasn't clear *why* you wanted to go on the expedition until later in the debate, where your 'honour the gods' thesis went a long way.
- Assembly Day 2: There was good clarity on your reasoning, but not specifically why you were against the agreement. Although the indirect approach makes sense for your character's strategies in reaching his objective, since you pretty much already reached them, a good preview for the speech would have been very welcome as several audience members were a little lost. The reminder to everyone that Hippocleides is wealthy and has slaves added to the successful logical appeals.
- Assembly Day 3: Again, very good logos in your speech and debate. Your thesis was clear (although a preview would have really helped here!) and your references to Sicily and to the law were effective (although the name of the law was

needed). Good facilitating in the debate with logical, historically accurate challenges to both Aristides and Herodion in the first debate. In the second debate, it was particularly effective to stay focused on the initiative to educate by council decision and argue that the Socratics can teach, but it got a little confusing when you also mentioned the need for public education.

- Assembly Day 4: Wonderfully poetic speech to your faithful followers, but this was too rushed, and without a preview; it wasn't clear what the full intention was for this speech. Similarly, the speech given to the full assembly was also rushed and a little unclear. In the debate you were making statements that should have drawn boos from others, but suspiciously there were none. Did you have any prearrangement with the democrats as well? Otherwise the emphasis on trying Socrates, and statement that a Socratic utopia is legitimate (as long as they're not arrogant rule breakers like Socrates) was good, but I think some people were confused on the argument about tyranny toward the end. But congratulations on getting Socrates executed, paving the way to an easy coup to overtake Athens!

Role: Aristocles

- Assembly Day 1: Your call to examples of past failures and a corrupt democracy provided excellent support that should have helped you reach your objectives, but it seems Hippocleides had gotten to the others first, so your argument was falling on deaf ears. This required some re-strategizing on your part in order to overcome this unforeseen dilemma. But you stayed strong with your 'down with the expedition' thesis anyway.
- Assembly Day 2: Very good previewing and signposting in today's speech, but you were too reliant on your notes, causing others to stop paying attention. Nevertheless, your speech contained excellent logos, and your emphasis on good, factual support was very effective as far as I was concerned. In the debate, your messages of look to the future and down with mythos were character-appropriate and clear. In the second debate you provided important support for Ion with his focus on culture, but the question about payment to attend the assembly was off the mark.
- Assembly Day 3: Good thesis, logos, and emphasis in your speech, but a preview was needed, and you needed to address the indeterminates directly. But you did well to re-emphasize and focus your argument. Your participation in the debate seemed similarly too well rehearsed and not flexible enough to change with the direction the discussion was going in. You provided a good reminder about slaves, but needed to focus the argument on elite women. Otherwise you provided a good, clear response to the challenge from Timon.
- Assembly Day 4: Great speech, but too reliant on notes…good focus on the charges against Socrates—very well researched. The impiety of Aristophanes was an excellent example. The move to no trial OR give Socrates a chance to clear his name was good, but needed to respond to the general sense of the crowd. You provided an excellent quote from Socrates, but mentioned he had already been convicted, which was confusing.

These notes from the individual students' participation in the debates focused on both content and performance in terms of their strategy and approaches in attempting to persuade others. In terms of contextual literacy EAP development, the notes here indicate that rhetorical strategies such as logos, ethos, pathos, and mythos may or may not have been used effectively through appropriate argumentation structuring and contextualization of the argument within the character role and historical period. Displays of content knowledge were important, but not to be done at the expense of proper contextualization (i.e., historical accuracy) of those displays. There was more of a focus on language maintained in the speech notes. Like the notes from the debates, the speech notes were summarized and shared with each student. Following are some examples from the notes on the same three students.

Role: Thrasybulus
Your speeches were well-focused but you needed to take your time—slow down so everyone can follow easily what you say and make notes of the important points, which you emphasized well, but rushed. There was some difficult vocabulary in your speeches that your audience struggled to follow. Always remember to check that your audience understands what you're saying. While previews also would have helped guide your audience, your thesis was always clear.

Role: Hippocleides
Your enthusiasm and dedication is what made your speeches so successful. While you often spoke rather quickly (which meant members of the audience were unable to follow) and there were moments lacking clarity or emphasis on the key ideas (understandably strategically vague) and speech previews were notably missing, these approaches were character-appropriate and effective in persuading your audience.

Role: Aristocles
Your careful research allowed you to form very well-supported arguments that were well structured and delivered. You were generally careful about articulating difficult language, but rushed when you appeared to be less confident. While some stronger emphasis on key ideas might have helped generate better-directed discussions, the speech was effective in directing the content of the discussion toward achieving your goals.

This level of observation was useful for identifying students' rhetorical moves, structured argumentation and use of supporting evidence. The findings are summarized in the following table showing the criteria for which the structured observation data were analysed (Table 1).

The structured observation notes provided valuable insights in consideration of the students' development of contextual literacy, maintaining a focus on the CLIL elements of the debate module. With the historical content providing boundaries for

Table 1 Criteria for analysis of structured observation

Engaging with rhetorical moves	Demonstration of interest in the topic	All students utilized this move in opening their speeches in order to focus the audience on their specific argument as a way of attempting to achieve their game objectives.
	Selective review of what is known	Most students used a single fact on which to build their argument in their speeches rather than reviewing all known relevant facts; however, students who provided a more extensive coverage of a review of the facts had more to draw on for the debates (although this appeared to happen inconsistently with the more prepared students who appeared to be nervous or shy).
	Establishment of a problem or gap to address	Most students successfully identified a problem, although most often based on a single fact; those students who reviewed more facts appeared to have persuaded their audience better in establishing the problem the way they wanted the audience to understand it.
	Focus on the currency of evidence	Very few students referred to the most up-to-date evidence (which, to remain in character, would have been 'word from the street'), occasionally referring to examples from *The Republic*, but more often referring instead to the general information from their character role sheets.
Using structured argumentation	Premises	All students made initial claims in support of their arguments, almost exclusively a single premise.
	Method of reasoning	Most students provided a single, specific argument based on logic, but some students attempted to use an emotional appeal to persuade their audience; some students faltered here, sometimes presenting logical fallacies.
	Conclusions	In all speeches, students concluded with the point they wanted their audience to understand and hopefully agree with them on, but the conclusion was often just a repetition of the premise rather than a point reached through the reasoning provided in the body of the speech; in the debates the points made in the speeches that were most problematic became the premises that were debated, and in most cases no conclusion was drawn as the students attempted to reason with each other until the end of the allotted time period for the debate.

the context, the students' language use was targeted for efforts made to persuade their audiences, including the audience's reception of and responses to the speeches, which depended largely on their ability to understand the speaker. Speakers who spoke too quickly or too softly, especially those with accents that were more difficult for the audience to understand, were encouraged to keep a balanced focus on the content and delivery. Structured observation notes were shared with students after each lesson so students could reflect on the notes in the delivery of later speeches and debates.

4.3   Students' Written Texts

The students' 1000-word written reflections were analysed using a thematic analysis based on the three main themes of the conceptual theory supporting contextual literacy EAP. All 12 students' reflections were found to contain evidence of all three themes, summarized as follows:

References to Culture Reflections on the role of culture in the English language were often concrete, with examples of the experience of the debates being associated with instances of disagreement or discord with people from other cultures. Many students focused on the experience of debating as a Western construct; students with backgrounds in the Americas described feeling 'advantaged' by this aspect, but also recognized that given the mixed audience, a purely Western (i.e., American) approach to the debate was ineffective, as it was their task to persuade the others, not bully them into agreement or defeat them. Several of the six students with more Japanese backgrounds described a feeling of 'disadvantage' as less vocal participants in the debates, but expressed an astute understanding of the value of recognizing the different cultural backgrounds of the group and using language appealing to those group members who could support them. Some Japanese-background students described the experience as 'good training' for assertiveness, and a 'good opportunity' to better understand approaches to persuading people from other cultural backgrounds.

References to History Students commented on how much they learned about democratic societies and ideologies from the content material. There were many references to a clearer understanding of who Socrates was and the impact he had on contemporary approaches to argument and persuading others. Many students were also critical of the material, recognizing the oversimplification of the use of the material for the purposes of the activities in class meant they could only use the experience as an introduction to the history content. Notable was the number of students who drew connections between the content topics of social justice and welfare that were significant in 403 B.C. and their continuing significance today, reflecting on the possibility that these topics were central to human existence and would continue to be debated and negotiated in different ways, depending on context.

References to Society The references to society were all related to the impact the experience of the debate module had on their understanding of how society functions and their role in society. Some students commented on "the failure of democracy" in modern society and contemplated the value of oligarchy, wondering if an oligarchy might not be a better description of the governments of Japan and the United States.

These summaries highlight the references to each of the three themes with a focus on a development of contextual literacy EAP. The references extended to thoughts about the role of the themes in the rhetorical functions of English, considering ways in which different cultures that use English influence the way rhetoric is used. For example, a Japanese-background student wrote (mildly edited for clarity):

> I feel like my Japanese way of using English is different from other people, especially the ones from America. I wanted to argue against their words like they did, but I guess it was my Japanese way that I didn't. Instead I told people what I prepared, and then let other people do a lot of talking. I listened to arguments, and waited until I heard enough to understand the whole picture. I tried to find compromise of their arguments to solve the problem. I think I missed some important chances to achieve my goals sooner because I was too gentle with my argument, but I still won because I achieved my goals. I think at first aggressive attitude is better, but later I saw aggressive speakers didn't achieve their goals. English compromise is stronger than shouting.

The role of history in shaping the English language was also a focus point with several examples provided. One international-background student reflected on the way English was used in the debates, wondering about how different it was from the way ancient Greek was used in 403 B.C.:

> I really liked learning the historical part of the debates, because it was interesting to see many of the topics are still relevant today. I tried to stay in character through the whole thing, but it was really hard. How did ancient Greeks make these arguments 2,000 years ago? Did they preview their arguments and provide supporting evidence like we had to? I think they probably did, and that's why we do those things now. Socrates was a very persuasive person, and there were the Sophists too. They figured out good ways of persuading that we still use. I think maybe we try to improve our strategies all the time, but it must always go back to those powerful ways of using clever language to win the argument.

The use of English in understanding society was a common point of reflection, with students considering how a democratic society means having equality, hearing what everyone has to say, and letting everyone be part of the decision-making process, regardless of English language proficiency. One English L1 international-background student found this aspect important:

> I was fascinated by the ways different people in the group tried to be democratic in the debates, encouraging the quieter students to be heard. The art of getting others to speak and make mistakes that you could use to win the debate was an important skill, and it didn't matter how good your English was, what mattered was the ability to create a balanced discussion. I thought this was something that only happened because we were told to do it, but then it felt very natural. People's arguments weren't stronger because their English was better, they were stronger when other people's arguments were weaker … [this] really showed me both the strengths and weaknesses of our democratic society, and how much it's not really a democracy.

The examples from the written reflections above were especially clear in illustrating the themes, but these were not common sentiments of the reflections. Instead, most students wrote about the learning experience in comparison with other, less critical pedagogies, and emphasized the nervousness they felt in facing a pedagogy such as RTTP. The following example from the Southeast Asian student highlights the processes of debate that the student thought was a particularly valuable aspect of the experience:

During the debate I was particularly motivated by the opposition who since the beginning already putting their best effort to bring us down. I felt like I had to match their enthusiasm. Searching for the flaws of the opposition's characters was done throughout the debates as I try to find loopholes of their ideas and opinions. At times it worked but not always. Strength in my performance I would say was facilitating. I did not see many other characters do that. I tried to bring people into the discussion, particularly the indeterminates, by calling their names and asking for their thoughts about the topic. Other strengths I could recall was by using a lot of Socrates' teaching into the argument. One memorable moment when I used the argument about women and men being equal in soul. I felt very satisfied after I successfully brought it out. This would not have been possible if I had not spent times to research about what is it actually was Socrates meant. I did it to contribute significantly in the discussion.

In this example, it is evident that in addition to qualities such as 'enthusiasm' and being strategic in 'searching for the flaws of the opposition', doing research in the process of persuading others was equally valuable. This idea was common in the reflections, showing that students were gaining not only academic and critical literacies, but a more comprehensive contextual literacy that gave them a deeper understanding of the objectives of the public speaking course.

5 Conclusion

The reflections from the students were overwhelmingly positive about the experience of learning public speaking through the CLIL pedagogy adapted from the Reacting to the Past series. The game selected, *The Threshold of Democracy: Athens in 403 B.C.,* proved to be particularly effective with its focus on the origins of Western civilization and rhetoric. Students learned valuable content about the history and culture that helped form the way rhetoric is used in shaping argument and debate in European languages. This was especially effective given the mixed group of students, as cultural backgrounds and English language proficiency played a much smaller role in their interactions with each other in developing contextual literacy EAP.

Supporting a 'contextual literacy EAP' means providing a valuable perspective on the increasing focus on the social and contextual aspects of academic and critical English literacy education. The focus on these aspects is in response to the perceived need to develop students' literacies to keep up with changing global trends in education and language use. This is especially evident in countries where English has a foreign language status but where it is being used by bi- and multi-lingual speakers. The use of CLIL pedagogies allows for contextual literacy EAP to develop through resourcing other languages, i.e., translanguaging, in the study of content that requires practicing the use of English for persuasive purposes. While academic literacy and critical literacy cover these concepts, it is significant to explore contextual literacy development as a way of understanding the learning and critical thinking that occurs in English language studies in an evolving global context.

As EMI programs are currently being developed in higher education in Japan and elsewhere, it is helpful to look at examples of good practice regarding the development of contextual literacy. In our globalized world, contextual norms are being challenged, and stereotypes of the differences between peoples of different cultural backgrounds are becoming increasingly irrelevant. As the students in this study showed, through engaging in a critical pedagogy such as that of the Reacting to the Past series that puts students at the centre and requires them to discuss, debate, problem-solve and compromise to find solutions, a balanced, global approach to using English rhetoric can create a more egalitarian classroom in which every student is better positioned to gain an equal development of contextual literacy.

Acknowledgements I am grateful to Dr. Hanako Okada, for introducing me to the Ministry of Economy, Trade and Industry announcement as reported by Reed (2010) and for her unwavering support in working with me on adapting the Reacting to the Past pedagogy for use in Japan.

References

Brown, H. G. (2014). Contextual factors driving the growth of undergraduate English-medium instruction programmes at universities in Japan. *The Asian Journal of Applied Linguistics, 1*(1), 50–63.

Brown, H. (2015). *Factors influencing the choice of CLIL classes at university in Japan.* ELTWorldOnline.com, 1–22.

Brown, A., Dashwood, A., Lawrence, J., & Burton, L. (2013). Embracing the Richness of Student Context in Pedagogy. In L. Burton, J. Lawrence, A. Dashwood, & A. Brown (Eds.), *Producing pedagogy* (pp. 74–92). Newcastle upon Tyne: Cambridge Scholars Publishing.

Bruton, A. (2013). CLIL: Some of the reasons why… and why not. *System, 41*(3), 587–597.

Coyle, D. (2007). Content and language integrated learning: Towards a connected research agenda for CLIL pedagogies. *International Journal of Bilingual Education and Bilingualism, 10*(5), 543–562.

Davidson, B. (1995). Critical thinking education faces the challenge of Japan. *Inquiry: Critical Thinking Across the Disciplines, 14*(3), 41–53.

Demetrion, G. (2001). Discerning the contexts of adult literacy education: Theoretical reflections and practical applications. *The Canadian Journal for the Study of Adult Education, 15*(2), 104–127.

Freire, P. (1970). *Cultural action for freedom, monograph series no. 1.* Cambridge, MA: Harvard Educational Review.

Galloway, N., & Rose, H. (2015). *Introducing Global Englishes.* Abingdon: Routledge.

Haberland, H. (2011). Ownership and maintenance of a language in transnational use: Should we leave our lingua franca alone? *Journal of Pragmatics, 43*(4), 937–949.

Hino, N. (2018). English as an international language for Japan: Historical contexts and future prospects. *Asian Englishes, 20*(1), 27–40.

Leedy, P. D., & Ormrod, J. E. (2005). *Practical research: Planning and design.* Upper Saddle River: Pearson Custom.

Lin, A. M., & Lo, Y. Y. (2017). Trans/languaging and the triadic dialogue in content and language integrated learning (CLIL) classrooms. *Language and Education, 31*(1), 26–45.

Lockley, T. (2014). Some learning outcomes and contextual factors of history as content and language integrated learning (CLIL) in a Japanese context. *Studies in Linguistics and Language Teaching, 25*, 165–188.

McKinley, J. (2013a). Displaying critical thinking in EFL academic writing: A discussion of Japanese to English contrastive rhetoric. *RELC Journal, 44*(2), 195–208.

McKinley, J. (2013b). Reacting to the past: A CLIL pedagogy. *The Language Teacher, 37*(5), 69–71.

McKinley, J. (2017). Identity construction in learning English academic writing in a Japanese university. *Journal of Asia TEFL, 14*(2), 228–243.

McKinley, J. (2018). Making the EFL to ELF transition at a global traction university. In A. Bradford & H. Brown (Eds.), *English-medium instruction at universities in Japan: Policy, challenges and outcomes* (pp. 238–249). Bristol: Multilingual Matters.

Mertler, C. A. (2008). *Action research: Teachers as researchers in the classroom*. Thousand Oaks: Sage.

Modiano, M. (1999). Standard English(es) and educational practices for the world's lingua franca. *English Today, 15*(4), 3–13.

Nikula, T., & Moore, P. (2016). Exploring translanguaging in CLIL. *International Journal of Bilingual Education and Bilingualism, 19*, 1–13.

Ober, J., Norman, N., & Carnes, M. (2015). *The threshold of democracy: Athens in 403 B.C* (4th ed.). New York: W.W. Norton & Company.

Pinner, R. (2013). Authenticity of purpose: CLIL as a way to bring meaning and motivation into EFL contexts. *Asian EFL Journal, 15*(4), 138–159.

Reed, W. (2010). *The blueprint of 21st century employability*. Daijob HR Club. Retrieved from hrclub.daijob.com/hrclub/?p=815

Rinnert, C., & Kobayashi, H. (2009). Situated writing practices in foreign language settings: The role of previous experience and instruction. In R. M. Manchon (Ed.), *Writing in foreign language contexts: Learning, teaching, and research* (pp. 23–48). Bristol: Multilingual Matters.

Rose, H., & McKinley, J. (2018). Japan's English-medium instruction initiatives and the globalization of higher education. *Higher Education, 75*(1), 111–129. https://doi.org/10.1007/s10734-017-0125-1.

Scribner, S. (1986). Literacy in three metaphors. In N. Stein (Ed.), *Literacy in American schools: Learning to read and write*. Chicago: University of Chicago Press.

Siegel, J. (2007). Creoles and minority dialects in education: An update. *Language and Education, 21*(1), 66–86.

Singh, M., & Shrestha, M. (2008). International pedagogical structures. In M. Hellstén & A. Reid (Eds.), *Researching international pedagogies: Sustainable practice for teaching and learning in higher education* (pp. 65–82). Dordrecht, Netherlands: Springer.

Sticht, T. G. (1997). *Functional context education: Making knowledge relevant*. San Diego: Consortium for Workforce Education and Lifelong Learning.

Swales, J. (1990). *Genre analysis: English in academic and research settings*. Cambridge, UK: Cambridge University Press.

Thompson, G., & McKinley, J. (2018). Integration of content and language learning. In J. Liontas & S. Abrar-ul-Hassan (Eds.), *TESOL encyclopedia of English language teaching*. New York: Wiley-Blackwell.

Learning by Design: Crafting the Knowledge Processes to Enable Pre-service Secondary Teachers to Design Authentic Learning

Helen CD McCarthy

Abstract It has been my experience working with university pre-service secondary teachers that some science, engineering, technology and mathematics (STEM) students are sceptical of having to study literacy units within their degree. Their reasoning is that there is no purpose for learning the teaching of literacy as they are far more concerned with honing their STEM subject content knowledge. This chapter will draw on the experiences of first-year secondary students who learned to apply a pedagogy of knowledge processes (Cope B, Kalantzis M: Pedagog Int J 4(3):164–195, 2009) or things you do to know. Knowledge processes are an activity type that represent a distinct way of making content knowledge by oscillating and weaving pedagogical repertoires (Freebody P, Luke A: Literacy as engaging with new forms of life: the four resources model. In: Anstey M, Bull G (eds) The literacy Lexicon, (2nd ed.). Pearson, Sydney, pp 51–66, 2003), including multimodal multiliteracies intentionally designed to help students to understand what they need to do in this world in order to know (Kalantzis and Cope, Literacies. Cambridge University Press, Cambridge, 2012). The point of sharing the pre-service students' testimonies is to reveal the transformatory processes they moved through: from healthy scepticism to openly revealing how the new order multimodal multiliteracies (The New London Group: Harv Educ Rev 66(1):60–92, 1996) had an impact on their capacity to develop engaging and authentic literacy pedagogies in ways they had not previously imagined.

Keywords Multiliteracies, Learning by Design, Multimodality, Knowledge processes

H. CD. McCarthy (✉)
School of Education, Curtin University, Perth, WA, Australia
e-mail: H.McCarthy@curtin.edu.au

T. Dobinson, K. Dunworth (eds.), *Literacy Unbound: Multiliterate, Multilingual, Multimodal*, Multilingual Education 30,
https://doi.org/10.1007/978-3-030-01255-7_6

1   Introduction

Even as a poverty-stricken PhD student with barely two shekels to rub together, I still could not resist the temptation. Stealthily I was perusing the lavishly crammed conference bookshop tables and lurking without intent when I saw it. Maybe it was the quiet blue cover that first alerted me amongst the conference loudness, but I know for sure it was that title word, the one proper noun, *Multiliteracies*, that definitely stumped me. It was 2000 and I had never seen nor heard that word before. Procuring the book, I read the compilation of chapters detailing a programmatic manifesto advocating multiliteracies with tacit clarity. Each of the 14 authors' words reverberated in my head as well as my heart. Never had I experienced anything so entirely affirming, validating everything I believed pedagogically about preparing students to participate in the yet uncharted twenty-first century. The manifesto provided a range of ways of making meaning, sensitive to a variety of socio-cultural contexts while integrating new communication demands and purposefully using multiple modes including digital media. Its agency inspired me and I felt an urgency to start preparation, to be primed and ready to participate with the learners of the new millennium. Decades earlier I had started working with undergraduate pre-service teachers and frequently heard colleagues express reluctance to tutor secondary students in literacy. They said secondary students, unlike primary and early childhood students, tended to be suspicious about why they were learning 'literacy'. Nodding their heads in shared collegial conspiracy, they consoled each other by saying, 'Let's see them in front of a class of Year 8s who don't share their love of physics, chemistry, mathematics or science and just wait until they have to teach students who cannot read, write or even spell *equation* much less "Pythagoras's theorem"'.

Subsequently, when I presented the first-year unit entitled Teaching Literacy in Secondary Schools in a bachelor of education course at an Australian university, without looking too hard, I recognised several of my colleague's claims. I sensed that the students, in a manner very unlike mitosis, were beginning to split into two extremely different cells. One cell comprised of humanities and social sciences (HASS) students who immediately identified literacy as complementary with their specialist subjects in a genuinely symbiotic way. The other cell comprised of the science, technology, engineering and mathematics (STEM) students who asserted that since they were content specialists, they were surprised and disappointed that they had to enrol in a core literacy unit. Each week as I walked into the workshop I could feel their churlish defiance. Acknowledging their open irritation spurred me on and I knew I had been given a consummate opportunity to demonstrate literacies, therein the multiliteracies manifesto, in ways they had not previously imagined.

My aim in this chapter is to provide a glimpse of what happened when these first-year pre-service secondary STEM teachers learned to apply a multiliteracies pedagogy known as Learning by Design, an intrinsic structure of four orientations known as knowledge processes: experiencing, conceptualising, analysing and applying. These processes 'are a map of the range of pedagogical moves that may prompt teachers to extend their pedagogical repertoires' (Cope and Kalantzis 2000, p. 186). This activity type represents a distinct way of making content knowledge by oscillating and weaving in pedagogical repertoires (Freebody and Luke 2003), including multimodal multiliteracies, intentionally designed to help pre-service teachers to understand what they need to do as active designers of meaning (Kalantzis and Cope 2012). It also introduces several of the dissenting voices who have been contributing to the new-millennium discourse regarding the role of education and the proficiency or readiness of schools to envisage and respond to students' shifting learning preferences. To understand the progression of this story, the chapter starts with a brief historical overview on how Learning by Design came about and why the timing of this impetus was a catalyst for great and necessary change.

2   Historical Background: The New London Group

In September 1994 a group of 10 highly experienced educators from various fields in several English-speaking countries came together. Courtney Cazden, Bill Cope, Norman Fairclough, Jim Gee, Mary Kalantzis, Gunther Kress, Allan Luke, Carmen Luke, Sarah Michaels and Martin Nakata met for a week in the small town of New London, New Hampshire in the United States of America. Unable to attend the September assembly, Joseph Lo Bianco attended subsequent meetings. As a result of long-term collegial involvement in education, and specifically the teaching of literacy, they recognised they were collectively experiencing a profound sense of apprehension as the new millennium loomed. One of their concerns was that irrespective of significant positive intervention regarding the teaching of language and literacy, major disparities on many levels continued to exist, served increasingly by neoliberal ideologies. Another concern related to the traditional pedagogical style of teachers, with the group suggesting that there were emerging shifts away from the didactic, teacher-centred style since it was proving to be increasingly less appropriate to learners and learning settings (Luke and Freebody 1999; Emmitt et al. 2010). Driving this emerging shift was the momentous global expansion of digital information technology and its resourceful capabilities within the massive substructure of computers interconnected via the Internet. Driven by enthusiasts and neophytes, this free, hugely imaginative, unprecedented network was taken up globally by users who began exploring a now borderless world like learners in a kindergarten of creativity, keen to collaborate and share their knowledge.

In New London, the group's strategic plan was to consider what they could do in literacy pedagogy based on "different national and cultural experiences" (Cope and Kalantzis 2000, p. 4). Having established from their experiences in their own countries that they shared the common apprehension that teachers and educators globally did not necessarily understand the socio-cultural implications, or anticipated the unparalleled impact of the emerging digital revolution. The group forecast that educators needed to actively respond to how learners were increasingly applying contemporary digital styles to language and literacy learning. As literacy specialists, the group recognised that they had a critical role in creating a prototype to guide educators on how to navigate these new demands in the changing learning environments and workplaces. Educators also needed to be savvy about the platforms from which learners were now beginning to operate. Teachers needed to become early adopters of this new transformatory literateness by designing learning in response to these diverse influences, enabling learners' to fully participate in the twenty-first century.

Cognisant there was a critical need for on-going dialogue to address the looming issues, the group continued to meet for another 3 years, becoming known as the New London Group. As the new millennium approached there was little doubt that the New London Group's astute initiatives in language and literacy teaching were both prudent and timely. Later in this chapter, using the group's keystone philosophies, the focus will move to the application of those knowledge systems created specifically by Bill Cope and Mary Kalantzis to develop the intrinsic structure used to design learning.

3 Multiliteracies and Multimodality Defined

The New London Group's perspicacious understanding of the multidimensional capacities of digital information technologies and Internet communication literacies was that firstly they were never again going to be static and secondly that modes of meaning-making representation were going to be far broader than language alone. This emphasis compelled them to assert that it was far more appropriate to redefine literacy in terms of 'multiliteracies':

> Multiliteracies: a word we chose because it describes two important arguments we might have with the emerging cultural, institutional and global order. The first argument engages with the multiplicity of communications channels and media; the second with the increasing salience of cultural and linguistic diversity (Cope and Kalantzis 2000, p. 5).

Correspondingly, as a result of the phenomenal global escalation of uptake by users within the now ubiquitous digital multimedia space, they argued that the shift from a one-dimensional mode (traditionally via writing or speaking) now created different social semiotic possibilities as multiple modes were being used to make patterns of meaning. According to Kress (2000), the decreasing complexity of writing was to be compensated for by the increasingly complex multimodal expressions used by learners in their communication practices through linguistic, visual, aural, gestural, spatial, kinaesthetic and synaesthetic literateness. Equally quick to see the benefits of embedding multimodal functions to enhance communication practices, users/learners became, in themselves, the catalyst for changing the semiotic milieu. Gee (2000), an early advocate of the multifarious possibilities that digital and information technologies presented, saw these possibilities:

> We are living amidst major changes, changes creating new ways with words, new literacies, and new forms of learning. These changes are creating, as well, new relationships, and alignments within, between, and among the spheres of family, school, business and science (p. 43).

Concomitant with Gee, the New London Group recognized that these emergent relational literacies increased through digital connectedness amongst local and global spheres. These relational literacies included crafted conscious mode and code switching and translanguaging as the diversity of global users communicated via English, the *lingua mundi*, or world language, and the common language or lingua franca for worldwide engagement. The term 'world Englishes' coined by

Indian linguist Braj Kachru stressed the idea of pluricentricity and diversity of Englishes in all their 'cross-cultural reincarnations' (2006, p. 447), implying users' ability to express culturally specific messages, performed in various social contexts or discourses (Gee 2000), applying appropriate communicative functions that serve different social, cultural and linguistic identities. 'English is also breaking into multiple and increasingly differentiated Englishes marked by accent, national origin, subculture style, and professional or technical communities' (Cope and Kalantzis 2000, p. 6). Therein the New London Group recommended that as a result of these communication practices, terms such as *multiliteracies* and *multimodality* were most appropriate to discuss both the emerging literacies and the new social practices and ways of participating as citizens: "Either way, the old literacy is no longer adequate, either to support decentralised governance along neoliberal lines or a civil society capable of making reasonable demands of its state" (Cope and Kalantzis 2009, p. 172). The multiliteracies approach advocated active citizenship, centred on equity within gender, race, ethnicity and disability. As a pedagogical paradigm it rejected neoliberal ideology that places education as an industry, schools as profit-seeking marketplaces and teachers as de-professionalised practitioners, reduced to facilitators of testing systems and surveillance mechanisms.

4   A New Millennium: The Equity Era or Not?

The New London Group were not alone in voicing concern that education and pedagogy had become increasingly centred on neoliberal ideologies positioned on patterns of exclusion or privilege controlled by a system following the user pays principle. Raewyn Connell (2013), one of Australia's leading social scientists and pubic intellectuals asserted that:

> Neoliberalism has a definite view of education, understanding it as human capital formation. It is the business of forming the skills and attitudes needed by a productive workforce—productive in the precise sense of producing an ever-growing mass of profits for market economy (p. 104).

As such, school systems sorted in an exercise of hegemony have the propensity to increase both privilege and poverty. Critical constructivist Henry Giroux (1992) advocated that pedagogy was not just something that went on in schools, but rather it had to be posited at the very centre of what should be about the discourse of social responsibility. He claimed that students from subordinate and marginalised groups continued to be silenced by exclusion and ideological distortions, ensuing that another 'whole generation of poor, young people of colour is being lost to the excruciating devastation of bad schooling, poverty, hopelessness and joblessness' (Giroux 1992, p. 4). Furthermore, Giroux called for educators to become engaged to create alternate public spheres. Titling these educators as 'border crossers', he warned they had to take up the dual task of not only creating new objects of knowledge but also addressing how inequities, power and human suffering were rooted in basic institutional structures. Having established that schools are anything but ideologically innocent, Giroux advocated the need to develop a pedagogy *of* difference and pedagogy *for* difference: 'If teachers can develop a pedagogy *for* difference, one which is characterized by an ongoing effort to create new spaces of discourse, to rewrite cultural narratives, and to define the terms of another perspective—a view from "elsewhere"' (Giroux 1989, p. 142) will provide students with the proficiencies to define their own identity and to find their own voices for exercising civic courage. He claimed it is the goal of educators to learn to take the perspective of the other, to deliberately submerge oneself into the others' world to eventually emerge, he hoped, transformed. Built into these processes is the underpinning necessity that the knowledge belonging to those of the margins and the periphery is a vital, intrinsic and natural part of the curriculum, insisting that culture and social practises 'no longer need to be mapped out or referenced solely on the basis of the dominant models of western culture' (Giroux 1992, p. 32).

> What is at stake here is not simply the issue of bad teaching, but the broader refusal to take seriously the categories of meaning, experiences, and voice that students use to make sense of themselves and the world around them. It is this refusal to enable speech for those who have been silenced, to acknowledge the voices of the other, and to legitimate and reclaim student experience as a fundamental category in the production of knowledge that the character of the current dominant discourse on the canon reveals it totalitarian and undemocratic ideology (Giroux 1992, p. 95).

He referred to the seminal works of Dewey (1916), who had also argued that a liberal education afforded people the opportunity to involve themselves in the deepest problems of society, to acquire the knowledge, skills and ethical responsibility necessary for 'reasoned participation in democratically organised public' (Giroux 1992, p. 97).

This reasoned participation aspiration is taken up in the next section: the changing lexicon. It explores what can occur when local and global communication connectedness and, utilising a *lingua mundi* of multiple Englishes, creates borderless socio-cultural fusion providing opportunities for individuals and communities to become democratically organised and participants for social change.

5   The Changing Lexicon

At the start of the new millennium there was a growing awareness amongst parents and teachers that learner behaviour was changing. This was demonstrated by students' self-motivated desire to learn how to operate computers to access digital information. As students' enthusiasm for the tool intensified, they began to work increasingly more independently. They used games to learn and problem solve and sought out online tutorials to know more. They became collaborators in completing complex projects, keen to stay on working and often on several tasks simultaneously. They began to supplement their assignments with a range of multimodal resources. So marked was this period that this age group of learners became known as the Millennials (Howe and Strauss 2000) or digital natives (Prensky 2001). While this transformation was not necessarily a challenge to the dominant discourse driven by the neoliberal user-pays ideology, it did give the illusion that there was a definite changing of the guard. The Millennials' ability to effortlessly access information due to their digital proficiency meant that they did not need to rely on traditional hegemonies to source knowledge. The intelligence was that the Millennials' modus operandi was synergetic and cooperative and most noted was their preference to share knowledge for free.

This observation was captured by Hedley Beare in *Creating the Future School* (2001) based on the changes to education that the main protagonist, a five year-old girl named Angelica who starts school in 2000, will see in her lifetime. Beare (2001) advocated that the goal of educators is to generate new knowledge systems and new ways of being in the worlds. He insisted that the word *world*, like *literacy*, needed to be used in the plural to best reflect the reality of the evolving creative learning environments. Another early adopter of aesthetic knowledge as central to learning that engages creativity as a generative force is one of Australia's foremost art educators and experienced researchers, Robyn Ewing (2010), who supported the increasing creativity of these promising multimodal multiliteracies methodologies. Ewing also called for the conceptual structure of emerging curriculums to remain central, advocating for teachers to:

1. share intellectual control with students;
2. look for occasions when students can work out part (or all) of the content or instructions;
3. provide opportunities for choice and independent decision-making;
4. provide a diverse range of ways of experiencing success;
5. promote talk that is exploratory, tentative and hypothetical;
6. encourage students to learn from other students' questions and comments;
7. build a classroom environment that supports risk taking;
8. use a wide variety of intellectually challenging teaching procedures;
9. use teaching procedures that are designed to promote specific aspects of quality and learning;
10. develop students' awareness of the big picture: how the various activities fit together and link to the big ideas;
11. regularly raise students' awareness of the nature of the components of quantity learning;
12. promote assessment as part of the learning process (Ewing 2010, p. 47).

The 12 pedagogical recommendations that Ewing identified squarely positioned the school to be a communal and non-hierarchical place where learning occurs within an appropriate negotiated space and within realistic timeframes in ways that are attentive of cyclical and/or seasonal variations. As a consequence, this learning environment fosters self-assuredness where teachers are not controllers but rather connectors, working in teams across multidiscipline, multiple-age groups and confident that 'the heart of the curriculum would shrink to a core of knowings essential to negotiating one's way around the global community of knowledge' (Beare 2001, p. 157).

Likewise, David Warner, who coined the term *knowledge era* in his 2006 text *Schooling for the Knowledge Era*, maintained that the knowledge era is an age of greater freedom of thought and access to information, regularly providing a broader and more complex view of the world that often occurs in real time. This global knowledge era rewards innovative, self-directed workers who can thrive in fast-moving, constantly changing environments. This sentiment is also endorsed by Patrick Slattery, Professor of Curriculum Development and Philosophy of Education at Texas A&M University, who suggested that the culture of the knowledge era is one that acknowledges the worldview of young people as different and that because their learning styles have developed considerably, 'individuals create a unique and often perplexing life-world in classrooms' (Slattery 1995, p. 103). In this new knowledge era, where people are linked locally and/or globally through an assortment of technologies, generating and processing significant amounts of information simultaneously with the intent to share data is a new phenomenon. One of Australia's most experienced educators, David Loader (2007) advised, 'It is now clear that as a result of this ubiquitous [digital] environment and the sheer volume of their interaction with it, today's [new generation] students think and process information fundamentally differently from their predecessors' (Loader 2007, p. 12). The implications of these developments were becoming broadly apparent in that schools had to be less prescriptive and more compatible with the new interface where 'the curriculum is far more divided and differentiated, the boundaries between learning, leisure and work are blurred and an influx of students from different cultural backgrounds is reshaping school populations' (Wadham et al. 2007, p. 248). They reported that young people 'cooperate in ways never before possible' (Loader 2007, p. 27) and are changing the way humans communicate by their ability to act together for shared purposes to effect change. They suggested group relationships are prioritised and socially engaging, motivated by the sense of connectedness through shared, often congenial and equitable experiences. This collaboration is a process 'wherein each individual becomes a participant in an epistemology of "emergence": they come to know through their part in things' (Wright 2008, p. 99). The key to emergence is that it often develops in ways not always anticipated, often serendipitously leading to complex evolutionary designs that are inherently reflexive and social: 'It changes people's lives because it creates new relationships and as a result creates new knowledge systems and new ways of being in the world' (Wright 2008, p. 100).

6   A Pedagogy for a New Millennium: Programmatic Manifesto for Multiliteracies

The attendant intrinsic configuration featuring new ways of being in the worlds (Gee 2000; Beare 2001) necessitated new pedagogies. Postulated some time earlier by the New London Group, their theoretical framework known as Learning by Design was a direct response in order to prepare for the now-accepted shift in educational and socio-cultural reality. The creation of their experimental programmatic manifesto for multiliteracies was underscored by an emphasis on diversity, multimodality and pedagogy. Built on notions of design for learning and meaning as transformation, their emergent multiliteracies program manifesto helps pre-service teachers and teachers incorporate richly embedded pedagogies focussed on *how* to teach as opposed to traditional didactic literacy teaching that has focussed predominantly on *what* to teach.

7 Application of the Multiliteracies Manifesto in an Australian Context: Learning by Design

While the multiliteracies program was instigated in several countries, the Learning by Design model was introduced to Australian educators as a result of a successful Australian Research Council grant that utilised the expertise of 50 schools and the knowledge of over 100 teachers in the late 1990s. Although Kalantzis and Cope are currently based at the University of Illinois at Chicago in the United States, they continue to work extensively with educators in Australia. Similarly, co-convenor and associate Rita van Haren returns to Australia from the University of Illinois regularly to coordinate the Learning by Design Multiliteracies Program and research in the Lanyon District of Schools in Canberra in the Australian Capital Territory, where the model has been successfully implemented across pre-primary to secondary programs. Later in the chapter I return to Rita van Haren's development of learning modules, where students take the Learning by Design model to build modules that are uploaded to share online via the text *Literacies* website (https://cgscholar.com/). But first, what is the Learning by Design model?

8 The Learning by Design Model

The fact you are still reading this is truly commendable and I applaud your steely resolve, but from here on in if you have not taught using this approach you may find the overview complicated or even difficult going. I would recommend that you persist with this practitioner's guide since learning to plan in this way will provide you with unbounded delightful teaching experiences where you will witness astounding student learning.

Learning by Design can be best defined as an intrinsic structure or act of construction that grew out of the multiliteracies program pedagogy and uses theory and practice to establish a set of organising ideas that help to create, discuss and plan what teachers must do to address learner diversity and lifeworld differences. It achieves this by integrating a mix of progressive, traditional and critical pedagogies by multiple modes of meaning making that may include multimodality practices through linguistic, visual, aural, gestural, spatial, kinaesthetic and synaesthetic literateness.

Teacher-centred didactic teaching is a process of transmission and, while this methodology does have a place in the repertoire of approaches, the objective of the Learning by Design orientation is transformatory. Kalantzis explains: 'A pedagogy of multiliteracies is characteristically transformative as it builds on notions of design and meaning-as-transformational. Transformative curriculum recognizes that the process of designing redesigns the designer. Learning is a process of self-recreation. Cultural dynamism and diversity are the results' (Cope and Kalantzis 2009, p. 184). The transformatory multimodal multiliteracies pedagogies pivot on four orientations, known in Learning by Design as the knowledge processes.

8.1 The Knowledge Processes

The knowledge processes are apportioned into four colour-coded orientations: experiencing (green), conceptualising (blue), analysing (red) and applying (yellow). These four orientations are then divided into eight elements: experiencing the known/experiencing the new, conceptualising by naming/conceptualising with theory, analysing functionally/analysing critically and applying appropriately/applying creatively.

8.2 The Placemat Template to Guide Designing

Pre-service secondary teachers use the four colour-coded template designed by Cope, Kalantzis and van Haren that is known as the placemat to guide their learning design. This is available to be reproduced: http://newlearningonline.com/learning-by-design/the-placemat. It is important to note that the knowledge processes are not prescriptive and do not need to be introduced in a particular sequence. The sequencing of the knowledge processes will depend entirely on the designer, who will map the learning progressively and in synchronisation with the students' learning requirements. However, because starting with the known and working towards the unknown sits well with good practice, most designers start with experiencing the known. Likewise, the boundaries between the knowledge processes are not set rigidly. For example, it can be difficult to conceptualise with theory without some overlap into analysing functionally. This is a good thing because often the same knowledge/content can be presented in a range of contexts. The following provides a working definition of each knowledge process.

8.3 Experiencing the Known

The objective here is getting the designer to draw on learner prior knowledge and experience, personal interests, life worlds, the everyday and the familiar, making connections to self and to other texts and establishing baseline knowledge.

8.4   Experiencing the New

This entails introducing and familiarising learners with the new experience by exposing them to texts (real or virtual), guest speakers, presentations and excursions and ensuring they can respond in open-ended, hands-on ways.

8.5   Conceptualising by Naming

This involves using experiential learning to define and draw out new concepts, ideas, themes, understandings and vocabulary and then identifying numeracy and literacy strategies.

8.6   Conceptualising by Theorising

This necessitates generalising and synthesising concepts and theories by linking and drawing them together, exploring them in more depth, deepening understanding and practising skills. It may include 'what if' scenarios.

8.7   Analysing Functionally

This encourages designers to examine the structure of multimodal texts and linguistic, visual, gestural, audio and spatial grammar in context. Examining function: What is it for? What does it do? What are the effects?

8.8   Analysing Critically

This insists designers interrogate purpose and audience, looking at how multimodal 'grammatical' choices position audiences therein and encouraging the examination of relevance, different perspectives and individual, social, cultural and environmental effects. This provokes courageous conversations about who gains and who loses and through whose cultural prism this viewpoint is generated.

8.9 *Applying Appropriately*

This means applying independently what has been taught and providing assessment opportunities. It involves transformation, reinventing or revoicing the world in a new way.

8.10 *Applying Creatively*

This engages the designer in pondering and creating interesting ways for learners to present their new knowledge by independently taking knowledge and capabilities from one setting and adapting them to a different setting and in this way creating a different way that had not been thought of previously.

9 Literacy Pedagogies Within the Knowledge Processes

The following section of the chapter describes how literacy comes into its own and fits within the design process. Adjoining to the knowledge processes are four literacy pedagogies: didactic, authentic, functional and critical.

9.1 *Didactic Literacy Pedagogy*

Aligned to didactic literacy pedagogy is conceptualising by naming and theorising. Didactic teaching turns on what the teacher says rather than what the learner does. The balance of agency weighs heavily towards the teacher. Teachers are in command of knowledge and their mission is to transmit this knowledge to learners, who, it is hoped, dutifully rote learn and absorb it. Students who succeed in this setting have learned to memorise and repeat the 'important points' of the lesson with little critical analysis.

While didactic teaching is not really consistent with the pedagogy of Learning by Design, it is used as one of a repertoire of strategies. There are clear times when students must learn specific content and, as didactic instruction is dependent on the teacher to provide all the required instruction, it is an effective manner by which to transfer knowledge to the learner.

9.2 Functional Literacy Pedagogy

Aligned to functional literacy pedagogy is analysing functionally and analysing critically. Functional literacy is an approach to literacy that focuses on the meaning of real-world texts and the ways in which different types of texts are structured to serve different purposes. A key insight of genre theory is that language occurs in a social context and that it is structured according to the purposes it serves in a particular context and according to the social relations entailed by that activity. In this element, reading and writing are closely linked.

Analysing functionally encompasses performing processes of reasoning, drawing inferential and deductive conclusions, establishing relationships between cause and effect and making logical connections. This guides learners to develop chains of reasoning and explain patterns in knowledge and experience.

The motives of analysing critically are knowledge making, cultural creation and communication. Learners are encouraged to interrogate the interests behind a meaning or action. This requires interpretation of the social and cultural context of a piece of knowledge. An important element of this orientation is reflecting meta-cognitively on the influence of one's own perspectives and processes of thinking.

9.3 Authentic Literacy

Aligned to authentic literacy is experiencing the known and experiencing the new. Learning that is authentic is grounded in the lifeworld of the learner; it is grounded in experience—often embodied experience—and aims at being relevant and meaningful to learners. Its practical application and benefits are apparent. This means it is not abstract or separate from the learner. Authentic literacy involves disciplinary knowledge and is focused on the connections between experiences, concepts, theories, reflection, inquiry and practical know-how, starting with the learner's own interests, experiences and motivations. In the case of literacies, whole-language and process writing are good examples of this approach, with their focus on student self-expression in writing and meaningful enjoyment of reading. Learning is most effective, according to experiential theories of learning, when it is socially situated, connects with learner identities and is meaningful to them; 'however, as a stand-alone pedagogy, it has also come under attack and found itself in retreat in recent decades' (Kalantzis et al. 2016, pp. 120–121).

Directly counter to didactic pedagogy, this approach is learner centred and focuses primarily on experiencing or learning by doing. Authentic literacy experiences are personally meaningful reading and writing occurrences with a focus on the processes of reading and writing rather than the formalities of rules and conventions.

9.4 Critical Literacy

Aligned to critical literacy are applying appropriately and applying creatively. This approach to literacy focuses on texts that communicate student interests and experiences and address challenging social issues such as discrimination and disadvantage. The essence of education is transformation of self and environment, which may be pragmatic (enabling learners to do their best in the given social conditions) or emancipatory (making the world a better place). Dimensions of critical literacies are to connect with lived experiences, to think critically, to take action-offer solutions, make others aware and participate. The differences between didactic and critical literacies are sharply differentiated. Didactic literacy focuses on formal rules, mechanical skills and training, and social reproductive values. It is passive and compliant. Critical literacies focus on personal and transformative education. They rely on shared democratic values that are active and participatory and their creative application is an extension within the learning design that sets the orientations apart from most other programs of learning.

To recap, the four knowledge processes are experiencing (known and new), conceptualising (by naming and by theorising), analysing (functionally and critically) and applying (appropriately and creatively). The four literacies are didactic, authentic, functional and critical. The focus in the next section of the chapter is on how the first-year pre-service teachers came to develop and design learning from their specialist content areas.

10 New Semester: Week One

I arrived early to the workshop room, pulled up the blinds to let in the dappled morning light and turned the data projector on. The opening slide exhibited a large welcome on the screen along with my name and contact details. I had all the resources we were going to be using throughout the semester on the table so students could see the hard copies, including the unit text: *Literacies* by Kalantzis and Cope (2012). In they came, some happy and chatting (could they possibly be the HASS majors?), but the majority of the group looked peeved. Clearly they had been talking amongst themselves about the unit and clearly they saw me as their nemesis who was taking up their time. Ignoring my smiling face, open upward palms in a friendly welcoming gesture, they arranged themselves around the room, some still on their mobile phones. When I used my trusty old non-verbal communication cue to start, nothing happened. I balked a little at being rebuffed then tried my cue to start again and still nothing happened. Being the mother of three university-aged teenagers, by the time I get to work in the morning I am hardly in the mood for dissidence. So as surreptitiously as one can possibly be with backpacks strewn all over the floor, I stepped carefully across the room and closed in on the noisy ringleader as he messed about. I am unashamed to say that I used my scary mother proxemics to get him seated and attentive. The rest followed his lead and settled in. Then I asked, 'OK, you mob, what's up?' Immediately they began to tell me that they had passed English in their final secondary school examination, so why did they have to do a core unit in literacy at university? In an adversarial tone they contended that since the majority of them were STEM students, where would teaching literacy 'fit' in their subjects? I listened attentively to their reasoning and I acknowledged their open irritation but I knew I had an opportunity to demonstrate literacies in ways they had not previously imagined. After a considerably candid discussion a truce of sorts was drawn. I got on with the unit learning objectives and went through the assessments tasks. Each assessment was designed to build onto the next and would culminate in the creation of a module of learning they could teach on their practicum. I returned to my presentation and clicked on the hyperlink and opened a sample of a module titled 'Pythagoras's theorem' designed by Rita van Haren, Rebecca O'Brien, Ed Cuthbertson and Cherie Connors. The module showed how students learn about Pythagoras's theorem and how to relate theory in real-life contexts. The designers apply their conceptual mathematical understanding by designing a multimedia presentation about how to teach Pythagoras's theorem to future Year 8 students. Using the sample from the unit text website, https://cgscholar.com/, the pre-service students could begin to see the feasible connections of how literacies within mathematics might potentially 'fit'.

11   Game Plan: How Learning by Design all Fits Together

Mindful that the first-year students were just beginning to embark on their language-learning teaching journey, I presented the information incrementally using a series of infographics. The instructions were set out: First they were to arrange themselves in small groups in their major area of study, with the option that they could also choose to select their minor area of study. Next they were to look closely at the Australian Curriculum Assessment and Reporting Authority's (ACARA) National Australian Curriculum to look for possible topics of learning they could teach in their second-semester practicum.

Second, they were going to use Glogster, the multimodal, interactive multimedia poster platform, as a visual prop to support their oral presentation, exhibiting how they applied each of the multimodal devices within their Glogster poster to demonstrate to their peers how they were going to apply the knowledge processes of experiencing, conceptualising, analysing and applying. Their peers were going to watch the presentation then offer compliments for areas of strengths and suggestions for areas needing improvement. Using these recommendations the group would then revisit their design and make the necessary amendments.

Third, they were going to use their placemat/Glogster plan as a framework to develop a module of learning using the Learning Element format found on the text website https://cgscholar.com/. This was to be submitted as their final compulsory assessment. If they desired they could go further and upload their module onto the online resource on Scholar. This was not a course requirement nor was there an expectation for them to do so.

When I had finished going through the unit assessment requirements I paused to check whether anyone had questions. The room remained silent. There was some head scratching followed by deep forlorn sighs. No one knew how to use Glogster and neither did they care to know its alleged interactive multimodal features. There was a reverberating grumbling about the stupidity of group work and oral presentations, and still they probed: 'So how does teaching literacy fit in all of this?'

So it came to be that for the first four weeks, each of the four specific literacy pedagogies were introduced. To be consistent, we agreed to use the ACARA National Australian Curriculum for Year 10 and each week we applied the same working question: How do you apply didactic, functional, authentic or critical literacy pedagogy to teach a core secondary area of study?

12 So how Do You Do that?

Using critical literacy as an example, the knowledge processes aligned to critical literacy are applying appropriately and applying creatively. This approach to literacy focuses on challenging social issues such as discrimination and disadvantage. Using mathematics as the subject area of study based on the ACARA National Australian Curriculum, focusing on Year 10, the pre-service teachers applied the elements that characterize critical literacy to the strands.

12.1 Year 10 Level Description Mathematics

The proficiency strands of **understanding, fluency, problem-solving** and **reasoning** are an integral part of mathematics content across the three content strands: number and algebra, measurement and geometry, and statistics and probability. The proficiencies reinforce the significance of working mathematically within the content and describe how the content is explored or developed. They provide the language to build in the developmental aspects of the learning of mathematics. The achievement standards reflect the content and encompass the proficiencies (ACARA, 2014).

Within the mathematics strands, the students were given the topic of statistics and probability, data representation and interpretation. The task to investigate is located in the content descriptors.

Content Descriptor Evaluate statistical reports in the media and other places by linking claims to displays, statistics and representative data. (Each content descriptor has a specific code: ACMSP253).

The students then chose one of a selection of elaborations.

Elaboration Evaluating statistical reports comparing the life expectancy of Aboriginal and Torres Strait Islander people with that of the Australian population as a whole (ACARA, 2014).

The students logged into Scottle, a national repository that provides Australian schools with more than 20,000 digital resources aligned to the Australian Curriculum. They began to research data sourced from the Australian Bureau of Statistics. The key words 'Australian Aboriginal and Torres Strait Islander people' and 'life expectancy' were applied in order to separate this group from other ethnicities in Australian society. A busy buzz began to fill the room with the sounds of students concurring and clarifying analysis of their data sets. Slowly the mood of the workshop shifted: the longer the students researched the statistical data the more circumspect they became. As they were scrutinizing pages of bar and line graphs, many of the students became perplexed as to what they were viewing. The statistical data they were reading seemed erroneous. Their surprise came discovering that male Aboriginal and Torres Strait Islander people die 13–15 years earlier than non-Aboriginal Australians. Aboriginal life expectancy is 15.1 years lower for Aboriginal men, and 13.5 years lower for Aboriginal women than other non-Aboriginal Australian women (ABS 2016).

They began to delve further, probing into the possible reasons why this statistic was so high, and in doing so accessed data from the Australian Institute of Health and Welfare 2015 *The health and welfare of Australia's Aboriginal and Torres Strait Islander peoples 2015* showing that Aboriginal and Torres Strait Islander imprisonment rates were 17 times the non-Indigenous imprisonment rate. The students deduced that the age group of the largest population of inmates incarcerated was between 24–39 years old, the group mostly likely to be parents. The pre-service teachers discussed how this would have an impact on the students they would be teaching, knowing that 29.8% of Aboriginal adults (18 years and older) in Western Australia reported high or very high levels of psychological distress in their lives. This impelled them to look further, and their research revealed that in Western Australia, according to the *Bringing them home: Report of the National Inquiry into the Separation of Aboriginal and Torres Strait Islander Children from their Families* 85% of the 438 clients surveyed by the Aboriginal Legal Service had spent at least part of their childhood in a foster home or mission after being forcibly removed from their parents. These children as a group suffered intergenerational trauma and were at a significant disadvantage compared with the general child population. They tended to have a very high level of emotional disorder, have a higher level of maladjustment compared to groups not in care, were more likely to suffer severe reading disability and delay in other language skills, and they tended to fail to learn the necessities of socialising with other people and made fewer new friends on leaving care. The effects of institutionalization have been found to persist into adolescence and later life (Australian Human Rights Commission 1997).

According to social demographers' predictions, the number of Aboriginal and Torres Strait Islander children enrolling in pre-primary will increase by 20% in 2020. It is certain that pre-service teachers will have Aboriginal and Torres Strait Islander students in their classes. Yet when the students were asked if they knew or socialised with Aboriginal or Torres Strait Islander peoples, in the three classes enrolled less than a third had even met an Indigenous person. The pre-service teachers, in carrying out a simple task involving mathematical statistics and probability data representation and interpretation, became cognisant of the deep division between non-Indigenous and Indigenous Australians in terms of social and economic conditions. Aware that an inequitable binary exists within the Australian population offered the students a chance to discuss what further proficiencies and cultural, socio-historic and linguistic knowledge they would need to gain in order to better understand Indigenous epistemological traditions.

With Learning by Design, the manner in which this statistical data is applied appropriately is to design a suitable format to make this data more transparent or visual, for example, by converting numerical data information to graphs or diagrams. Usually this is where the process ends, but with the knowledge processes, the students are required to take this data further in order to ask how this important statistical information can be applied creatively. The challenge the students now faced was how they were going to bring attention to the data in ways not normally presented, or in this case presenting contentious data creatively and imaginatively. The students began to look at a range of modes and mediums to develop pedagogical strategies that provided distinctive ways to highlight the message of the inequitable conditions experienced by a particular group of citizens within the broader Australian society. They designed tasks that required the learners to sensitively consider the message they were sending, including short animated films, scripts, slam poetry, info graphics and digital posters. The students (in particular the STEM students) could now appreciate the interdependent relationship between critical literacy and mathematics.

The following section is designed as a practitioner's guide - the things you do to know - and focuses on the construction and phases engaged to accommodate the four knowledge processes and the four literacies.

13   Using Learning by Design Planning Phases

There are five major planning phases in Learning by Design for the pre-service teachers as designers to work through: ideation, mapping, sequencing, reviewing/ aligning and publishing.

13.1   Ideation Phase

The ideation phase is the percolating up of great ideas. It is the broad-brush, big-picture start of designing based on the learning objectives of the curriculum. It is the incubation of design and is usually done on large sheets of butcher's paper using four colours of post-it notes. Colour-coded post-it notes help to ensure that all the knowledge processes have been included. This is the phase where the Learning by Design placemat comes in. Students are encouraged to print out the template on A3 sheets, cut and glue them together, and colour code the orientations.

Post-it notes are effective because they can be pulled off and put wherever there is a smudging of orientations. The other good thing about post-it notes occurs later, when the pre-service students present their Glogster with their module design to the whole class in the workshop, their peers can jot down suggestions while they are watching and donate them at the end of the presentation, making the experience very collegial.

13.2   Mapping Phase

The mapping phase is the coming together of all the collaborators to discuss the ideas, concepts, processes and procedures of the evolving module. This is a deeply reflective stage where the pre-service teachers reflect on and understand things they need to know as active designers of meaningful learning (Kalantzis and Cope 2012), such as what the pupil is going to learn and how they are going to learn it. The placemat is vital in this phase to ensure that all ideas are gathered and documented.

13.3   Sequencing Phase

The sequencing phase is where the designers ensure that the order of the lessons flows cohesively and there is a strong sense that it fits together. One strategy is to use colour-coded paper dots to ensure that the orientations are evident. This stage is important in making sure that there is a diversity of pedagogies and repertoires and that they are suitably multimodal.

13.4   Reviewing and Aligning Phase

The reviewing and aligning phase is where the designer keeps going back to the questions: How can I be sure the learner is learning what I am teaching? How can I be sure that I have designed learning that is going to be achieved? At this stage, pre-service teachers/designers check their construct again against the curriculum and ensure they are meeting all the learning outcomes.

13.5   Publishing Phase

The publishing phase is the stage where students get to upload their learning module on the Scholar website with a shared community of collaborators of learners and sharers. There are two aspects to the particular format of documentation using the

Learning Element: a prospective aspect (planning before you teach) and retrospective aspect (rewriting after you teach and saving best practices to a knowledge bank). Doing it this way effectively enabled the pre-service teachers to clearly map what both they and the students they were doing. This planning prompts smooth transition, starting with the known—what the students already know—to knowing the right time to introduce to them new learning content using the most appropriate pedagogical strategy.

14 The Learning Element

The Learning Element format is located on the website https://cgscholar.com/ Transforming Learning and Assessment. The layout is divided into two sides: one side that speaks in the language of teacher professional talk (so learning designs can be shared with colleagues) and the other side that speaks directly to learners in the language of the classroom (so learners can access a Learning Element and take a relatively autonomous role in their learning) (Cope et al. 2000). It is important at this stage to visit the website to see how the samples are designed as the key pedagogical information is set out under five main headings:

1. Learning focus: Curriculum area and learning level.
2. Knowledge objectives: Intended learning outcomes and links to mandated standards.
3. Knowledge processes: Activities, marked up for the kind of knowledge making required of the learner (below), sequenced appropriately and with a range that accommodates learner diversity.
4. Knowledge outcomes: Formative and summative assessment processes.
5. Learning pathways: Recommended follow-on activities such as other learning elements.

15 Challenges Faced

At the start of their learning, the pre-service teachers experienced many difficulties, seldom coming up with activities that were thought provoking and appealing or best suited to achieve the learning objectives. To assist students to oscillate their pedagogical repertoires and bring active engagement and interest to the learning they were given a teaching tool: a checklist of a range of multimodal applications known as the Lanyon Cluster Toolkit. This valuable tool was developed by classroom practitioners in the Learning by Design Multiliteracies Program and is available for designers on the Learning Element website https://cgscholar.com/.

When the students first began to work with the knowledge processes, they also found the concept problematic because they thought they were designing a lesson plan. They started to write on their Placemats information such as:

9:00 am Students arrive
9:01 am Students sit down, get out their calculators
9:05 am Ask students to get out their homework
9:10 am Give out worksheet

Other notions that challenged them were that:

1. learners collaborating and negotiating with teachers would take equal ownership and lead the design of their learning with their own ideas and suggestions to design the module of learning,
2. learners' prior knowledge was an integral part of the development of the design,
3. the planned work would take a longer period of time than one period of 45 min, and
4. knowledge could be presented in multiple modes and in multiple literacies.

As students progressed through the semester, they began to apply a deeper understanding of their role as designer. The following students' testimonies demonstrate the quality of this reflective practice as they moved through the five planning phases.

Student A Testimony
Topic: Genetics and inheritance

Purpose and big ideas: After completing this learning element, students should have a developed knowledge and understanding of how meiosis and mitosis work, develop an understanding of genetics and inheritance and have researched and shaped an opinion on some of the social and ethical issues involved in the areas of genetic research, gene therapy, and gene manipulation and modification.

Ideation phase: I used the ideation phase as a brainstorming session, utilising curriculum references and teaching strategies to develop multimodal activities that would deliver content to the students whilst trying to facilitate students' creative thinking and inspire freedom of thought. Students could then use the information learnt to develop their own opinions and views on ethical and social issues related to the topic of genetics and inheritance.

Mapping phase: Using the placemat, I moved my learning activities around to find out whether the activities suited the knowledge processes. If they were not a match with the knowledge processes, I reassessed whether they were worth using or needed restructuring. Once I was happy with the activities that I felt would be most beneficial, I moved them around the placemat to find which learning process they suited best. Some activities overlapped and could fit into a number of processes, so I began thinking about sequencing to help fit them into the best category.

Sequencing: I looked over the different activities and the processes within which they were categorised and after some rearranging I found the best sequence for the learning activities to flow well and link in an appropriate order.

When reading the student's comments I could imagine the ruminating and higher order thinking he was engaged in. In my experience, this internal monologue is very uncharacteristic in first-year university student writing, which made it stand out as an exemplar. I then picked up the next assignment and it too was filled with reflective expressions of how the student had worked through the sequencing phase for a long time to ensure relevance and connectedness in the learning material.

Student B Testimony

During the ideation phase, I used my Glogster script outlining the four knowledge processes, or 'things you do to know', as inspiration to generate ideas for teaching the theory of evolution by natural selection, often a difficult topic to teach as it can conflict with cultural views and many misconceptions.

I chose to address the year 10 curriculum standard of 'science understanding: The theory of evolution by natural selection explains the diversity of living things' (ACCSU185) through a variety of lesson ideas and multimodal learning and expression to allow for learner differences and learner needs.

During the sequencing phase I began by refining my ideas to the most interesting and multimodal activities that worked together in a logical process in order to allow for an engaging classroom environment for students of diverse abilities.

I compared ideas for each of the eight orientations together and played with various chronologies of activities. This was easy to do using the sticky notes, which were already colour coded to knowledge process, and the strip of paper to change places and replace ideas while ensuring I included all knowledge processes.

For example, I felt that analysing the data immediately after completing the experiment would also provide a good foundation for students to build upon with more formal naming and theorising through conceptualising, so I changed the order of activities quite a lot. I also found it difficult deciding on an appropriate activity for applying appropriately so had both included in the sequence for a while before I decided on the activity that best joined conceptualising and analysing.

During the reviewing and aligning phase I reviewed my learning activities to ensure they addressed curriculum descriptors for year 10 science, rewriting each step to ensure a logical flow and identifying objectives for each activity.

My learning outcomes are as follows:

- Discuss the theory of evolution by natural selection and other culturally relevant theories of creation (ACARA, ACSIS208) (e.g., class discussion and word wall activity)
- Demonstrate correct scientific procedure when conducting an experiment (e.g., through the 'natural selection modelled' experiment).
- Relate genetic characteristics to survival and reproductive rates (ACARA, ACCSU185)
- Summarise the concept of evolution by natural selection using multimodal presentation (e.g., final summative assessment of teaching year 7 students the theory of evolution by natural selection).

The knowledge processes provided a planning schema for the pre-service students to create their content-specialist modules. On completion, many elected to upload their work onto the Scholar website. This was another unexpected breakthrough: to see the students who were initially very annoyed about having to work in groups keen to be collegial and collaborative. They had gained ideas from the online samples, especially the work of Rita van Haren, as well as from a vast collection from strangers and felt a reciprocal desire to give back.

16   End of the Semester: Transformation Complete

The interesting outcome of enduring so much torment from the secondary pre-service STEM teachers' reluctance to 'doing' literacy was that I felt fortunate to observe them move through their stages of resistance to eventually reach a state of equilibrium. I respected their scepticism and conviction at the start of the semester that literacy had no place in their STEM subjects; likewise, I respected their gradual appreciation that Learning by Design represented a unique way of making content knowledge by oscillating and weaving pedagogical repertoires (Luke et al, 2003). They got it because they could see for themselves that as pedagogy it was rational, inventive and exploratory for learners to develop a sense of wonder, think originally and imaginatively. They left the final workshop knowing that they had the knowledge to design a wide-ranging and engaging plan of learning in their chosen subject with the guidance and support from hundreds of teachers and fellow students online.

Afterword

I was striding across the campus the other day and heard someone yelling my name. I stopped and out from the enmeshed throng of multi-coloured shapes and cacophony of human traffic came one of the third-year students. He had just completed his practicum and enthusiastically shared with me that he had used Learning by Design to create his programs. He told me that in all honesty he had not 'gotten it' when he was in his first year because he was too interested in messing around but now he said, 'I get it because it is a great way of thinking about building context and content knowledge. Sorry I was such an arsehole.' I smiled. As he walked away he called back, 'Hey, Helzey. Thanks.'

References

Australian Bureau of Statistics (ABS). (2016). *Aboriginal and Torres Strait Islander life expectancy.* Retrieved from http://www.abs.gov.au/websitedbs/D3310114.nsf/home/Statistical+Data+Integration+-+Case+Study:+LIfe+Expectancy

Australian Curriculum, Assessment and Reporting Authority [ACARA]. (2014). *Foundation to year 10 curriculum: Language for interaction* (ACELA1428). Retrieved from http://www.australiancurriculum.edu.au/english/curriculum

Australian Human Rights Commission. (1997). *Bringing them home: Report of the national inquiry into the separation of aboriginal and Torres Strait islander children from their families.* Retrieved from https://www.humanrights.gov.au/publications/bringing-them-home-report-1997

Australian Institute of Health and Welfare. (2015). *The health and welfare of Australia's Aboriginal and Torres Strait Islander peoples 2015.* Cat. No. IHW 147. Canberra: AIHW. Retrieved from https://www.aihw.gov.au/getmedia/584073f7

Beare, H. (2001). *Creating the future school: Student outcomes and the reform of education.* London/New York: Routledge Falmer.

Connell, R. (2013). The neoliberal cascade and education: An essay on the market agenda and its consequences. *Critical Studies in Education, 54*(2), 99–112.

Cope, B., & Kalantzis, M. (2000). Designs for social futures. In B. Cope & M. Kalantzis (Eds.), *Multiliteracies: literacy learning and the design of social futures* (pp. 203–234). London: Routledge.

Cope, B., & Kalantzis, M. (2009). "Multiliteracies": New literacies, new learning. *Pedagogies: An International Journal, 4*(3), 164–195.

Cope, B., Kalantzis, M. & van Haren, R. (2000). *Transforming learning and assessment* Retrieved from http://newlearningonline.com/scholar

Dewey, J. (1916). *Democracy and education.* New York: Macmillian.

Emmitt, M., Zbaracki, M., Komesaroff, L., & Pollock, J. (2010). Language and learning. In *An introduction for teaching* (5th ed.). Oxford: South Melbourne.

Ewing, R. (2010). *Curriculum and assessment: A narrative approach.* Melbourne, VIC: Oxford University Press.

Freebody, P., & Luke, A. (2003). Literacy as engaging with new forms of life: The four resources model. In M. Anstey & G. Bull (Eds.), *The literacy lexicon* (2nd ed., pp. 51–66). Sydney: Pearson.

Gee, J. P. (2000). New people in new worlds: Networks, the new capitalism and schools. In B. Cope & M. Kalantzis (Eds.), *Multiliteracies: Literacy learning and the design of social futures* (pp. 43–68). London: Routledge.

Giroux, H. (1989). Schooling as a form of cultural politics: Towards a pedagogy of and for difference. In H. Giroux & P. McLaren (Eds.), *Critical pedagogy, the state, and cultural struggle* (pp. 125 Freebody–151). New York: State University of New York.

Giroux, H. (1992). *Border crossings: Cultural workers and the politics of education.* London: Routledge.

Howe, N., & Strauss, W. (2000). *Millennials rising: The next great generation.* New York: Vintage.

Kachru, B., Kachru, Y., & Nelson, C. (2006). *The handbook of world Englishes.* Malden, MA: Blackwell.

Kalantzis, M., & Cope, B. (2012). *Literacies.* Cambridge: Cambridge University Press.

Kalantzis, M., Cope, B., Chan, E., & Dalley-Trim, L. (2016). *Literacies* (2nd ed.). Cambridge: Cambridge University Press.

Kress, G. (2000). Design and transformation: New theories of meaning. In B. Cope & M. Kalantzis (Eds.), *Multiliteracies: Literacy learning and the design of social futures* (pp. 153–161). London: Routledge.

Loader, D. (2007). *Jousting for the new generation: Challenges to contemporary schooling.* Melbourne: ACER Press.

Prenksy, M. (2001). Digital natives, digital immigrants. *On the Horizon, 9*(5), 1–6.

Slattery, P. (1995). *Curriculum development in the postmodern era*. New York: Garland.

The New London Group. (1996). A Pedagogy of multiliteracies: designing social futures. *Harvard Educational Review, 66*(1), 60–92.

Wadham, B., Pudsey, J., & Boyd, R. (2007). *Culture and education*. Frenchs Forest, NSW: Pearson Education.

Wright, D. (2008). The mythopoetic body: Learning through creativity. In T. Leonard & P. Willis (Eds.), *Pedagogies of the imagination: Mythopoetic curriculum in educational practice* (pp. 93–106). Chicago, IL: Springer.

Pre-service Teachers' Literacy Abilities: An Exploration Amidst the Criticisms

Jennifer Howell and Von Sawers

Abstract The literacy skills of pre-service teachers and the perceived wider 'literacy crisis' in schools and higher education has been the focus of much discussion and debate, both in the media and in research for a long time. There is a perception that students who begin teacher education programs have low level skills in literacy, and that the programs they are enrolled in are failing to develop their skills, hence resulting in poorly equipped teachers and poor language practices in classrooms. This chapter will examine the history of this discourse; identify the publications it has been based upon and determine the validity of its conclusions. This background will contextualise the results from an empirical case study in which the participants were pre-service teachers enrolled in a common first year unit within the Bachelor of Education (Early Childhood Education and Primary) programs in an Australian university. The project sought to identify the scope and breadth of literacy skills that the students present with as they *begin* their pre-service teacher program. The findings from this case study can be used to better understand and identify how the critical discourse regarding their skills has emerged, and offer insights into the perceived crisis itself.

Keywords Pre-service teachers · Literacy crisis · Teacher education · Literacy skills

1 Introduction

The literacy skills of pre-service teachers and the perceived wider 'literacy crisis' in schools and higher education has long been the focus of much discussion and debate, both in the media and in research (Snyder 2008; Williams 2007; Buckingham et al. 2014). This has led to a renewed focus on the literacy skills of teachers and how these skills are identified and then developed within pre-service teacher education

J. Howell (✉) · V. Sawers
School of Education, Curtin University, Bentley, Australia
e-mail: Jennifer.Howell@curtin.edu.au; Yvonne.Sawers@curtin.edu.au

© Springer Nature Switzerland AG 2019   113
T. Dobinson, K. Dunworth (eds.), *Literacy Unbound: Multiliterate,*
Multilingual, Multimodal, Multilingual Education 30,
https://doi.org/10.1007/978-3-030-01255-7_7

programs. This has resulted in the requirement for all graduates to pass a national literacy and numeracy proficiency test prior to applying for teacher registration. There is a perception that students who begin teacher education programs have low-level skills in literacy and that the programs they are enrolled in are failing to develop their skills, hence resulting in poorly equipped teachers and poor language practices in classrooms. The accreditation pathway for pre-service teacher programs has been revised and the rigor around this process has been carefully redeveloped into a more detailed and scaffolded process. Central to this has been the focus on how literacy and numeracy is developed across the degree program. These changes have all arisen from a rather negative position and set of beliefs regarding the literacy skills and abilities of practicing teachers (Rowe 2005; Buckingham 2017) and the public concern about pre-service teacher literacy that this generates (Teacher Education Ministerial Advisory Group Final Report 2014). The evidence for these beliefs and statements is at best sketchy and largely anecdotal, yet the debate has continued and resulted in a highly critical discourse.

This chapter will examine the history of this discourse, identify the publications it has been based upon and determine the validity of its conclusions. It will also suggest that at the heart of this discourse is a misunderstanding of the term *literacy* and that a new definition is needed that is more mindful of the types of skills required to be active participants in the current digital age. This background will contextualise the results from an empirical case study in which the participants were pre-service teachers enrolled in a common first-year unit within the early childhood education and primary education bachelor of education programs in an Australian university. The project sought to identify the scope and breadth of literacy skills that the students present with as they begin their pre-service teacher program. This data could then be used to better understand and identify how the critical discourse regarding their skills has emerged. The findings from this case study will make two contributions to the ongoing debate surrounding literacy: firstly they will offer a redefinition of literacy that moves beyond the current traditional definitions that have recently dominated and constrained discourses. Secondly, they will provide a voice for the pre-service teachers themselves who have been the voiceless subjects of this discourse.

2   Literature Review

This review of the literature seeks to explore the discrete areas that underpin the focus of this chapter. Initially it will explore definitions of literacy and chart the evolution of this term. It will then examine the current 'literacy crisis' and the factors influencing this situation and finally it will conclude with an examination of formal teacher preparation programs.

2.1 Defining Literacy

In recent times the definition of literacy has broadened and the boundaries of literacy have expanded and become more complex. Language use is not rigid with one set of rules (Williams 2007). The definition of the term *literacy* has continued to evolve from a basic definition of being able to learn a set of discrete skills considered important for reading and writing to the more complex understandings of multiple and critical literacies, which include understanding of the impact of home, culture, technology and global diversity (Kalantzis and Cope 2012).

The skills needed for effective literacy have been debated over the years. One view is that literacy teaching in English-speaking countries should involve the systematic teaching of phonic skills, where the relationship between sounds and written symbols is taught explicitly and some whole words are taught by sight (Rose 2006; Rowe 2005). Understanding this alphabetic principle enables children to use this knowledge to apply strategies and become successful readers (Emmitt et al. 2014). The systematic teaching of phonics has been widely adopted as an essential part of a balanced view for teaching literacy (Winch et al. 2010). However there has also been deep criticism of a style of teaching phonics known as synthetic phonics instruction. Proponents of synthetic phonics have based their commitment on a small study in Clackmannanshire, Scotland, that has been highly criticised for its poor research methods. The findings have influenced English government policy, and synthetic phonics has been implemented through mandated curriculum and other compliance mechanisms (Goouch and Lambirth 2016). The accountability regime includes assessment of both university departments and schools where short-notice inspections are undertaken to ensure resources and teaching only embrace a systematic synthetic approach to teaching phonics (Ellis and Moss 2014). In Australia, Buckingham (2016) outlines the simple view that for all children to read systematic synthetic phonics must be taught.

Literacy is multifaceted and is also a social practice (Klein and Unsworth 2014) that enables people to make meaning for functional and particular social purposes and contexts (Luke 2000). Access to literacy is not neutral. It is steeped in culture. Literacy practices are shaped by the various contexts of participants and involve much more than decoding words. Freire and Macedo (1987) explained it well with the title of their book: *Reading the Word and the World*. One set of literacy skills and one set of social skills were not deemed to be enough. Literacy can be viewed as part of enculturation through commonly accepted ways of behaving (Gee 1992). Literacy can be described as powers of literacies and the literacies of power (Kalantzis and Cope 1993).

The impact of elements such as home, culture, technology and global diversity has led to the emergence of a new conceptualisation of literacy as *multiliteracies*. Multiliteracies involve multiple modes of meaning-making: written, visual, oral, gestural, spatial and tactile. Changes in technologies have facilitated these new literacies (Cope and Kalantzis 2000), and the ability to be proficient in all modes of meaning-making is seen as fundamental to people's lives. Employment opportunities, personal growth, and participation and engagement in civic life can all be transformed through literacy (Kalantzis and Cope 2012).

The global and digital world is rich with information, which requires sophisticated critical literacy and thinking skills, commentary and response (Snyder 2008). Critical literacy supports learners as active citizens and agents of making meaning (Kalantzis and Cope 2012). A critical perspective, which comes from an author's ideology and beliefs about power, inequality and injustice, includes the analysis of texts for layers of meaning (Emmitt et al. 2014). Critical literacy teaching is planned around the voice and agency of learners. Text can be scrutinised for the multiple voices portrayed or the voices left out. Learners engage with real-world issues as they actively make meaning in their contexts (Kalantzis and Cope 2012).

2.2 A Literacy Crisis

Broader views of literacy have attracted criticism and have contributed to the emergence of a discourse around a crisis as well as the negative views in the media. Rowe, in Caroline Milburn's article, 'Battle Lines', *The Sydney Morning Herald*, September 2008, stated that higher education providers are 'puddling around in postmodernist claptrap about how children learn to read' and not focusing on the evidence from many significant reports such as Rowe (2005) and Rose (2006). More negative headlines in mainstream media such as 'Trainee teachers have failed a new national literacy and numeracy test' (Marszalek 2015), 'Poor teachers beget poor students' (Buckingham 2016) and 'Trainee teachers fail spell, maths test' (Martyn-Jones 2017) all contribute to perception of a major problem.

Snyder (2008), in her book titled *The Literacy Wars*, believes that literacy is far more than decoding; rather, it includes a repertoire of social practices, which confirms the concept of multiliteracies. Literacy is a shared enterprise between a teacher and a learner. Snyder states that to improve literacy education there is no single answer, instructional approach or package that will be effective for all, especially when learners are very culturally diverse. One universal method does not exist, and prescribed lessons are not a quick fix in the diverse cultural and economic realities of today's world. Snyder argues that holding teachers responsible for the poor performance of students ignores all the other contributing factors over which teachers have no control. Concentrating on the method also distracts from another key issue: that of access to quality programs and the lack of equitable sharing of economic and social capital (Luke 1998). Research into teacher preparation programs have largely ignored how best to teach diverse student populations and how to reduce societal inequalities by preparing teachers to deal better with the effects of poverty on children (Cochran-Smith et al. 2015).

According to Gee (2000), the two sides of the literacy debate are about those who understand literacy to be a discrete ability to read and write and those who make meaning from their repertoire of grammatical resources to create social languages and discourses that are contextual and involve thoughts, beliefs, values, acts and interactions. Gee argues that in our hypercompetitive world the skills people need are socio-technical, flexible and adaptable, involving an understanding of consumer workplace identities and values so that products and markets can be designed accordingly. The narrow view of literacy as the ability to read and write 'won't purchase much' (pp. 412 and 418) in the world according to Gee.

One of the many tensions in teacher education (Lloyd 2013) is the attitude of deficit toward the personal literacy and numeracy skills of entrants to teacher education, which is entwined in policies across state and federal jurisdictions resulting in a push for entrants to be in the top 30% of the population for literacy and numeracy skills. The discourse of deficit and denunciation in literacy teacher pre-service education has been in many reports including *Literacy in teacher education: Standards for pre-service programs* by the Queensland Board of Teacher Registration (QBTR 2001) and the Masters report, *A shared challenge: Improving literacy, numeracy and science learning in Queensland primary schools* (2009). Both of these outline extensive problems with the personal literacy skills of pre-service teachers. This has resulted in the Australian government commissioning the Australian Council for Educational Research to prepare and conduct the Test of Literacy and Numeracy for Initial Teacher Education Students, which started in 2016 and must be passed prior to completion of their final teaching practice and graduation. According to Connell (2009), we are steeped in a time of reform where teachers are measured against competency standards and all teaching needs to be auditable for teacher registration. Teacher's individual achievement is gauged against the highly regarded Australian Institute for Professional Standards.

As criticism and responses are published, what is emerging is a call for a new approach to the conceptualisation of the teaching of literacy. Honan et al. (2013) believe teacher educators must prepare pre-service teachers for two contrasting circumstances. Firstly, they must be prepared to teach in a digital world and be highly capable in broad digital literacies. Secondly, they must be equipped to pass the highly political pre-registration tests, which reflect a very narrow set of literacy skills and understandings. They found in their study that pre-service teachers were capable of demonstrating a broad and complex range of literacy skills including digital and traditional literacies. Benefits were also gained from undertaking multimodal assessment opportunities to develop and extend their knowledge about text type conventions.

The QBTR's (2001) review of the research and reports into pre-service programs investigated first-year pre-service teacher's own views about literacy teaching, their own personal literacy and their English teaching skills. The findings showed that in spite of the participants being in the first year of their course, the majority believed they had knowledge of English that was appropriate to teach literacy to children. However, there was disparity between the opinions and views of senior school staff about beginning teachers' literacy capabilities and the students' self-reflections. In another study by Louden and Rohl (2006), most early service teachers viewed themselves as having either *fairly adequate* or *very adequate* literacy skills, whereas it was reported in Rowe (2005) that senior school staff saw beginning teachers as lacking in the capacity to be effective teachers of reading.

A key critic of the teaching of literacy and teacher quality, Jennifer Buckingham, a Research Fellow at The Centre for Independent Studies, together with Justine Ferrari and Tom Alegounarias wrote a commercial research paper titled, 'Why Jaydon Can't Read: A Forum on Fixing Literacy' (Buckingham et al. 2014). In this paper Buckingham identifies the billions of dollars of Australian public money spent unsuccessfully trying to improve the literacy levels of children across Australia. Buckingham again in 2017 asks why, after so much targeted literacy funding spent and many programs tried, do the 2017 National Assessment Program for Literacy and Numeracy (NAPLAN) tests indicate little progress from the time NAPLAN began in 2008?

Adoniou (2017) sees the problem of declining NAPLAN achievement as not one of funding but of funding the right children in the right ways to support their development. Adoniou also believes that upon investigation, children are doing well in the simple basics of reading and writing, through using simple books, simple structures and vocabulary; however, there is a need to raise expectations of students' achievement to include rich literature and complex language to enhance opportunities for young people to grow to be literate. The over focus of the 'back-to-basics' movement is creating another type of crisis.

It has been argued that the two main causes of the current literacy crisis are pre-service teacher education programs and government policy (Louden and Rohl 2006). Louden and Rohl's (2006) study, 'The perceptions of pre-service teacher preparation for literacy teaching in Australian schools', indicated that beginning teachers were not confident about their own abilities and knowledge and believed they had not been adequately prepared to teach literacy. More evidence was cited from the National Inquiry into Teaching Literacy (NITL), which examined 34 four-year primary education degree courses and found that the majority had less than 10% of their courses focused on the teaching of reading. They also recommended that given the importance of literacy, teacher education courses should have this as their key objective.

This second apparent cause of the literacy crisis, government policy, was also identified by Buckingham et al. (2014). The cyclic nature of policy making affects the allocation of resources, which, according to Buckingham, are often used for untried and under evaluated programs. The gap between research and teaching is not the fault of teachers but policy and academic leadership. The profession and policy makers have not responded quickly enough to key evidence, they argue. They go on to suggest that open discussion amongst teachers about better practice is limited because they are rightly defensive due to the unhelpful and unwarranted political attacks on their teaching as a whole. No evidence has been presented to support either of these observations (Buckingham et al. 2014).

Popular press articles regularly describe pre-service teachers as deficient in literacy or blame the low level of entry score (Australian Tertiary Admission Rank [ATAR]) to some Australian universities. These observations are based on narrow conceptions of literacy and neglect to report pre-service teachers' strengths (Honan et al. 2013). These views are not sustainable empirically, but they remain largely unquestioned. Snyder (2008) stated that public opinion has had more influence on policy than research, and many policy makers and people outside of education still hold a very narrow view of literacy. Honan et al. (2013) set out to examine the capabilities and expertise of pre-service teachers in all forms of literacy including digital and new literacies. The participant pre-service teachers navigated their way through the demands of personal, academic and professional literacies during their undergraduate courses.

2.3   Teacher Preparation Programs

There is no single and unified perspective on teacher education (Massengill Shaw et al. 2007). The issues around literacy for universities are about determining the level of personal literacy capability of course entrants, their development and understanding of the content knowledge of literacy and their capacity to teach literacy on exit from their pre-service teachers' program in line with the graduate standard set by the Australian Institute for Professional Standards.

Pre-service teachers self-efficacy is influenced heavily by the role models they encounter (Johnson 2010). Hudson (2012) found that beginning teachers valued practice more than theory and that university preparation needed to include more literacy teaching practice on teaching practicums, particularly in the areas of reading and spelling. This research concluded that for universities to support beginning teachers more effectively these issues should be addressed and embedded in the university coursework (Hudson 2012; Edwards-Groves 2011; cited in O'Neill and Geoghegan 2011). This was supported in research by O'Neill and Geoghegan (2011), who found that there pre-service teachers were less confident in teaching grammar and phonics and that more course time should be spent on how to teach specific elements of literacy instruction and that there should be more opportunities to apply skills in authentic classrooms through continuous access. There are also advantages for teaching English grammar as part of the pre-service teachers' course (Carey et al. 2015).

Lack of confidence to teach phonics was also supported further by the work of Barnsley-Fielding (2010) who found that pre-service teachers' required explicit education in phonemic awareness and that they felt ill prepared to teach beginning reading. However, Honan et al. (2013) dismiss these claims and criticise the study for being too narrow and portraying pre-service teachers as incompetent, ignorant and weak. Knowing about phonemes does not relate to personal literacy but as a component of literacy teaching content.

A distinction needs to be made between pre-service teachers' own literacy and their ability to teach literacy. It is reasonable to expect pre-service teachers to have high levels of literacy and be multiliterate. Some content knowledge needs to be taught, therefore, particularly about new literacies (QBTR 2001, p. 49). Survey data indicated that pre-service teachers rated themselves higher and better prepared to teach literacy than their supervising teachers did. It was also difficult for pre-service teachers to make the links between university learning and classroom practice (QBTR 2001, p. 64). Pre-service teachers in one survey stated that university lecturers made assumptions that they had a good understanding of language just because they were enrolled in the course, and this tested their preparedness to teach when they went on practicum where their limited explicit knowledge of language became a problem (QBTR 2001, pp. 64–65).

The gap between theory and practice according to Buckingham et al. (2014) can be attributed to a lack of engagement by the profession with evidence and data from empirical research. Ideologies and practices are set which rule out any opportunities for change. Alegounarias lists many concerns about teachers and their practices, which include their lack of confidence and the limited backgrounds of the students (e.g., most students come from a humanities background not maths and science). This can come together to promote an 'anti-science or an anti-evidence culture' (Buckingham et al. 2014, p. 16) amongst literacy teachers.

This review of the literature has explored the three related areas that underpin the focus of this chapter, the literacy skills of pre-service teachers and the wider issue of a perceived 'literacy crisis' in schools and higher education. The review examined how literacy is defined, factors that have led to the current perception of a crisis and the role of literacy in teacher preparation programs. The following section will present the findings of a case study that sought to examine some of these issues in further detail and provide a voice to the pre-service teachers themselves. It sought to present an alternative position to the current debate that skills of pre-service teachers have been undermined by definitions that have no currency or applicability within the generation in which they are being applied. These findings and the resulting discussion will present an alternative discourse regarding the literacy skills of pre-service teachers, one that is less critical, more constructive and more optimistic.

3 The Case Study

The case study involved 170 undergraduate pre-service teacher education students enrolled in two cohorts of bachelor of education programs (early childhood education and primary education) in an Australian university. Cohort 1 was enrolled in 2016 and Cohort 2 in 2017. These two groups were combined to represent one pool of participants. The guiding aims of the project were:

- to examine the literacy habits of a cohort of tertiary students,
- to explore the literacy expectations of the cohort, and
- to understand the conceptualisations of the cohort regarding their own personal literacy skills and abilities and their impact on their development as a teacher.

The methodological framework guiding the project was a qualitative ethnography that adopted an empirical case-study design, which allowed for a closer examination of one specific culture-sharing group, in this case, two cohorts of undergraduate students enrolled in literacy units within a pre-service teacher education program. The two cohorts were comprised of first- and second-year students enrolled in two of three literacy units within the program. This was purposeful as it allowed a snapshot of students at two perspective points within the three required literacy units, which in turn allowed for observations to be made. Data was collected via a paper-based questionnaire that was distributed and collected over a period of 2 weeks during a university semester.

The students were invited to participate via email and verbally during scheduled workshops that were part of the normal teaching and learning activities for the unit. The two units represented two developmental points within the bachelor of education program. The respondents were first and second year students, from the early childhood and primary programs. The potential participant pool was approximately 470, (i.e., the total number of students enrolled in the units) and the total number of responses collected was 170, representing a response rate of 36%. The questionnaire had a written consent mechanism and all responses were anonymous with no personal details or identifying information collected thereby ensuring anonymity. The questionnaire comprised eight questions; two questions were multiple choice and the remainder were open-ended questions. The analysis was a combination of the collation of answers and thematic analysis using MaxQDA©, which allowed for the emergence of codes from the data. The unit of analysis was logical phrasing, and a code was allocated to the first theme that emerged in the phrase. The total number of coded units was 1046.

4   Findings

For purposes of clarity and organisation, the findings will be presented and organised under each question as they were presented in the questionnaire.

1. In your own words how would you define literacy?

The majority of students identified literacy as being associated with reading and writing ($n = 98$), followed by it being viewed as the act of communicating ($n = 58$) or as language itself ($n = 34$). For example:

> Literacy is the ability to read and write. It is conveying your message in a textual form using different language in a different context. [Coded: Literacy is reading and writing]

> I would define literacy as being able to effectively communicate with others and within society. [Coded: Literacy is communication]

> Being literate means that one has the ability to use various components of language in everyday situations. Strong literacy skills means that a person understands how to speak in a range of situations, how to use language to convey meaning and how to understand language through a variety of different modes. [Coded: Literacy is language]

These results showed that the respondents were sorting themselves into two distinct groups: those who viewed literacy in a more traditional manner with it being limited to reading and writing (i.e., concerned with text) and those who viewed it as an action, such as being able to communicate. These three response types, as shown in Table 1, clearly attracted the most results; however, the next grouping of results was interesting, as it appeared to be associated with the second group, which viewed literacy as associated with communication. Some of the respondents associated literacy with being able to function ($n = 18$) or interactions with others ($n = 16$).

2. In your daily life what are some of your personal literacy habits for each of the following: reading, writing, talking, watching?

The literacy habits of the respondents were interesting to examine, as there was a growing number of digital or communicative habits evident in their responses. Reading was largely viewed as something associated with study or university work. Some respondents identified reading as reading fiction, whilst many viewed reading as being associated with social media (e.g., Facebook, Twitter). For example:

Read newspapers online, novels, fact and fiction [Coded: reading]

Pre-readings for university, assignments, Facebook, magazines [Coded: reading]

Writing was a broad mix of communicative writing (e.g., email, tweets and text messages) and university-related tasks. For example:

Note taking, communication (social networking, texting, emailing), letters/notes [Coded: writing]

Beyond university I don't really write. [Coded: writing]

Talking was viewed as a social pursuit with no connection to study or their professional worlds, which might be indicative of the more colloquial word 'talking' being viewed as an informal action rather than something students associated with more formal contexts such as work or study. For example:

Table 1 How literacy is defined

Defining literacy	$n = 232$
Literacy is reading and writing	98
Literacy is language	34
Literacy is communication	58
Literacy is textual	2
Literacy involves interactions with other people	16
Literacy is being able to function	18
Literacy is personal	2
Literacy is multi-literacies	4

Family, friends, peers, orally in a face-to-face manner and via telephone [Coded: talking]

I adjust my speech to context. Being bilingual I not only change my language but also the conventions I use. [Coded: talking]

The items coded as 'watching' were as expected and concerned television, videos and web-based content. For example:

Watching television shows, movies and YouTube videos [Coded: watching]

These responses were fairly predictable; however, it was clear that students' typical habits were not being identified as being concerned with literacy per se but were just seen as communicative acts. Students did not appear to have made the connections between these activities and being literate.

3. Please choose from the list below the best description of your personal literacy skills, for example, reading, writing, spelling and grammar.

The phrasing of this question was purposeful, as the various aspects associated with literacy and being literate, reading, writing, spelling and grammar, were clearly listed in an attempt to get the respondents to carefully consider their skills across these domains. Interestingly, none of the respondents self-selected *Poor skills* in literacy; however, external to this project, the university requires all students to undertake a compulsory post-entry English language assessment during their first semester of study. On average, 10–15% of students do not do well on this assessment, which is a written essay task, and are then required to undertake a six-week language-focused support program. It would have been interesting to include a question asking respondents if they had been told they were required to undertake this intervention program and correlate this with the results presented in Table 2. The majority of respondents self-identified themselves as having *reasonable skills* in literacy ($n = 49$), closely followed by the more tentative response of *some skills* ($n = 21$). Hence, the cohort felt that they were literate but varied in their perception of how literate they were across the different identified domains. Of particular interest were those who self-identified themselves as having *high-level skills* ($n = 9$). Further information is required to truly clarify these results, and focus groups are needed to analyse these self-ratings, which might be a direction of future research. High levels of confidence might explain these results; alternatively, they might be linked to the respondents' personal understandings of what it means to be literate.

Table 2 Self-rated assessment of personal literacy skills

	Poor Skills	*Some skills*	*Reasonable skills*	*High-level skills*	*No answer*	*Total*
Cohort 1		10	21	4	1	36
Cohort 2		11	28	5	5	49
						85

Table 3 Feelings of
preparedness to teach literacy

Sense of preparedness	n = 150
Very confident/very prepared	36
Confident + some areas of concern	46
Worried about grammar/language/phonics	14
Reasonably confident	16
Confidence depends on year level I am teaching	10
Not confident and/or underprepared	28

4. Thinking about your own literacy skills, how prepared do you feel to step into a classroom to teach a literacy-based lesson?

The responses to this open-ended question resulted in 150 coded items, as shown in Table 3. The spread was quite revealing and largely expected considering the members of the cohort were either in Year 1 or 2 of a pre-service teaching degree. The number of respondents who felt very confident and very prepared to teach literacy ($n = 36$) was surprising considering the low number who self-identified as possessing high levels of literacy skills in Question 3 above (Table 2). For example:

> My confidence is quite high—I just lack the resources and planning. [Coded: very confident]

Perhaps the pre-service teachers did not feel they needed to be highly skilled in order to teach literacy or at least viewed their required fluency in literacy to be higher than that of their students. As would be expected in a cohort in the early stages of their development as teachers, the majority felt either reasonably confident ($n = 16$) or confident with some areas of concern ($n = 46$). For example:

> I would feel reasonably confident; I just need to learn more on ways to teach children.

> I would be happy to teach a literacy-based lesson, but I would have to read up on grammar elements and sentence structure. [Coded: confident + some areas of concern]

Contrary to the results presented in Table 2, a significant number felt unprepared to teach literacy ($n = 28$). For example:

> Probs [sic] not very confident. Mainly because I wouldn't know what to teach to who and how in-depth to go. [Coded: unprepared]

This result shows the respondents are unable to make a connection between their own personal literacy skills and the skills required to be able to teach literacy. The skills they personally possess to be able to function and the high level of proficiency required to be able to teach literacy appear to them to be unrelated. It was clear that there were specific areas of concern identified by the students, with a number ($n = 14$) identifying grammar, language and phonics as being areas of weakness or aspects they did not yet feel confident to teach. For example:

> Reading and phonics I feel confident. Writing and grammar on the other hand are not very strongest points. [Coded: specific areas of concern]

Table 4 The importance of teacher literacy skills

The importance of teacher literacy skills	n = 168
Very important	150
Important	10
Somewhat important	2
Not important	0
No answer	2

Table 5 Why teacher literacy skills are important

Teacher literacy	n = 148
Important so you can teach students literacy	62
Needed to be able to function in society	16
Important skill or core skill	64
Involves knowing what to learn or what is important	4
Students and parents expect fluency in teachers	2

Alarmingly, confidence for some of the respondents was dependent upon the year level they might teach ($n = 10$), which does not reflect an appreciation for the required level of expertise needed to be an effective teacher regardless of year level. This result might be explained by the cohort themselves being either Year 1 or 2 of their four-year pre-service degree.

5. How do you rate the importance of teacher literacy skills? Please explain.

This question contained two parts, a multiple-choice question and an opportunity for respondents to clarify their answer further

The results shown in Table 4 clearly show that all respondents identified literacy skills as being either important ($n = 10$) or very important ($n = 150$). These results whilst being an accurate reflection of their beliefs might also be skewed as the respondents were participating whilst being enrolled and studying a literacy unit within their program, hence their answer might have been unduly influenced by the content of the unit. Their explanation or further clarification of their chosen answer is presented in Table 5.

It is clear from the further information that the pre-service teachers provided to explain why they had identified literacy as either an important or very important skill for teachers that the respondents considered it to be a core skill ($n = 64$). This result correlates with the results presented in Table 4 and is as expected from a pre-service teacher cohort as they began to link skills and literacy with effective teaching ($n = 62$). It was revealing that a number of the respondents associated fluency in literacy with being able to function effectively in society ($n = 16$), and to a lesser degree being literate enabled them to know what is important to learn ($n = 4$). This indicates an association being made between literacy and the ability to participate fully in the wider world. Only two respondents ($n = 2$) identified the expectations of parents and students regarding the literacy abilities of teachers. This result might be

Table 6 Expectations
regarding literacy content

	$n = 172$
Grammar + writing	2
Develop my personal literacy skills	38
How to deliver engaging literacy lessons	2
The what and why of content areas	4
Technical aspects	22
How to teach literacy	104

explained by the influence of the title of the research project on the participant information sheet: 'Listening to pre-service teachers: One university's response to the perceived literacy crisis in pre-service teacher education programs'. It could also have been a genuine observation.

6. What do you expect to learn about literacy in your four-year pre-service education program?

The responses to this open-ended question resulted in 172 coded items, which were then further coded into the descriptors presented in Table 6. The majority of respondents expected that during their pre-service teacher education program they would be taught how to teach literacy ($n = 104$). If this response is contextualized with the results presented in Table 1, it could be surmised that participants expected to be taught how to teach reading and writing. This is supported by the following examples:

> The technical aspects of literacy skills, expected ages that particular skills are developing, proven techniques for teaching skills
>
> By the end of my degree I expect to understand and be able to teach literacy myself in a confident manner.
>
> How to teach children in terms of writing, listening, reading and speaking [Coded: how to teach literacy]

The next most common group of coded responses was concerned with the development of their own personal literacy skills ($n = 38$). This is consistent with the second definition of literacy identified in Table 1 pertaining to language, communication and interactions with other people. For example:

> I want to improve my literacy skills so that I am knowledgeable so that I can pass on my knowledge to my students. [Coded: personal literacy]

The remaining answers were concerned with specific aspects, such as grammar and writing ($n = 2$), the syllabus (i.e., content areas; $n = 4$) and pedagogy ($n = 2$).

7. What could you do to improve your personal literacy skills?

Interestingly, the results from this question (shown in Table 7) were consistent with the answers collected in Questions 1 and 6. There was a persistent view of literacy being concerned with either reading and writing or communication. The majority of students identified reading and spelling ($n = 76$) or writing ($n = 44$) as actions in which they could engage to improve their own personal literacy skills. For example:

Table 7 Strategies to improve personal literacy skills

	n = 200
Watching videos	2
Act on feedback	4
Speaking/oral practice	10
Study more	42
Grammar	22
Writing	44
Reading + spelling	76

Table 8 Opinion regarding media criticisms

	n = 144
Have not heard anything	8
Sometimes true	16
Cause by low ATAR scores	4
Teachers need higher levels	44
PL or more training is needed	26
Teachers should be assessed before employment	6
Should not be teaching if true	4
Disagree: Not possible to graduate	12
This is correct	16
Can still be a good teacher	8

> Read more different types of texts it broadens my vocabulary and to see the different type of language used in the text

> Reading and writing more in my own time and not just when I have to for uni

> Improve on my spelling and general writing skills [Coded: reading and spelling]

These results were closely followed by more practice in grammar ($n = 22$) and speaking or oral practice ($n = 10$). For example:

> Read to myself, siblings and out loud more often. Practice grammar that I struggle with/ sometimes do wrong [Coded: reading and oral practice]

This would indicate the more traditional definition of literacy, which involves being concerned with reading and writing, was starting to emerge as being the dominant view. The act of communicating effectively was beginning to feature less prominently. In contrast, these results could be viewed as indicating that the participants felt that they were effective communicators.

8. You might have heard in the media a lot of criticism about teachers having low levels of literacy. What do you think about this?

The results to Question 8 of the survey (Table 8) were expected but also revealed that pre-service teachers training to enter the same profession were more critical of practicing teachers. There was a consensus that teachers needed higher levels of literacy than the public ($n = 44$) in order to be able to effectively teach. For example:

> I think that literacy is very important in education therefore teachers should have high literacy standards. [Coded: require higher levels]

The students felt that if this were true, then teachers should be offered more teacher education or professional learning opportunities to improve their literacy skills ($n = 26$). For example:

> I think that all teachers are trained to have literacy skills but there are some who are always continuing to improve them. I think all teachers should attend a class to make sure their skills are up to date. [Coded: require professional learning]

Some respondents felt that the media criticism about teachers having low levels of literacy was either correct ($n = 16$), sometimes true ($n = 16$) or not true ($n = 12$). They reasoned that it would not have been possible for Bachelor of Education or Graduate Diploma in Education students to graduate if their literacy levels were not sufficient for the job.

> I think it's true that teachers have low levels of literacy but they are not considering the whole of literacy, just the writing section of literacy. [Coded: correct]

> I believe this can be true at times so it is important to ensure all students are provided with a teacher who has appropriate levels of literacy. [Coded: sometimes true]

> I don't agree with it as they wouldn't be able to graduate from their degree if they have low levels of literacy. [Coded: disagree]

> The media is notorious for exaggerating and antagonizing people and most teachers have a satisfactory level of literacy. That being said, some teachers are not equipped with the necessary level of literacy needed to effectively teach students and that is a problem which needs to be resolved, ideally through professional development programs. [Coded twice: disagree and professional learning]

There were a small number of participants who had not heard anything about this issue ($n = 8$), whilst some did not state whether or not they had heard of these criticisms and felt that regardless of the literacy level teachers possess, they could still be good teachers ($n = 8$).

> Low levels of literacy doesn't mean that a teacher isn't able to teach well, though the teacher should still have a fair level of literacy at least. [Coded: still an effective teacher]

Some adopted a more punitive position. They felt that if literacy skills were not at the level they needed to be then teachers should be assessed in literacy prior to being employed ($n = 6$). These low literacy skills could have been a result of the lowness of the ATAR score necessary for entry into teaching programs ($n = 4$) in Australia. In cases of low literacy, teachers should not be allowed to teach ($n = 4$).

> I think that unfortunately this is becoming a trend. The lower expected ATAR for entry to teaching would inevitably have this effect in Australia; other factors obviously play a part

too but I think this will have a negative impact on future students' skills. If a teacher doesn't know sufficiently, how could they teach it? [Coded: caused by low ATAR]

There was a great deal of difference in these answers that might need to be examined further, but as a gauge to the response of pre-service teachers to this broader issue of criticism around the perceived literacy skills of teachers, these answers do represent a breadth worthy of further investigation.

5   Discussion

The results from this single case study appear to align with the growing body of research examining the literacy crisis. The respondents' view of literacy was broadly polarized: those who viewed it as reading and writing (a traditional conceptualisation) and those who viewed it as a communicative act. This result neatly surmises the two opposing positions in the literacy crisis itself, and until a consensus is reached on what it means to be literate, it will persist. Respondents were very digitally literate, relying heavily on digital tools and modes of communication, as would be expected from such an age group; however, it was apparent that everyday communicative acts were not being associated with literacy. Literacy was seen as something different or separate from these, and this perception in both the students involved in the project and the broader community is most pronounced. It lies at the heart of the difficulties in addressing literacy skills and abilities in schools. If individuals were able to see the connection between their personal communicative acts and literacy and pay more attention to the substance of those acts, then perhaps the literacy crisis might begin to be viewed differently and abate. As Klein and Unsworth (2014) attest, literacy is a multifaceted social practice, and herein lies the truth in connecting the practices and lived experiences with the theoretical concept of what it means to be literate.

As shown in earlier research, the students self-rated themselves as being reasonably literate. This is an expected result, as they have been through 12 years of formal schooling, having been reasonably successful through that experience and having managed to obtain an ATAR score for entry into a program of study. Expecting a different result would not have been realistic. This confidence, and the result it rewarded them with (i.e., a place in university), would explain the high levels of self-rated literacy skills expressed by the respondents. They did identify some areas of concern, which were aspects usually associated with traditional conceptions of literacy such as grammar, spelling, reading and writing. These were the same areas or skills they employed in their everyday routines. Unwittingly, they were demonstrating fluency and ability in these areas, yet their failure to recognise this as being a persistent disconnect between behaviours, practice and literacy was interesting to see emerge from the data. A distinction needs to be made between pre-service teachers own literacy content knowledge and their ability to teach literacy.

Unsurprisingly, respondents in this study placed a high value on the literacy skills of teachers, viewing them as a core requirement, and this aligned with their view that their studies would develop their own personal skills and expertise in technical aspects. The explicit identification of wishing to develop their own personal literacy skills could be viewed in two ways: an insecurity in their own skills perhaps due to the broader discussion surrounding their future profession or a personal desire to be more proficient or improve in some specific aspect. This requires further research to analyse and examine. When asked how they could improve, they defaulted to very traditional strategies such as more studying, writing, reading and spelling, which aligns with their definition of literacy being largely concerned with reading and writing.

Regarding the 'literacy crisis' itself, the majority of respondents agreed on the importance of having teachers with high levels of literacy. It would have been interesting to turn this question around to match the definitions of literacy that emerged from the data sets and inquire whether they meant fluency in reading and writing or communication in general. It was also of interest to see how many agreed with the perceived crisis. Since the majority of pre-service teachers were recent school leavers, this answer might have been either the result of recent experiences or observations in the school system itself or a repetition of the media position that has been widely disseminated.

6   Conclusions

This chapter has explored the literacy skills of a cohort of pre-service teachers in one Australian university and the perceived wider issue of the 'literacy crisis' in schools and higher education as the broader context in which they are situated. What has emerged from the data collected in this case study is the need for a new approach to conceptualising and teaching literacy. There appear to be two competing perspectives held by students: that literacy is the very traditional act of reading or writing or that it is a communicative act. Added to these two perspectives is the polarization of the wider community—schools perceiving pre-service teachers as not having the required 'hard skills' to teach literacy, and the media viewing literacy in a traditional manner as pertaining to aspects such as grammar or phonemic awareness. This muddle and mess has resulted in a perceived crisis, yet the underlying premise that pre-service teachers are lacking literacy skills is not correct. As Honan et al. (2013) attested, teacher educators must prepare pre-service teachers for two contrasting circumstances. Firstly, they must prepare them to teach in a digital world and be highly capable in broad digital literacies. Secondly, they must equip them for the narrow set of literacy requirements of the highly political pre-registration tests. Perhaps a solution would be to either redefine what is meant by literacy or uncouple the discrete areas within literacy, as has happened with STEM (science, technology, engineering and mathematics) and teach these as separate subjects. Assuming that content being covered under the guise of literacy might no longer suffice, explicitly framing lessons around the discrete areas of literacy, such as grammar, writing and phonics would be more correct. When we say someone is not fluent in literacy, what we really mean is that they are not fluent in a specific aspect. We would like to suggest that the generalist arguments and framing of literacy around one term has led us to this point of misunderstanding and perceived crisis.

References

Adoniou, M. (2017, August 5). *NAPLAN results show it isn't the basics that are missing in Australian education. The conversation.* Retrieved from https://theconversation.com/naplan-results-show-it-isnt-the-basics-that-are-missing-in-australian-education-82113

Buckingham, J. (2016, August 4). Poor teachers beget poor students. *The Australian financial review.* Retrieved from https://search-proquest-com.dbgw.lis.curtin.edu.au/docview/1808367339?accountid=10382

Buckingham, J. (2017, August 3). NAPLAN results show that core learning skills are in retreat. *The Weekend Australian.* Retrieved from http://www.theaustralian.com.au/opinion/naplan-results-show-core-learning-skills-are-in-retreat/news-story/64c08f0017967cd14b9e8399e1ba32ee

Buckingham, J., Ferrari, J., & Alegounarias, T. (2014). *Why Jaydon can't read: A forum on fixing literacy* (144). Retrieved from the Centre for Independent Studies website: http://www.cis.org.au/publications/issue-analysis/article/5080-why-jaydon-cant-read-a-forum-on-fixing-literacy

Carey, M., Christie, M., & Grainger, P. (2015). What benefits can be derived from teaching knowledge about language to preservice teachers? *Australian Journal of Teacher Education, 40*(9). https://doi.org/10.14221/ajte.2015v40n9.2

Cochran-Smith, M., Villegas, A., Abrams, L., Chavez-Moreno, L., Mills, T., & Stern, R. (2015). Critiquing teacher preparation research: An overview of the field, part II. *Journal of Teacher Education, 66*(2), 109–121.

Connell, R. (2009). Good teachers on dangerous ground: Towards a new view of teacher quality and professionalism. *Critical Studies in Education, 50*(3), 213–229 https://doi.org/10.1080/17508480902998421.

Cope, B., & Kalantzis, M. (2000). *Multiliteracies: Literacy learning and the design of social futures.* London, UK: Routledge.

Edwards-Groves, C. (2011). Connecting students to learning through explicit teaching. Retrieved from http://www.myread.org/explicit.htm

Ellis, S., & Moss, G. (2014). Ethics, education policy and research: The phonics question reconsidered. *British Educational Research Journal, 40*(2), 241–260. https://doi.org/10.1002/berj.3039.

Emmitt, M., Zbaracki, M. D., Komesaroff, L. R., & Pollock, J. (2014). *Language and learning: An introduction for teaching* (6th Ed.). South Melbourne, Australia: Oxford University Press.

Fielding Barnsley, R. (2010). Australian pre-service teachers' knowledge of phonemic awareness and phonics in the process of learning to read. *Australian Journal of Learning Difficulties, 15*(1), 99–101. https://doi.org/10.1080/19404150903524606.

Freire, P., & Macedo, D. (1987). *Literacy: Reading the word and the world.* South Hadley, MA: Bergin & Garvey.

Gee, J. (2000). Teenagers in new times a new literacy studies perspective. *Journal of Adolescent & Adult Literacy, 43*(5), 412–420.

Gee, J. P. (1992). *The social mind.* New York: Bergin & Garvey.

Goouch, K., & Lambirth, A. (2016). *Teaching early reading and phonics: Creative approaches to early literacy.* London: Sage.

Honan, E., Exley, B., Kervin, L., Simpson, A., & Wells, M. (2013). Rethinking the literacy capabilities of pre-service primary teachers in testing times. *Australian Journal of Teacher Education, 38*(10), 48–63.

Hudson, P. (2012). How can universities support beginning teachers. *Journal of Higher Education Theory and Practice, 12*(3), 50–59.

Johnson, D. (2010). Learning to teach: The influence of a university- school partnership project on pre-service elementary teachers' efficacy for literacy instruction. *Reading. Horizons, 50*(1), 23–45.

Kalantzis, M., & Cope, B. (1993). *Histories of pedagogy, cultures of schooling. The powers of literacy: A genre approach to teaching writing* (pp. 38–62).

Kalantzis, M., & Cope, B. (2012). *Literacies.* Port Melbourne, Vic: Cambridge University Press.

Klein, P., & Unsworth, L. (2014). The logogenesis of writing to learn: A systemic functional perspective. *Linguistics and Education, 26*, 1–17 https://doi.org/10.1016/j.linged.2013.12.003.

Lloyd, M. (2013). Troubled times in teacher education: 2012–2013. Australian government Office for Learning and Teaching. Accessed February 2, 2017 from www.olt.gov.au/resource-troubled-times-Australian-teacher-education

Louden, W., & Rohl, M. (2006). Too many theories and not enough instruction': Perceptions of pre-service teacher preparation for literacy teaching in Australian schools. *Literacy, 40*(2), 66–78 https://doi.org/10.1111/j.1467-9345.2006.00440.x.

Luke, A. (1998). Getting over method: Literacy teaching as work in "new times". *Language Arts, 75*, 4.

Luke, A. (2000). Critical literacy in Australia: A matter of context and standpoint. *Journal of Adolescent & Adult Literacy, 43*(5), 448–461.

Marszalek, J. (2015, December 1). Trainee teachers have failed a new national literacy and numeracy test. *The Courier Mail.* Retrieved from http://www.couriermail.com.au/news/one-in-10-trainee-teachers-have-failed-a-new-national-literacy-and-numeracy-test/news-story/e6262e379ce95b9ad28522ad5cd6416e

Martyn-Jones, L. (2017, March 10). Trainee teachers fail spell, maths test. The Herald Sun. Retrieved from http://www.heraldsun.com.au/news/trainee-teachers-fail-spell-maths-test/news-story/699f620d52abcf082d23f89bb42f523b

Massengill Shaw, D. M., Dvorak, M. J., & Bates, K. (2007). Promise and possibility. Hope for teacher education: Pre-service literacy instruction can have an impact. *Reading Research and Instruction, 46*, 223–254. https://doi.org/10.1080/19388070709558469.

Milburn, C. (2008, September 8). Battle lines. *The Sydney Morning Herald.* Retrieved from http://www.smh.com.au/national/education/battle-lines-20080804-3pnl.html

O'Neill, S., & Geoghegan, D. (2011). First year pre-service teachers' views about literacy: Exploring the breadth and depth of their pedagogical needs. *International journal of pedagogies and learning, 6*(3), 187–205.

Queensland Board of Teacher Registration. (2001). *Literacy in teacher education: standards for pre-service programs: a report of the literacy in teacher education working party.* Toowong, Qld: Board of Teacher Registration.

Rose, Jim. (2006). *Independent review of the teaching of early reading: Final report.* London: Department for Education and Skills.

Rowe, K. (2005). National inquiry into the teaching of literacy (Australia). Retrieved from Australian Council for Educational Research website: http://research.acer.edu.au/tll_misc/5/

Snyder, I. (2008). *The literacy wars. Why teaching children to read and writing is a battleground in Australia.* Crows Nest, Australia: Allen & Unwin.

Teacher Education Ministerial Advisory Group Final Report. (2014). Action now: Classroom ready teachers. Department of Education and Training. Retrieved from https://docs.education.gov.au/node/36783

Williams, B. T. (2007). Why Johnny can never, ever read: The perpetual literacy crisis and student identity. *Journal of Adolescent and Adult Literacy, 51*(2), 178–182.

Winch, G., Johnston, R., March, P., Ljungdahl, L., & Holliday, M. (2010). *Literacy: Reading, writing and children's literature* (4th Ed.). South Melbourne, VIC: Oxford University Press.

Students' Perceptions of the Use of Video Recording in Additional Language Oral Assessments

Qian Gong, Kyoko Kawasaki, Wai Ling Yeung, Grace Zhang, and Toni Dobinson

Abstract This study adds resources to the current research on computer-aided second-language (L2) learning by focusing on a relatively under-explored area of online oral assessment using video recording. It fills the gap of existing literature by looking into the area through the lens of students' perception. Drawing on data collected through questionnaires and interviews of students enrolled in Chinese and Japanese language programs at Curtin University, this study found that video-recorded oral assessments facilitated L2 learning by improving learners' motivation and encouraging self-reflection. The study also sheds light on the importance of technical and teamwork guidance in maximising learning outcomes. Data variations between beginners and advanced learners who participated in this study gave weight to the argument that a 'one-size-fits-all' approach is not effective in online language learning, so facilitators may need to carefully evaluate the level of learners' language competence when they are incorporating online components into their programs.

Keywords Language learning · Video recording · Reflection · Collaboration

Q. Gong (✉) · G. Zhang · T. Dobinson
School of Education, Curtin University, Perth, WA, Australia
e-mail: Q.Gong@exchange.curtin.edu.au; Grace.Zhang@exchange.curtin.edu.au; T.Dobinson@curtin.edu.au

K. Kawasaki
School of Social Sciences, University of Western Australia, Perth, WA, Australia
e-mail: kyoko.kawasaki@uwa.edu.au

W. L. Yeung
Independent Researcher, Perth, WA, Australia

1 Introduction

Oral proficiency constitutes an important part of language learning. However, unlike written assessments, which the learners can review and make corrections to, oral assessments often create anxiety. In particular, presentations in front of an audience put stress on students. The power imbalance between assessors and learners can create interactive events which are intimidating and threatening for some students. Moreover, the anxiety of speaking in another language in front of an audience or classmates can also affect the performance of students. Perhaps because of this, extant studies have shown that technology can be perceived by students to be useful and to increase their enthusiasm and motivation for learning a new language (Gu and Xu 1999; Guo 2013; Erben et al. 2013). Specifically, the integration of video into additional language instruction has been perceived by students to have a positive impact on their learning, including motivating students to take control of their study, promoting collaborative work, and facilitating reflective practices (Newhouse and Cooper 2013).

Despite the fact that technology-aided language learning has been promoted by universities, the introduction of technology has also brought issues and challenges to students and teachers (Lee 2005; Murday et al. 2008). Reliance on logging into a computer can be inconvenient for some students, and concern has been raised for health issues such as eye strain and stronger self-discipline needed for commitment to regular hours in a non-monitored environment (Murday et al. 2008). In addition, technical glitches in the classroom may sometimes hinder the smooth running of lessons (Al-Musawi and Abdelraheem 2004; Chia and Ellis 2003, Murday et al. 2008). There can be a general sense of reluctance on the part of teachers to use technology-aided assessment due to their own lack of computer literacy or that of the students (Bani Hani 2014; Scheffler and Logan 1999). Attitudes of students and teachers towards technology may also be less than positive (Khine 2001; Norris et al. 2003; Penuel 2006) and resources may be insufficient, including infrastructure and support offered by the schools (Norris et al. 2003; Penuel 2006; Weikart and Marrapodi 1999). In addition, there may be a shortage of time for preparing instruction sheets with computer technology (Brown and Warschauer 2006; Lee 2005), and teachers' perceived expectancy of success and their valuing of technology use also plays a role in the adoption of technology in classrooms (Becker 1994; Wozney et al. 2006). While the successful implementation of technology in learning depends on all these factors, another essential factor is the students' perceptions of the usefulness of technology in learning.

This study adds to current research on technology-aided additional language learning by focusing on a relatively under-explored area: online, video-recorded oral language assessment. The exploration of this area fills a gap in existing literature by looking at oral language assessment from the students' point of view. Drawing on data collected through questionnaires and interviews with students enrolled in Chinese and Japanese as an additional language at one Australian university, this study examines students' perceptions of the role of video-recorded assessment in motivating them to complete oral tasks and to be reflective upon their performance. It also considers the implications of this for teachers of additional languages who wish to implement technology-aided assessment. The study found that students in general perceived that video-recorded oral assessments helped facilitate language learning by improving student motivation and encouraging self-reflection on performance. The study also shed light on the role of task authenticity in technology-aided language learning and the importance of technical and teamwork guidance in optic learning outcomes. Data variations between beginners and advanced language learners who participated in this study give weight to the argument that a 'one-size-fits-all' approach will not be effective in online language learning, so facilitators may need to carefully evaluate the level of learners' language competence when they are incorporating online components into their programs.

This study has breadth and depth in so far as it involves two taught languages (Japanese and Chinese), assessments devised in different formats (speech, role play, storytelling and documentary) and student participants with different language proficiencies (beginner, intermediate and advanced learners).

2   Theoretical Foundations

Throughout the last three decades, a variety of technologies such as computers and audio and video devices have become integral to the language-learning classroom. Teachers have also been experimenting with mobile phone applications, internet resources and network-based social computing technologies such as blogs, internet forums and discussion boards. Previous studies have frequently revealed that various aspects of technology increase students' enthusiasm and motivation for learning a new language (Gu and Xu 1999; Guo 2013; Ilter 2009; Kim 2008; Lee 2005; Murday et al. 2008). One of these aspects is the flexibility that technology offers. That is, students can access learning materials and tasks with fewer limitations in terms of time and space (Almekhlafi 2006; Lai and Kritsonis 2006; Lee 2005; Murday et al. 2008), and they appreciate the chance to work at their own pace and to choose materials depending on their personal academic progress (Murday et al. 2008; Zapata and Sagarra 2007).

Another aspect of technology-aided instruction and assessment that fosters student motivation is constructive feedback received online (Gu and Xu 1999; Hafner and Miller 2011; Lee 2005; Shih 2010). In Gu and Xu's (1999) study, students expressed satisfaction with the constructive feedback they received in different forms (written and oral, formal and informal, and individual and group) and from different sources (peers, teachers and e-mail partners). Online feedback encouraged students to do revision both before and after they submitted their assignments. Computer-assisted language learning technology has also been shown to contribute to students' improvement in additional language macro skills (listening, speaking, reading and writing) (Almekhlafi 2006; Deckhinet 2008; Heins et al. 2007; Lee

2005) and micro skills such as grammar, vocabulary and pronunciation (Zapata and Sagarra 2007).

Several studies (Brown 1997; Jahnke 2010; Presby 2001) have reported more balanced participation among students in online situations. Students might feel too intimidated to participate in class, not because they are incompetent in the language, but because of their shyness. The researchers found that the online delivery mode of learning encourages less extroverted learners to participate confidently in discussion. Collaborative learning has been shown to be an area where technology has made a particularly positive impact. Several studies have reported that a collaborative spirit can be fostered more easily with technology than in a traditional classroom (Brown 1997; Dekhinet 2008; Gu and Xu 1999). Collaborative learning has occurred in language courses that focus on writing using wiki (Kessler and Bikowski 2010) and online discussion forums (Nor et al. 2012) and on activities that combine speaking and writing through telecollaboration (Bueno-Alastuey and Kleban 2014). This is true even for beginners or students with lower proficiency in the target language (Chang and Windeatt 2016).

2.1 Issues and Challenges of Using Technology in Language-Learning Instruction

Investigations of how technology can benefit students' learning of another language have been plentiful; however, there is also evidence that raises questions about the efficacy of this tool. In Murday et al.'s (2008) study, students complained that they had to log into a computer whenever they needed to have more practice or to revise previous lessons and asked if they could use printed materials such as books and worksheets instead. The complaints stemmed from health concerns, as students stated that staring at a computer screen for prolonged periods of time caused them eyestrain. Lee (2005) also found that, despite the fact that online discussion has been considered to be an effective learning tool, her students experienced difficulties communicating in this mode because they could not see the faces of those with whom they were communicating.

Technical difficulties experienced in the classroom can be another major obstacle to steady progress in learning. Al-Musawi and Abdelraheem (2004) and Murday et al. (2008) reported that students complained about technical glitches such as network interruptions and pages that did not load correctly frequently occurring in lessons, while Chia and Ellis (2003) recounted student frustration with slow computer speed, which resulted in a reduction of the popularity of technology among students. An overall lack of technical support to deal with these problems can be a major hindrance to teachers adopting technology in the classroom (Al-Senaidi et al. 2009).

It is frequently reported that the quality of teacher education may not be sufficient for teachers to extensively use technology in the classroom (Al-Senaidi et al.

2009; Meskill et al. 2002). Kessler's (2007) survey showed that while TESOL professionals seemed to feel confident in computer-assisted language learning, they did not show much confidence about integrating it into their classroom instruction, particularly on aural and oral skills, due to their lack of formal training.

2.2   Integration of Video Into L2 Instruction

Video recording as a learning tool has been integrated into classroom instruction to improve constructive learning for many years now. McNulty and Lazarevic (2012) identified three levels of video integration in L2 classrooms. At a basic level, video materials can be used for simple viewing of and listening to L2 content to elicit discussion or communication in the classroom. This level is considered to be a passive element of a language classroom as it has limited impact on promoting students' classroom engagement (McNulty and Lazarevic 2012). Video recordings can also be used for self-reflection and assessment, such as identifying students' pronunciation errors and providing constructive feedback. More challenging video tasks in language classrooms involve language learners as creators of video scripts and video content. Shrosbree (2008) highlights this approach as one of the most effective ways for promoting collaborative learning and communication among language students.

From passive viewing to the students' production of video materials, there is a whole array of techniques and methods for including video technology in classroom learning and teaching. Hafner and Miller (2011) reported on a semester-long English for science and technology (EST) course at a university in Hong Kong. A major component of the course was a student-centred digital video project in which students created and shared a scientific documentary. The students in the course had upper-intermediate English language proficiency and were divided into groups of three to conduct a science project using English. The course was evaluated from the students' perspectives through questionnaires, focus group interviews and blog comments. Findings suggested that the digital video project and associated technological learning environment provided students with opportunities to take control of their learning as autonomous learners.

Another study by Shih (2010) on video-based blogs established an effective blended teaching and learning model combining online and face-to-face (FTF) instructional blogging for an English public speaking course at a university in Taiwan. Shih's (2010) findings endorsed the notion that blended learning gives students more motivation, improves their skills in public speaking, equips students with computer skills and encourages reflective practices.

Common features for video-assisted projects highlight enhancement of motivation in autonomous learning, resulting in ample opportunities for self-reflection, collaboration and receiving corrective feedback. What can be unique in using video is the ability to see and hear oneself. This feature not only develops students' language abilities but also their presentation skills. Because making presentations is a common practice not just in additional language classrooms but also in other subject areas, acquiring good presentation skills is a crucial part of today's education. Using videos as a reflective tool at practice sessions can help to instil more confidence into students and readiness for their new language-learning experience. Video-assisted classes are often task or project based. This provides a more global approach for learning, as it allows multimodal (writing, reading, speaking and listening) skills to be practised in sequential steps (pre-video activities, video filming and post-video activities). This requires multiple skills (language skills, collaboration skills, searching skills, technical skills etc.) to be practised repeatedly and in doing so produces better learning outcomes through learners' continuous self-reflection and self-correction.

2.3   Learners' Perspectives on Technology Integrated Instruction

Lee (2005) investigated web-based language instruction that utilised the Blackboard course management system (CMS). A CMS allows language educators to create task-based activities that promote the learning of an additional language through interaction and collaboration amongst learners (Lee 2002). Lee (2005) researched how this management system affected the learning of an additional language and how students perceived learning in that particular context. In another similar study, 35 tertiary students enrolled in a third-year Spanish course participated in two online activities: an online essay and an online discussion. At the end of the course, a survey and interview were conducted to elicit students' views on using the web-based course. The results of the survey revealed that the students believed that online activities enhanced the development of their Spanish skills. The commonly used Blackboard platform created a learning community where the individual's learning is formed as a result of corrective involvement from the group. Lee quotes a student who reported that 'it was very helpful for me to be able to use my Spanish through chatting in my group. Often we helped each other to come up with ideas or solve grammar or vocabulary problems'.

In this collaborative working space, individuals also need to be accountable to the group. Students confirmed that daily essay writing online was very challenging and a bit stressful at the beginning, but became a rewarding experience by the end. One student commented:

> At the beginning I was sceptical about using Blackboard for writing assignments. But after a few weeks, I got used to it and found the online writing very rewarding because I could focus on specific topics, and I wrote about my own perspectives and personal experiences concerning these topics. The topics were very interesting to me. I have never written so many essays in Spanish. I believe my writing skills have improved. (Lee 2005, p.148)

Good topic choices that were relevant to their lives helped them to keep their motivation high for the assignments. Overall, the students' experience of web-based learning changed the way they viewed the role of internet technology in language learning. This was corroborated by Lee (2005), who inferred that it was important that learning be a personalised experience and that web-based instruction facilitated by the Blackboard platform was well suited to the students' needs and benefited their learning of the new language.

2.4   The Use of Video in Oral Language Assessments

Not a lot has been written about the use of video in oral second-language assessments in terms of student perceptions. One piece of research by Newhouse and Cooper (2013) in which students learned Italian, however, was conducted over 3 years and examined several approaches to using digital technology to assess oral performance. The first component was a portfolio of sub-tasks that included a video-recorded oral presentation, a computer-based exam, a video-recorded interview, and an online exam that included oral audio recordings. Findings suggested that online assessment of oral performance appeared to be an equally effective way to facilitate assessment when compared with traditional methods. Moreover, the benefits of this mode were convenience, the possibility of access from a variety of locations and the fact that recorded assessments could be kept as a reliable first-hand record of student output (Swanson and Early 2008a, b). Interestingly, though, both students and teachers in the study reported preferring the use of audio-visual recordings and online performance tasks for revision more than for summative assessment.

Another study by Guo (2013) found that video recordings can be a useful tool in improving students' classroom oral presentation skills because students perceive this resource to improve their learning. In her study, Guo set up an experimental group, which engaged with aspects of using video recordings, and a control group, which was denied the chance to use video recordings. The experimental group reported that watching videos of their performances facilitated improvement in this task because they could rehearse, review and repeat the performance. The control group, however, reported: 'It is extremely difficult to assess yourself without being able to review video data' (p. 96).

The benefits of video recording students in their oral assessments have been listed by Lewis (2016), who states that one big advantage of students recording themselves is that they have an opportunity to have several attempts at the task and can therefore make use of the technology as a rehearsal. Using technology as a mode of assessment also caters to the many different learning preferences that different students might have. Moreover, students may demonstrate a higher level of commitment to the task and be more invested when their face is attached to a recorded piece of work and they are not just a name on a test sheet. The time taken to assess students orally can also be cut down by using video-recorded assessments, and markers can delay feedback to a time that may be more convenient for them (Swanson and Early 2008a, b). The use of recorded oral assessments for speakers of

English as a first language as well as speakers of English as an additional language has become very common in the area of health sciences in recent years. In particular, the virtual learning environment and the use of avatars as interlocutors who carry out conversations with those being assessed has been found to be effective (Bánszki et al. 2018). This virtual learning environment has a realism that can provide immersion through 'a sense of authenticity and identification with the environment' (Whitton 2010, p. 41). The avatar can be used to address the issue of variability in interviewer styles and the inequity that may arise from this if some interviewees are given more linguistic turns than others (Norton 2013). An avatar can be pre-programmed to give all test takers the same opportunities to speak and motivate students to engage more with the unit learning activities (Müller and Habel 2012).

Once adapted to the students' context, it will simulate authentic communication, elicit real performances and mimic authentic social interaction (Leung and Lewkowicz 2006) in a non-threatening learning environment, which can all be recorded. Results from a research project underway at one Australian university suggest that students prefer interacting with the avatar and being video-recorded while doing so to simulations carried out by real actors or with actual patients because they feel safer and less self-conscious when interacting with the avatar. In the article that emerged from this study, however, findings reported that although students in the experimental group found the recorded virtual learning environment beneficial, they also found it more challenging than students in the control group who did their oral assessment face to face and not online (Bánszki et al. 2018).

The above literature survey has attempted to show that technologies in various forms can be a useful tool in developing an additional language and, in particular, in the assessment of oral language development, despite some ongoing challenges. Research findings have shown several positive aspects of technology-aided learning, including greater flexibility in learning modes, stronger motivation to engage in learning when boosted by constructive feedback received online, and the opportunity for collaborative learning. Video-recording technology, now widely available and easily accessible, can be effectively blended into language classrooms to improve students' macro skills, including speaking skills. However, there is much less research available on how video recording can be used for assessing oral skills and even less on both how students perceive blended learning and implications for the integration of blended learning into L2 instruction. This action-research project aims to contribute to the understanding of video-recorded assessment by implementing a specially designed assignment to students at different levels of language proficiency and soliciting their feedback through surveys and interviews with a view to integrating student feedback into the use of video as an assessment tool.

3   Methodology

The design of this project is in line with action research. Action research has six key characteristics: a practical focus, the educator-researcher's own practices, collaboration, a dynamic process, a plan of action and sharing research (Creswell 2008). This research project, in principle, addresses a practical problem identified by language teacher-researchers at one university. These teachers aim to work collaboratively to integrate technology-aided tasks into the Japanese and Chinese language course curriculums in the future using the findings presented in this chapter.

The study involved collecting both qualitative and quantitative data from students using interviews and survey questions. To begin with, students filmed their assessment task with a video camera for six Chinese and Japanese language units offered through the Department of Asian Languages at one Australian university. Project-based work provides language learners an opportunity to go out of the classroom and try out what they have learned in the classroom in real-life situations. The processes of filming and editing the videos can allow students the chance to review their speaking performance in the additional language. Five unit coordinators teaching Chinese and Japanese at different levels designed and implemented assignment tasks. The sequence of student activities used in the 6 units (Chinese 212, Chinese 311, Chinese 322, Japanese 111, Japanese 312 and Japanese 342[1]) were writing a script, practising an oral presentation, filming a performance and sharing a video. The videos were first uploaded to YouTube and embedded in blog posts on Blackboard, the online learning management system employed at the university in question, so that they could be viewed in class and outside the classroom. Students were encouraged to view other students' videos and leave comments on the blog (in English in beginners' units and in the language being studied in other units). Tasks chosen were dependent on language level. There were three types of tasks: role-play, speech and documentary. Specifically, Chinese 212 students were provided with an advertisement for a new customer service officer to work at a local tourist information centre. Students then wrote a speech to talk about why they thought they were suitable or unsuitable for the job vacancy. This speech was videoed.

In Chinese 312, students were asked to tell a story based on a sequence of four pictures depicting a young man looking for a date online and video the story telling. The assessment for Chinese 322 was to make a video of a role play of unsuccessful cross-cultural communication. Japanese 111 required students to make a video of a role play of a pair of students greeting and introducing themselves to each other. The assessment for Japanese 322 was to video a speech about a mysterious event of some kind. In Japanese 342, students formed a group and did some research on a topic then made a visual report that could be either a news report or a short documentary designed for television. The reason for involving participants who were

---

[1] All first-year units are 111 (Semester 1) and 112 (Semester 2), second-year units are 211 (semester 1) and 212 (Semester 2), third year units are 311 (Semester 1) and 312 (Semester 2), and final-year units taken in either the third or fourth year are 321 (Semester 1) and 322 (Semester 2). Japanese 342 is an advanced course.

studying different languages in different units with different tasks was to examine the perceived usefulness of video-recorded assessments independent of the content or language level of the students.

According to the classification that McNulty and Lazarevic (2012) put forward in their study, this project involves the most sophisticated use of video technology in a language classroom, as it is based on language students themselves as creators of video scripts and video content. Our aim was to elicit the students' perceptions on whether the video-recorded assessment was more helpful for assisting learning than face-to-face feedback. In order to examine students' experiences with the recorded oral assessment, all 86 participants completed a multiple-choice written survey, but only 41 of these then went on to do a one-on-one, face-to-face, semi-structured oral interview after the tasks were complete. The units, type of tasks and the number of students involved are shown in Table 1 below.

The survey used a Likert scale, and students were asked to choose their response to the given statement from five choices: *strongly agree, agree, neither agree nor disagree, disagree,* or *strongly disagree,* to which numerical scores of 1–5 were assigned, according to the level of agreement. The highest score, 5, was assigned to the response *strongly agree,* and the lowest, 1, to *strongly disagree.* The responses for each statement were aggregated and the mean score and standard deviation (SD, discrepancy among participants) from each unit and those for the combined data of all units were calculated. A mean above 3 was interpreted as positive and below 3 was seen as negative. The semi-structured interviews were conducted individually without audio or video recording, but the responses to each question were noted down at the site of the interview.

Table 1 Unit information

	Level	Task	Total enrolment in the unit	Number of returned surveys	Number of interviews
Chinese 212	Beginner stage 2	Speech	27	21 (78%)	21[a] (78%)
Chinese 311	Intermediate	Role play	14	6 (43%)	0 (0%)
Chinese 322	Advanced	Role play	12	12 (100%)	2 (17%)
Japanese 111	Beginner stage 1	Role play	69	24 (35%)	10 (14%)
Japanese 312	Intermediate	Speech	20	10 (50%)	4 (20%)
Japanese 342	Advanced	Documentary	20	13 (65%)	4 (20%)
TOTAL			162	86 (53%)	41 (25%)

[a]Instead of individual oral interviews, Chinese 212 students were given the same open-ended questions as were given in the oral interviews so that they could write their answers when they completed the multiple-choice survey

4   Findings

This section examines the quantitative data from the survey and the qualitative data from the interview and open-ended questions in the survey. In order to discuss the effects of the project on the students' perceptions of the value of recording oral assessments for their language development, we identified three areas to examine: (1) mode of the oral assessment task, (2) task engagement and (3) reflection and student-centred learning.

4.1   Mode of the Oral Assessment Task

The statement in the written survey to which students were asked to respond was 'It was easier to perform in front of the camera than in class'. The mean and SD for this question for each class are shown in Table 2.

The findings showed that the overall responses were moderately positive except for two Chinese units. Interestingly, on average, students in Japanese classes gave positive responses with smaller SDs and students in Chinese classes gave more negative answers with bigger SDs, which indicates a high level of difference amongst the responses of students studying Japanese and those studying Chinese, especially in more advanced levels of the language course. Interviews found that although many students felt that performing in front of the camera was less intimidating than performing in class, most people thought filming was more time consuming, not only because it involves technical tasks, but also because students were tempted to redo the video after viewing what they had produced. The survey shows that the majority of the students attempted filming more than four times (55%). Four students who participated in the interview answered that they needed more than 20 takes. One student said in the interview that perfection is not expected for the class performance, but it is expected for the video production. Another commented that it would be a nightmare for a perfectionist to produce a video. This mode of presentation gives students opportunities and motivation to practice repeatedly until they can perform the role to their satisfaction. Students, especially those who are not used to speaking in the target language, responded positively to this mode of presentation, presumably appreciating the many chances to rehearse that it offered.

Table 2 Responses to the statement 'It was easier to perform in front of the camera than in class'

	Ch 212	Ch 311	Ch 322	Jap 111	Jap 322	Jap 342	Total
Mean	3.43	2.67	2.30	3.50	4.05	3.92	3.38
SD	1.36	1.63	1.40	1.18	1.16	1.08	1.35

Table 3 Responses to the statement 'The project has effectively engaged me in language learning'

	Ch 212	Ch 311	Ch 322	Jap 111	Jap 322	Jap 342	TOTAL
Mean	4.00	3.67	3.00	4.00	3.85	3.61	3.81
SD	0.83	1.15	1.41	0.72	1.00	1.19	0.99

4.2   Task Engagement

One of the higher positive responses in the survey related to engagement. The statement presented in the survey was 'The project has effectively engaged me in language learning'. The mean and SD for this question for each class are shown in Table 3.

In both languages, the mean scores of the beginners' responses to this statement were higher than the more advanced learners', with the SD of responses from beginner students being the smallest. The mean gradually decreased and the SD widened in more advanced language level learners, as shown in Table 3. In other words, most of the beginner students felt that they were engaged in the project, but at higher levels fewer students felt they were engaged. That is probably due to the diversity of the language skills in classes of more advanced proficiency levels. At the beginner's level, most students have no previous knowledge of the additional language and they start at about the same linguistic level. In addition, the tasks for the project did not require a wide range of words and expressions in the additional language. Students attempted to create natural and meaningful scenes with a limited set of expressions. For many students, this was the first meaningful communication for them outside the classroom. A few students commented positively about going out of the classroom for a real life experience in their interviews. On the other hand, in the advanced level units, the language competence of the students and skills required for the projects were more diverse, which may have resulted in less favourable student responses. The fact that they have been with their classmates longer may also mean that they feel less threatened by face-to-face presentation in front of their peers. Having experienced many different techniques and teaching tools during their language learning career they may also have found the videoing technique less novel or remarkable. In the interviews, many confirmed that the project was fun and entertaining, however, confirming the ability of the recordings to facilitate students' engagement.

4.3   Reflection and Student-Centred Language Learning

The statement that attracted the most consistent responses from the different Chinese and Japanese units was the one on self-reflection. Most students agreed with the statement 'The project helped me to notice my weaknesses'. Table 4 below shows that the mean scores are all around 4 and the SDs are relatively low, ranging from 0.59 to 1.28. Also, those students who participated in the interviews all agreed that

Table 4 Responses to the statement 'The project helped me to notice my weaknesses'

	Ch 212	Ch 311	Ch 322	Jap 111	Jap 322	Jap 342	Total
Mean	4.05	4.00	4.20	3.91	4.05	3.85	3.94
SD	0.59	1.1	0.63	0.97	0.63	1.28	0.97

Table 5 Responses to the statement 'Watching my own performance is a good exercise'

	Ch 212	Ch 311	Ch 322	Jap 111	Jap 322	Jap 342	Total
Mean	3.71	3.83	3.5	3.79	3.6	3.31	3.64
SD	0.9	0.98	1.09	1.1	1.17	1.25	1.06

they noticed what needed to be corrected or improved in their use of the additional language. This awareness led some students to practise their language repeatedly and make more attempts at filming, as mentioned above.

Students commented that watching their own performance not only helped them to notice language inaccuracies but also boosted their confidence. Some students in the interview used the word 'proud' to describe their feelings and others suggested that they found speaking in a foreign language 'interesting' and 'amazing'. Even if students did not like their performance, many thought watching and reflecting upon their own language speaking performance was a good exercise. Table 5 below shows the response scores for the statement 'Watching my own performance is a good exercise'. The scores are not very high, but still on the positive side. Again, advanced language level units showed lower scores with bigger SDs.

One comment common to all students from advanced language level units was that the project provided a good writing exercise. Although the aim of the project was to improve oral performance, since performances were pre-prepared rather than spontaneous, with students taking time to write detailed scripts and edit them with the use of different resources, the integrated skills of writing, listening and reading were also practised. Lower-level language students also commented that they used a wide variety of resources. One student specifically stated that she used 'the beginning to the end of the textbook'. Students were aware not only that they could attempt the recording many times, but also that the assessors of their performance could watch the same video repeatedly. This led the students to attempt to write high-quality scripts rather than relying on the entertainment factor of the live performance.

An important aspect of student-centred learning is collaboration. The response to the statement 'Collaboration with my partner enhanced my learning' is shown in Table 6 below. Again, the students with the lowest level of proficiency in the additional language showed the most positive responses. Interestingly, the actual task for Chinese 212 was an individual speech, but many responded positively to the statement with a very small SD. Quite a few students in this unit also commented that the best aspect of the project was collaboration or 'helping each other'. Since the task involved filming, each student needed someone to film their speech. This extra step seems to have created an opportunity for collaboration. Students at the

Table 6 Responses to the statement 'Collaboration with my partner enhanced my learning'

	Ch 212	Ch 311	Ch 322	Jap 111	Jap 342	Total
Mean	3.71	3.17	3.58	3.83	3.23	3.61
SD	0.56	1.33	1.16	0.96	1.25	1.02

lower proficiency language levels operating with a minimum of language skills stated that collaboration had had a positive effect on their learning experience, as shown in Table 6.

5 Discussion

This discussion explores three questions: (1) What is the principal reason for the overall positive feedback from students who participated in the video-recorded oral assessment study? (2) In what way can a mixed response from advanced additional language learners to some survey questions be explained? (3) What are the implications of this study for teachers of languages who use technology-aided assessment?

5.1 *Importance of Task Authenticity to Language Learning*

The overall positive feedback from student participants is consistent with findings of other research (Radinsky et al. 2001) on the importance of task authenticity to learning. According to Radinsky, authentic learning tasks provide real-world relevance as well as personal meaning to learners; they are crucial factors that motivate learners to learn well.

An online video project for assessing language skills is an example of a learning task simulating a real-life situation. Task authenticity describes the degree to which a learning task resembles activities outside of the classroom. It involves problem-solving practices similar to those undertaken by people in the real world (CTGV 1990). The learners are required to decide what needs to be discussed or presented in their own contexts (Nikitina 2011). They also have to determine how to convey the message in a way that includes an effective use of the technology. The online environment is considered ideal for facilitating collaborative learning and learner reflections (Reeves et al. 2002). When this environment is integrated with a student-developed video project, it offers a medium for a range of sophisticated and rich representations that allow learners to use their language skills in a way closer to their life experience outside the classroom (Potter 2005). Although, the speeches in the video are planned and scripted, thus only semi-authentic, the video-making task gives an opportunity for the learners to recreate a scene from the real world and run a simulation. The tasks for the more advanced language learners also require students to view their peers' work and give feedback in the target language. This particular part of the activity is authentic in that students are engaging in real-life communication using the target language. The positive evaluations received from students who participated in this survey, therefore, particularly for the survey questions about 'engagement', 'reflection' and 'student-centred learning', can be interpreted as recognition of the effectiveness of a video project as a semi-authentic additional language-learning activity for conducting oral assessment.

Kearney and Schuck (2006), in their study of student-developed digital video projects, go one step further to point out the importance of an audience. Students' anticipation of screening their videos in front of a real audience gave students an extra incentive, not only to make a worthwhile video, but also to use appropriate language and humour. This resonates with some of the comments collected in interviews with students who participated in this study. Many students said they preferred to make a video than to give a live presentation. They believed that the video alternative reduced their anxiety and improved their performance.

5.2   The Discrepancies in Responses of Beginners and Advanced Language Learners

The findings of this study also point to some differences between beginners and advanced learners in the way they evaluated the effectiveness of the video project as a learning task. Due to the limited scope of the survey used in this study, it is difficult to ascertain whether the disparity in findings is due to an inadequacy in the language participants' ability to report what they felt, task-related issues or participant-related issues such as personality or preferred approaches to learning language. When the findings of this study are looked at more closely it is not difficult to see that the more advanced language learners were slightly more reserved in their assessment of the video project as effective. The advanced learners were students who had achieved a reasonable level of success in their acquisition of another language. Some of them had studied abroad in Japan or China. Others had extensive experience communicating with speakers of Chinese and Japanese as a first language through informal language-exchange arrangements. The fact that they were more experienced learners who may have developed a larger repertoire of language learning strategies over the years may explain why they were less enthusiastic in endorsing the video project as a preferred mode of collaborative learning, but they would not hesitate to acknowledge the value of the video project as an effective tool for reflective learning. A future study could probe this phenomenon further by employing more in-depth interviews with students about their reasons for their responses.

5.3 Implications for Implementing Technology-Aided Assessment

This study has identified several important aspects of technology-aided assessment that have pedagogical implications:

- The video assignments used in this study, in their current formats, are adequate for the beginners' level Japanese and Chinese language learners. They provide novice language learners with an engaging and less threatening environment to improve their language skills. Further adjustment and refinement can be achieved through aligning the assignment with assessment practices for authentic tasks. Self and peer assessment is an important part of such practices. In this study, peer assessment was conducted by asking students to share their videos on a blog. The integrating of the video project with an e-portfolio assessment would be another effective way of promoting self-assessment. It would also allow teachers to observe the production process and provide frequent, well timed feedback.
- All video projects in this study required students to use the virtual classroom on Blackboard instead of face-to-face interactions where learners can use their first language to communicate and clarify. While the virtual classroom is useful and provides a unique platform for language learners to conduct the kind of communicative activities they may come across outside of the classroom, it does not necessarily mean that virtual classroom learning can completely replace face-to-face interactions in classrooms or elsewhere. The findings in this study showed that the more advanced level language learners tended to prefer participating in a real rather than virtual community and engaging directly with members of the target communities. There seems to be no substitution for an in-country experience of studying, living and working in the target language countries.

6 Conclusions and Implications

While the existing literature indicates that, in general, technologies in various forms can be beneficial to learning a new language (Gu and Xu 1999; Guo 2013; Hafner and Miller 2011; Ilter 2009; Kim 2008; Lee 2005; Murday et al. 2008; Sato et al. 2017; Shih 2010), oral assessment in the form of video recording is an under-explored research area. This study goes some way towards investigating the area through the lens of students' perceptions. The empirically based findings in this study report the perceptions of students with different levels of language competence and their experience with blended assessment methods.

The findings indicate that video-recorded oral assessments conducted in this study were considered by students to be effective tools for helping them to develop their additional language. On the whole, students felt more confident to perform in front of the camera than in front of their teachers or peers. They reported being more engaged in learning and collaborative study and more able to self-reflect on their language performance. While students felt generally positive about the video-recording approach, however, there were some discrepancies in terms of degree of agreement. Of the five survey questions, students were most enthusiastic about the greater level of engagement and reflective learning (e.g., noticing one's language areas needing improvement) that the video tasks promoted, but slightly less enthu-siastic about the collaborative opportunities the video tasks afforded.

The virtual classroom helped students to perform oral assessment tasks at least as effectively as traditional face-to-face interview tasks. The other important finding was the discrepancy between the reported experiences and evaluations of recorded oral assessment tasks by learners with different levels of additional language com-petence. The pattern was that students at the beginners' level appeared to be more positive and energised by the project than the advanced learners. Reasons for this are probably complex and multifaceted, but one of the possible reasons could be that the advanced language learners had already had extensive online and computer-aided experience and had already been exposed to wide-ranging learning modes, making them less easily impressed by technology-aided tasks and more critical of the tasks than the beginners for whom the tasks were a novelty. Nevertheless, the advanced learners endorsed the video project as a preferred mode of oral assessment in general.

The implications of this study are twofold. Firstly, the findings of this study are consistent in principle with the findings of previous studies on roles of technology in language learning. The fact that studies of different areas of online learning and different sets of data generate similar results indicates that technologies appear ben-eficial in principle for some learners of additional languages. Secondly, the differ-ences between the beginners and the advanced Chinese and Japanese language learners observed in this study suggests that language teachers and instructors who utilise technology-assisted language teaching and learning tasks for oral assessment may need to take the level of language competence of their students into account; that is, a 'one-size-fits-all' approach may not be effective in achieving optimal learning outcomes. These findings suggest that online video assessment may help motivate learning and encourage self-reflection. However, more technical and team-work guidance may be required to maximise the learning outcomes.

The size of this study means that it can only be used as a springboard for further enquiry, and its findings should be treated as tendencies and guidelines only. To extend this present study, further research on video-recorded oral assessment could drill down into teachers' perceptions of this tool. A comparison of the results of this study and those of a future study which employs more qualitative data collection methods might also provide a fuller picture of the usefulness of video-aided online assessment tasks.

Acknowledgements We thank Yuko Asano-Cavanagh for help with data collection, Aki Kaneko for help with literature review, John D. Ball for proofreading and all the students who participated in this research project. We acknowledge with gratitude the eScholar grant awarded by Curtin University in 2012.

References

Almekhlafi, A. (2006). The effect of computer assisted language learning (CALL) on United Arab Emirates English as a foreign language (EFL) school students' achievement and attitude. *Journal of Interactive Research, 17*(2), 121–142.

Al-Musawi, A., & Abdelraheem, A. (2004). E-learning at Sultan Qaboos University: Status and future. *British Journal of Educational Technology, 35*(3), 363–367.

Al-Senaidi, S., Lin, L., & Poirot, J. (2009). Barriers to adopting technology for teaching and learning in Oman. *Computers & Education, 53*, 575–590.

Bani Hani, N. A. (2014). Benefits and barriers of computer assisted language learning and teaching in the Arab World: Jordan as a model. *Theory and Practice in Language Studies, 4*(8), 1609–1615. https://doi.org/10.4304/tpls.4.8.1609-1615.

Bánszki, F., Beilby, J., Quail, M., Allen, P. J., Brundage, S. B., & Spitalnick, J. (2018). A clinical educator's experience using a virtual patient to teach communication and interpersonal skills. *Australasian Journal of Educational Technology, 34*(3), 60–73.

Becker, H. J. (1994). Computer-based integrated learning systems in the elementary and middle grades: A critical review and synthesis of evaluation reports. *Journal of Educational Computing Research, 8*(1), 1–41.

Brown, A. (1997). Designing for learning: What are the essential features of an effective online course? *Australian Journal of Educational Technology, 13*(2), 115–126.

Brown, D., & Warschauer, M. (2006). From the university to the elementary classroom: Students' experiences in learning to integrate technology in instruction. *Journal of Technology and Teacher Education, 14*(3), 599–621.

Bueno-Alastuey, M. C., & Kleban, M. (2014). Matching linguistic and pedagogical objectives in a telecollaboration project: A case study. *Computer Assisted Language Learning, 29*(1), 148–166.

Chang, H., & Windeatt, S. (2016). Developing collaborative learning practices in an online language course. *Computer Assisted Language Learning, 29*(8), 1271–1286.

Chia, C. S. C., & Ellis, M. (2003). PRC students' experience with independent learning at the National Institute of Education, Singapore. In *Proceedings of the independent learning conference 2003*.

Creswell, J. W. (2008). *Educational research: Planning, conducting, and evaluating quantitative and qualitative research*. Upper Saddle River: Pearson/Merrill Prentice Hall.

CTGV (Cognition and Technology Group at Vanderbilt). (1990). Technology and the design of generative learning environments. *Educational Technology, 31*(5), 34–40.

Dekhinet, R. (2008). Online enhanced corrective feedback for ESL learners in higher education. *Computer Assisted Language Learning, 21*(5), 409–425.

Erben, T., Ban, R., Jin, L., Summers, R., & Eisenhower, K. (2013). Using technology for foreign language instruction: Creative innovations, research, and applications. In T. Erben & I. Sarieva (Eds.), *Calling all foreign language teachers: Computer-assisted language learning in the classroom* (pp. 13–36). New York/London: Routledge.

Gu, P., & Xu, Z. (1999). Improving EFL learning environment through networking. In R. Debski & M. Levy (Eds.), *World CALL: Global perspectives on computer-assisted language learning. Improving EFL learning environment through networking* (pp. 169–184). Lisse: Swets & Zeiltlingers.

Guo, R. X. (2013). The use of video recordings as an effective tool to improve presentation skills. *Polyglossia, 24*, 92–101.

Hafner, C., & Miller, L. (2011). Fostering learner autonomy in English for science: A collaborative digital video project in a technological learning environment. *Language Learning and Technology, 15*(3), 68–86.

Heins, B., Duensing, A., Stickler, U., & Batstone, C. (2007). Spoken interaction in online and face-to-face language tutorials. *Computer Assisted Language Learning, 20*(3), 279–295.

Ilter, B. G. (2009). Effect of technology on motivation in EFL classrooms. *Turkish Online Journal of Distance Education (TOJDE), 10*(4), 136–158.

Jahnke, J. (2010). Student perceptions of the impact of online discussion forum participation on learning outcomes. *Journal of Learning Design, 3*(2), 27–34.

Kearney, M., & Schuck, S. (2006). Spotlight on authentic learning: Student developed digital video projects. *Australasian Journal of Educational Technology, 22*(2), 189–208.

Kessler, G. (2007). Formal and informal CALL preparation and teacher attitude toward technology. *Computer Assisted Language Learning, 20*(2), 173–188.

Kessler, G., & Bikowski, D. (2010). Developing collaborative autonomous learning abilities in computer mediated language learning: Attention to meaning among students in wiki space. *Computer Assisted Language Learning, 23*(1), 41–58.

Khine, M. S. (2001). Attitudes toward computers among teacher education students in Brunei Darussalam. *International Journal of Instructional Media, 28*(2), 147–153.

Kim, H. K. (2008). Beyond motivation: ESL/EFL teachers' perceptions of the role of computers. *CALICO Journal, 25*(2), 241–259.

Lai, C., & Kritsonis, W. A. (2006). The advantages and disadvantages of computer technology in second language acquisition. *National Journal for Publishing and Mentoring Doctoral Student Research, 3*(1). Retrieved from http://files.eric.ed.gov/fulltext/ED492159.pdf

Lee, L. (2002). Enhancing learners' communication skills through synchronous electronic interaction and task-based instruction. *Foreign Language Annals, 35*, 16–23.

Lee, L. (2005). Using web-based instruction to promote active learning: Learners' perspectives. *CALICO Journal, 23*(1), 139–156.

Leung, C., & Lewkowicz, J. (2006). Expanding horizons and unresolved conundrums: Language testing and assessment. *TESOL Quarterly, 40*, 211–234.

Lewis, J. (2016). *Seven benefits of video-based assessment.* Retrieved from file:///F:/Journal%20 articles%20and%20submissions/Springer%20edited%20book%20-%20chapters%20 etc/7%20Benefits%20of%20Video-Based%20Assessment%20_%20D2L%20Australia,%20 New%20Zealand%20&%20Asia.html

McNulty, A., & Lazarevic, B. (2012). Best practices in using video technology to promote second language acquisition. *Teaching English with Technology, 12*(3), 46–61.

Meskill, C., Mossop, J., DiAngelo, S., & Pasquale, R. (2002). Expert and novice teachers talking technology: Precepts, concepts, and misconcepts. *Language Learning and Technology, 6*(3), 46–57.

Müller, A., & Habel, C. (2012). Gaming to learn: Language in a clinical context. In C. Nygaard (Ed.), *Transforming university teaching into learning via simulations and games* (pp. 123–138). Oxfordshire: Libri Publishing Ltd.

Murday, K., Ushida, E., & Chenoweth, A. (2008). Learners' and teachers' perspectives on language online. *Computer Assisted Language Learning, 21*(2), 125–142.

Newhouse, C. P., & Cooper, N. G. (2013). Computer-based oral exams and Italian language studies. *ReCALL, 25*(3), 321–339.

Nikitina, L. (2011). Creating an authentic learning environment in the foreign language classroom. *International Journal of Instruction, 4*(1), 33–46.

Nor, N., Hamat, A., & Embi, M. (2012). Patterns of discourse in online interaction: Seeking evidence of the collaborative learning process. *Computer Assisted Language Learning, 25*(3), 237–256.

Norris, D. M., Mason, J., Robson, R., Lefrere, P., & Collier, G. (2003). A revolution in knowledge sharing. *Educause Review, 38*, 15–26.

Norton, J. (2013). Performing identities in speaking tests: Co-construction revisited. *Language Assessment Quarterly, 10*(3), 309–330.

Penuel, W. R. (2006). Implementation and effects of 1:1 computing initiatives: A research synthesis. *Journal of Research on Technology in Education, 38*(3), 329–348.

Potter, J. (2005). 'This brings back a lot of memories': A case study in the analysis of digital video production by young learners. *Education, Communication & Information, 5*(1), 5–23.

Presby, L. (2001). Seven tips for highly effective online courses. *Syllabus, 14*(11), 17.

Radinsky, J., Bouillion, L., Lento, E., & Gomez, L. (2001). Mutual benefit partnership: A curricular design for authenticity. *Journal of Curriculum Studies, 33*(4), 405–430.

Reeves, T., Herrington, J., & Oliver, R. (2002). Authentic activities and online learning. In A. Goody, J. Herrington, & M. Northcote (Eds.), *Quality conversations: Research and Development in higher education* (Vol. 25, pp. 562–567). Jamison: ACT: HERDSA.

Sato, E., Chen, J. C. C., & Jourdain, S. (2017). Integrating digital technology in an intensive, fully online college course for Japanese beginning learners: A standards-based, performance-driven approach. *The Modern Language Journal, 101*(4), 756–775.

Scheffler, F., & Logan, J. (1999). Computer technology in schools: What teachers should know and be able to do. *Journal of Research on Computing in Education, 31*, 305–325.

Shih, R. (2010). Blended learning using video-based blogs: Public speaking for English as a second language students. *Australian Journal of Educational Technology, 26*(6), 883–897.

Shrosbree, M. (2008). Digital video in the language classroom. *The JALT CALL Journal, 4*(1), 75–84.

Swanson, P., & Early, P. (2008a). Digital recordings and assessment: An alternative for measuring oral proficiency. In A. Moeller, J. Theiler, & S. Betta (Eds.), *CSCTFL report* (pp. 129–143). Eau Claire: Central States Conference on the Teaching of Foreign Languages.

Swanson, P., & Early, P. (2008b). Technology for oral assessment: Recapturing valuable classroom time. In C. M. Cherry & C. Wilkerson (Eds.), *Dimension: Proceedings of the southern conference on language teaching* (pp. 39–48). Valdosta: SCOLT Publications.

Weikart, L. A., & Marrapodi, M. (1999). The missing link: The technology infrastructure. *Computers in the Schools, 15*(2), 49–60.

Whitton, N. (2010). *Learning with digital games: A practical guide to engaging students in higher education*. New York: Taylor & Francis.

Wozney, L., Venkatesh, V., & Abrami, P. C. (2006). Implementing computer technologies: Teachers' perceptions and practices. *Journal of Technology and Teacher Education, 14*(1), 173–207.

Zapata, G., & Sagarra, N. (2007). Call on hold: The delayed benefits of an on-line workbook on L2 vocabulary. *Computer Assisted Language Learning, 20*(2), 153–171.

A Rich Mix: What Is English? Integrating Literature, Literacy, Language and Multimodal Dimensions of Meaning-Making in the UK Secondary School English Classroom

Alison Douthwaite

Abstract This chapter proposes a new tripartite model of critical voice development for secondary English literature education. It argues that English teachers need a revised, cohesive theory around criticality development that can both account for new practices with technology and mesh productively with existing disciplinary conventions. The chapter reports on attempts to meaningfully integrate iPad usage into the study of literary texts, exploring the experiences of two classes producing multimodal responses to literary texts. Drawing on Kress' scholarship on multimodality and reader-response theories, it argues that multimodal response can increase motivation, engagement and originality by acknowledging students' cultural agency and giving them access to a broader range of semiotic modes. It highlights ways in which task design encourages students to draw on traditional disciplinary skills. The chapter also explores how the engagement demanded by embodied approaches to learning can have an impact on students' sense of identity and belonging in both positive and difficult ways, underscoring the social and intersubjective dimensions of literacy development. By enabling closer attention to complexity of criticality development through literary study, the tripartite model may develop our understandings of under-recognised aspects of this process, offering teachers greater scope to imagine productive new ways of working with technology in English literature classrooms.

Keywords English literature · Criticality · Multimodality · Literacy education · Secondary education · Educational technology · Mobile technologies · Reader response

A. Douthwaite (✉)
Department of Education, University of Bath, Bath, UK
e-mail: A.Douthwaite@bath.ac.uk

© Springer Nature Switzerland AG 2019
T. Dobinson, K. Dunworth (eds.), *Literacy Unbound: Multiliterate, Multilingual, Multimodal*, Multilingual Education 30,
https://doi.org/10.1007/978-3-030-01255-7_9

1   A New Synthesis: Developing Students' Critical Voices

Using mobile technologies to enable students to produce multimodal rather than verbal texts presents a challenge. Though teachers may have some ideas about the potential value of the activity, they are going into uncharted territory. Assessment criteria, which increasingly direct classroom activities and teachers' evaluations of students' progress, are no longer obviously relevant. Even when productive activities using the technology can be envisaged, the burden of finding justification for them may prevent teachers from using them (Pandya 2012). When students produce texts containing images, emojis and photographs, for instance, the learning may be worthwhile but not easy to assess, making it harder for teachers to argue for it in an era driven by showing evidence of progress. With the monitoring of learning and progress often relying heavily on looking through students' exercise books, time spent producing digital responses may seem hard to justify to teachers who are concerned about being seen as doing their best by their students by complying with school policies. Teachers need a theory and language to help them make sense of and talk about these new practices with technology in ways that mesh with and usefully broaden existing educational discourses.

As a teacher, I felt confident and justified in judging and grading students' learning in essay form or through their verbal contributions. The lack of criteria for judging multimodal texts, however, left me unsure how to respond to or evaluate them. As students created them, I found I made certain interpretations about what they were trying to say or do, but that I needed to ask and discuss it with them to feel confident that I was making a fair assessment. It seemed that multimodal responses to literature needed to be part of a bigger conversation—they needed to be talked about and discussed for them to be part of an ongoing process of learning rather than simply being another product of learning. The multimodal texts the students made were not 'ideal for judging the value of the process' (Pandya 2012, p. 183).

Seeing these texts as students' voices in other modalities directed my efforts to know how to approach them. The notion that we are developing students' voices would no doubt feel quite familiar to most English teachers. Through essay writing and discussion, we traditionally try to encourage the adoption of new vocabulary, disciplinary terminology and rhetorical strategies. 'Voice' also captures an essence of the 'personal response' literature teachers encourage, the nurturing of individual expression and personal interpretation. Considering this, broadening the notion of voice to encompass other forms of representation and expression offers a useful way of considering the multimodal work students produce. Similarly, 'critical' is a word that teachers are likely to feel familiar with. Though there seems to be no agreed definition of the term (Moore 2013), it appears regularly on English assessment criteria to describe the reflective, analytical and interpretative nature of the responses sought from students. It is also an 'educational ideal' at university level though again with no clear agreement amongst academics of exactly what it entails (Moore 2013). The following section outlines the theoretical perspectives I draw on in trying to shape this new synthesis.

1.1   Critical Voice and Reader Response

Rosenblatt's reader-response theory (Rosenblatt 1995) has been a key theoretical influence on English teachers' notions of what it means to teach and read literature (Goodwyn 2012). Her transactive model of reading highlights the important role of the individual's subjective response in making meaning from a literary text in a 'reciprocal, mutually defining relationship'. The aim of engaging with literary texts is to experience and interpret. The text only comes to life, as it were, in the mind of the reader. Developing literary understanding then entails individuals developing a growing awareness of their personal responses and the factors that led them to have these: the associations, personal experiences and emotional reactions to features of the text. This implies that developing increasingly 'critical' responses involves building greater metacognitive awareness and self-awareness.

The literature teacher's role is to encourage students to voice their responses or reflections and articulate how these grew from the text. This way they can also see how others made different meanings. Criticality, it implies, is developed as individuals consider a broader range of perspectives: those of peers, other authors, the teacher and critics. It also grows as students develop greater understanding of themselves and of other people and the way they see texts and the world.

Another useful concept from reader-response theory is the idea of readers adopting stances to a text. Rosenblatt suggested that readers may adopt a different stance depending on whether they were looking to find answers or information in a text (efferent stance) or looking to experience and explore the text (aesthetic stance). Langer (2011) later developed this idea into a fuller model of literary reasoning. She identifies four notional 'stances' she has observed students adopt in relation to a text that help them build more complex responses in a process she argues is 'recursive rather than linear'. Criticality develops, she suggests, as students become increasingly able to adopt the full range of stances to develop richer 'envisionments'.

The stances suggest that the process of interpretation involves both immersive and distanced stances.

1. Being outside and stepping into an envisionment
2. Being in and moving through an envisionment
3. Stepping back and rethinking what one knows
4. Stepping out and objectifying the experience

While these stances focus only on the transaction between individual and text, Langer specifies that successful 'envisionment-building classrooms' 'encourage different points of view because multiple perspectives enhance interpretation' (Annenberg Foundation 2017). So the theory suggests a process through which students are learning about literary texts and ways of thinking, but are also becoming more themselves, more autonomous. They are finding their own voice, but this is done through engaging them with the voices of others.

This appears to theorise the interaction between student and text rather separately from the interactions between the students themselves and between the students and the teacher. While discussion and perspective sharing are framed as a pedagogical approach, reader-response theories appear to see the process of literary meaning-making as distinct and different from this. As Yandell (2013) highlights: 'agency in this model lies with individuals who remain oddly abstracted from the social' (p. 37). He argues for the acknowledgement of the reading of literature as 'an irreducibly social process' where the learning is situated 'in the social interaction between people, not merely in the mind of the learner' (p. 179).

This reframing of the process suggests a transactive process, not just between text and individual, but between the three factors: text, individual and others. Engaging with the voices of others then is not just a means to develop the individual's critical voice, but another strand of critical voice development.

1.2 Critical Voice and Classroom Talk

Certainly, research into classroom interaction suggests that certain forms of talk have greater impact on students' reasoning skills (Mercer and Littleton 2007). Engaging in 'exploratory talk' helps students develop improved criticality in terms of their ability to offer reasons, suggest alternatives, challenge and justify in a collaborative and constructive way. Explicit instruction in ground rules in how to talk productively, they suggest, can help students develop their criticality as they undertake group work.

Research into classroom talk suggests that this educationally useful style of interacting does not happen frequently in classrooms and requires explicit training if students are to engage in it. My question then is if this style of interaction, this way of participating, is a fundamental part of successful learning, should it not be considered part of the same educational aim, rather than as a separate training in order to be able to learn?

As an educational aim, developing critical voice could be broad enough to encompass styles of interaction with text and styles of interaction with other people. It is as much about the stances you are able to take with other people and their ideas as it is about the stances you are able to take with text.

If the point of studying literature is not just to develop students' literary interpretation but also their ability to deal with other perspectives and be reflective and explicit, then our aims are social. Students' ability to engage in these forms of social interactions may be as important to their progress as their literary interpretation. Recent research into students' use of multimodal responses to literature in an ESL classroom supports this idea. Early and Marshall (2008) concluded that although the multimodal aspects of the work appeared to 'support the growth of these ESL students' interpretation and appreciation of English literature', the students would have benefitted from 'language to help them wade through the negotiations' (p. 389). Viewing the English teachers' aim as developing students' critical voices perhaps enables a more holistic and coherent sense of what we are trying to achieve.

1.3   Critical Voice and Multimodality

With this in mind, how might we address the challenge that multimodality poses to the English curriculum? Kress (2003) argues that 'a linguistic theory cannot provide a full account of what literacy does or is' (p. 35). The increasing dominance of screen-based communication and the rise of the visual are seemingly problematic for a subject whose focus is on print-based literary texts, written literary analysis and face-to-face discussion.

However, Kress' theories complement reader response in key ways. His view of learning chimes with Rosenblatt's transactive model: Kress describes it as 'the shaping of the subjectivity of the maker of signs' (2003, p. 39). He describes the process of making meaning from reading as occurring 'at the moment when the "taken meaning" is integrated into the existing totality of all meaning in the brain' (ibid). This echoes Langer's (2011) notions of an envisionment: 'the world of understanding a particular person has at any given time', which is made up of 'images, questions, disagreements, anticipations, arguments, and hunches that fill the mind during every reading, writing, speaking or listening experience' (p. 9).

Kress's (2003) social semiotic perspective on meaning-making adds further detail to the socio-cultural model of learning with literature proposed by reader-response theories. He defines meaning as 'the result of [semiotic work] whether as *articulation* in the outwardly made sign, as in writing, or as *interpretation* in the inwardly made sign as in reading' [emphasis in the original] (p. 37). This offers an important clarification of the relationship between the two aspects of critical voice development, the personal and the social, or the internal and the expressive. The transactive process theorised by Langer and Rosenblatt is further developed by Kress' observation that the meanings individuals express are necessarily shaped by their perception of the social situation and what communication in that environment involves. It is not simply a transaction between reader and text, but also involves the transformation of semiotic resources. Individuals make their own meanings internally, but the expression of this involves transforming an existing form by combining it with this new meaning.

Firstly, this highlights that the inner meaning-making that occurs when we read literature is multimodal in nature. Kress highlights that meaning is 'spread across modes' and not just contained in the verbal. Though the process of reading printed text may seem rather monomodal, in that the 'message' is carried in print, Kress' notions of transduction or synaesthesia can help us see the role of other senses in this process. Kress suggests a synaesthetic element to sense making, where meaning from various modalities is combined to form a whole. The whole power of literature is for words to make us feel sensations, visualise places, experience emotions. To imagine or engage with literature involves 'investing static words and images with action and sound'. The inner world of imagination involved means that the 'two-dimensional texts can, in fact, be characterised as having the range of dimensions or modes recognised in media and multimedia texts' (Bearne and Styles 2003, p. xiv).

To develop the self-awareness and metacognition required when developing students' critical responses to literature, we have to engage them in recognising, acknowledging and unpicking these associations, looking inwards. It is important to pay attention to the sensations they felt, to the visualisations they had, as they are all important strands of becoming increasingly perceptive and reflective.

Secondly, Kress (2014) highlights the effort involved in externalising this inner meaning-making. The way the students' response to literature can be externalised or articulated depends on the semiotic resources available to them. It will always involve what Kress terms 'translation' and 'transduction' in that they may have to find words to express the image they imagined, for instance, or a gesture to convey the emotion they felt when they identified with a character. In this way, their response is 'critical' in that they are selecting 'apt' resources, from what they have available, to best communicate their meaning. This is what Kress terms 'design': the individual selection of signs and forms readers use to convey their message to one another.

So, an individuals' ability to articulate their meaning will depend on what they have to hand: a pencil, their voice alone, a screen to show things. It will also depend on their interpretation of what they feel the listener, or audience, expects. When the teacher asks a question, for instance, students' responses will be shaped by their awareness of expectations such as whether they can get out of their chair to enact their response, whether they can pick up a marker and draw on the whiteboard, or whether they are expected to form an answer in words. In this way, their participation in conveying a response, in whatever form, is, as Kress (2014) suggests, motivated and is arguably therefore 'critical'. It is critical in so far as any response has had to be shaped. It may not be consciously critical. That is to say, it may not necessarily have involved them in conscious or abstract reflection on these processes, but the selections are not arbitrary.

Indeed, while Langer (2011) outlines ways that discussion, group work and writing can be used to support the development of 'envisionments', she also identifies factors that mitigate against this. One pertinent limitation is that

> thoughtful responses cannot always be offered verbally, either in writing or speech. Therefore, we need to provide opportunity for alternative response options (e.g. drawing, dance, music and other forms) and sometimes accept the reality that lack of response does not necessarily indicate lack of understanding. (p. 41)

The difficulty of communicating these synaesthetic elements of sense-making means 'fruitful discussions can be inhibited by a lack of common language' (ibid). This is important to know in the classroom. English literature assessment criteria can give a sense of what a polished 'critical voice' might sound or look like at a particular level. A 'critical' response to literature in this framing is likely to be one in which students use Standard English, use the conventions of literary analysis, such as quotation, language analysis and depersonalisation to talk about the 'reader's response'. However, in the broader conception of critical voice development I have been exploring, the grasp of these conventions is but one aspect. This is in part because a multimodal text will draw on conventions from other types of text and on other grammars and genres.

In this chapter, I therefore propose a tripartite model of critical voice development that integrates three key areas:

1. Critical voice as evolving self-awareness (metacognition, agency)
2. Critical voice as participation and engagement with other voices (text, audience, addressee)
3. Critical voice as grasp of conventions and expectations (discipline, norms, genres, movements

This proposed model of critical voice development could be evaluated through indicators relating to these key areas, as illustrated in the table below (Table 1).

Table 1 Indicators of critical voice development through literature

Self	Others	Disciplinary conventions
Evolving self-awareness, metacognition, agency	Participation and engagement with voices of others	Grasp of conventions and expectations; disciplinary, literary, norms and genre knowledge
Relating to personal experience	Questioning, seeking clarification or explanation	Providing textual evidence
Expressing emotional reactions and opinion	Being sceptical	Using literary terminology
Commenting on impact on self	Bringing a new perspective to bear	Giving supported, reasoned judgements
Making analogies	Noticing inconsistences or incoherence	Making comparisons to other texts
Metaphorical thinking	Empathising, putting self in somebody else's shoes (peer, author, character, idealised reader)	Commenting on impact of language
Reflecting on own thought processes	Developing, building, refining an argument	Making connections: verbally, visually, parody, synthesis
Reflecting on or modifying own perspective	Hypothetical thinking	Evaluating: making meaning from across multiple sources, modes, viewpoints
Suspending judgement, being tentative, expressing uncertainty, provisional view of knowledge	Dealing with differing views, resolving conflicts	
Putting responses forward	Relating contributions to those of others	
Confidence and assertiveness	Influencing others	
	Encouraging others' contributions	

2   Background

The following sections draw on data gathered in two English classrooms in the same secondary school in the UK. The school is a state-maintained comprehensive in a rural area with approximately 1500 students. In 2013, it invested in a set of 20 iPads as part of a school improvement drive to try to reinvigorate teaching and learning. After initially offering parents opportunities to buy iPads through the school, paying in instalments, they more recently launched a bring your own device initiative.

The first piece of research took place in 2014. The iPad work here was planned around the scheduled scheme of work on *Romeo and Juliet*, which aimed to prepare students for General Certificate of Secondary Education (GCSE) questions on how an extract should be performed. Though 'effective written analysis' was the main focus, the unit sought to foster creativity and engagement with the play more broadly. The class teacher felt the students were 'visual learners' and wanted them to grapple with the language and meaning themselves. The class comprised 28 Year 10 students. This class was identified by the school as a 'C-D borderline class', which is a label given to groups of students deemed to be at risk of underachieving by failing to achieve a GCSE C grade. Although grades A* to G counted as 'passes', achieving a C grade was used as an indicator in league tables to judge school performance and often as a threshold grade for entry to certain courses and professions. Many of the students were also in 'literacy booster' classes as the school felt that their underachievement in terms of language might jeopardise their success in other GCSE exams the following year.

After working with their teacher to devise an initial activity, I then independently devised two further tasks during the unit. The first was led by the class teacher and involved pairs of students using the application 30hands to produce multimodal response to the prologue. These presentations contained keywords from the prologue, recordings of the students reading their selected lines from the script and an image to represent the meaning of the lines they had chosen. The second and third tasks were led by me due to teacher illness. The second required them to use voice, gesture and facial expression to alter meanings. They worked in groups to record themselves speaking one line in 3 different ways in order to alter the implied meaning. They then combined this with photographs of themselves in an appropriate pose for each tone. Finally, they filmed themselves performing a short extract of the play. In each instance, the intention was to follow the creation of these texts with a viewing and discussion in the classroom. It was this aspect that proved most problematic.

The second piece of research was with another Year 10 class in the same school. It spanned two terms during which the students studied three literary texts: *The Curious Incident of the Dog in the Night Time*, *The Merchant of Venice* and *A Christmas Carol*. With the aim of developing the students' critical voices, I worked alongside their class teacher to devise a range of learning activities involving students making multimodal responses to literature. Working in groups of three or four with one iPad, students collaborated to produce multimodal responses to a task.

These texts were projected, shared and discussed with the whole class. The examples below are taken from pilot data for this study, so the findings are the result of an initial analysis and indicate the directions the research is taking rather than the comprehensive final findings of the full study, which is not yet complete.

3   Critical Voice Strand 1: Developing Self–Awareness

This section draws on critical incidents (Francis 2006; Harrison and Lee 2011) during work on *Romeo and Juliet* that suggest that the multimodal texts students made enabled a window into their emerging representations of the texts to themselves: their 'envisionments' (Langer 2011). This seemed to be particularly helpful in relation to students who rarely spoke in class or those who struggled with reading but did not typically engage the teacher's attention for help with this, as it offered students an alternative way to 'voice' their responses, externalising them in such a way that they and others could discuss them. I also draw on examples that suggest that the embodied and visual aspects of the work appeared to play a role in students' developing self-awareness in terms of metacognition, identity and agency.

There was some evidence that the work prompted student reflection and greater efforts to articulate their thoughts. After task one, where students made multimodal representations of lines from the prologue, different groups projected their slides to the whiteboard for class discussion. One group produced two slides for their given line: 'and the continuation of their parent's rage, which but their children's end naught could remove.'

Slide 1 featured a Google image of a middle-aged man and a woman, shouting at each other angrily. The woman's hands are clamped over her ears, her mouth open wide as if shouting. The man's hand is extended, palm open in a gesture of frustration as if he is trying to make a point. Across the image, between the two figures, in large purple font they had added the words 'Parents Rage'.

Slide 2 contained a close-up photograph of two hands in the foreground, one on top of the other. In the background a blurred face can be seen, suggesting a figure lying in bed with their arm extended forwards. The hand covering that hand seems to belong to somebody standing higher than them, seemingly standing next to the bed.

When the second slide was projected, a student called out 'I don't get it.' The teacher challenged the group, asking 'why the picture?' One group member said it was because of the 'crossing hands'. Another added, 'there's a child there. It's dying and they can't help.' The third group member said 'it kind of works, kind of doesn't. If the child is ill, maybe it's all the grief.' Together, they really tried to articulate a critical response. They highlighted the features of the image that were significant to their interpretation: the crossed hand and the child in bed. The final comment shows a realisation that they have not fully made sense. The tone is quite tentative and reflective, showing that they are open to the idea of other interpretations. They add the emotion of 'grief', which is not mentioned in the line, demonstrating an understanding, on some level, that an angry conflict situation is stopped because of grief at something bad happening to their children.

This was a group of students who did not often contribute in class discussion unless put on the spot by the teacher. They had no experience of public display of their work and had never made this kind of multimodal response in their English lessons before. This exchange, to me, evidenced an engaged attempt to make meaning from a challenging text and to communicate and discuss that meaning. Not only did a class member have enough interest to ask for an explanation, but everyone in the group spoke up in a joint attempt to explain, each highlighting different aspects of the image to try to get their viewpoint across.

Their verbal explanations are not polished and coherent. The image they have chosen for their first slide suggests they may have interpreted the phrase 'parents' rage' to mean an argument between mother and father, rather than the inter-family feud between the Capulets and Montagues that the play deals with. For the class teacher, this led to a degree of uncertainty over the work's value. He felt it just showed us 'that these students can't do what we know they can't do'. He felt the lesson was 'fuzzy' and voiced concerns that we had gone about it 'backwards' and should have taught the students more about the text before getting them to make the multimodal responses.

My role as a researcher caused me to see this in a different light. I could relate to his concerns. As a colleague, I felt the same anxieties about how we could support these students to 'better' understand and about exam results. However, making these multimodal responses gave us a different window into the students' meaning-making. It showed the struggles they were having making sense of short chunks of Shakespeare's language, offering opportunities to intervene and help them. I interpreted his feeling that we should have given more input first as evidencing either a desire for their responses to have been more correct or an acknowledgement that they needed more guidance, as their interpretations were revealing flaws in interpretation. Rather than seeing this as positive evidence of students grappling with meaning for themselves, he appeared to feel that they had not been taught enough to produce a satisfactory product. It was simply more evidence of their underachievement.

After three separate sessions of multimodal text making, I discussed the work with the students to get their perspective on the value of the experience. A range of comments appear to support the idea that the multimodal work prompted greater reflection. Carly, for example, said that the 30hands work was good because 'it made you think about what you're actually doing.' When I asked Roxy if the work was challenging or easy, she replied, 'it made you think.' Referring to task three, the performance task, she said she felt this was because 'you're like speaking the words, so you like think about it a bit.' Carly built on this saying 'yeah, cos like when you're writing it down, you don't really take it in, well I don't really take it in... It makes you like think about what you're actually doing and then, like, how you're doing it.'

One student appeared to acknowledge that the creative work the students undertook positively influenced her critical response to the play, though of course she did not use these words. Discussing task two, which was not based upon the text but on students delivering lines to convey different attitudes, Julianne expressed that the enactments of the phrases helped her when it came to the Shakespeare analysis in the mock exam, 'because when we erm did Shakespeare um like there's some angry parts in it so like when we expressed the angry parts it came out similar.' Together their comments suggest that the acts of creating and recording themselves prompted reflection and metacognition, thinking 'how you're doing it'. This student seems to be acknowledging that physically doing things with their own bodies and voices helped them later in making personal sense of the text.

In addition to encouraging metacognitive work, students' comments suggested that it may foster expression in a way that encourages a sense of agency. For instance, during task two, students had to convey a line in three different ways by photographing themselves enacting it and recording themselves speaking it. The behaviour of one group of girls was markedly different to previous lessons I had observed. They were working with the line 'where are you going?' Normally quiet and drawing little attention to themselves in class, this group eagerly called me over at regular intervals, proud to show me what they had done. In the rush of the lesson, I was not too sure how to respond to the addition of their final slide (Fig. 1). The visual was accompanied by the line delivered in a Jamaican accent, asking 'where ya gwin maaan?' The visuals of the drugs and alcohol, the materialism of the slogan, the awkward racial stereotype and misogyny of the tiny roller-skating waitress all made me uncomfortable but the girls were keen to share, not trying to disturb the other students by showing it to them. They did not seem to feel any sense of its oddness. Reflecting later on why they had done this, I could see that, as the task required, they were communicating attitude through tone and visual means.

In later focus-group discussion, I asked them how they made it and what made them come up with the idea. Holly said, 'we just thought it would be something different.' Abigail added 'we wanted to do something and nobody else in the class would do it.' This desire to be unique, to have attention paid to their work, was not something I had experienced from them before. It seemed to be a form of agency enabled by the fact they could harness their slightly subversive energies and their

Fig. 1 Enacting and delivering lines, Slides 1–3

knowledge of popular culture in creative ways to both comply and push the boundaries—something there is little scope for in an essay where informal tone would be inappropriate and links to popular culture irrelevant. Describing their use of their own application, Snoopify, to make the slide, they said 'it was like between Holly and Abigail's idea. And like, I said I could try and do a voice of it and then I thought of the app that I had on my iPad.' The negotiated creativity they described reveals the extent of their collaboration to develop an idea and find resources to achieve their designs. The approach allowed for genuinely collaborative creativity and fostered originality in responses.

Importantly, the iPads allowed them to draw on other semiotic resources to make meaning. The girls' options, as white female students in school uniform, to visually represent the attitude they had in mind was quite limited. The iPad enabled them to quickly find and use other resources, in a form of bricolage (Lévi-Strauss 1962/1974) or assemblage (Jocson 2012) in order to get the job done. This resonates with the suggestion that 'assemblages can position young people as producers of knowledge to expand larger discourses of history, culture and politics' (Jocson 2012, p. 300). By allowing them to draw on resources and cultures from outside the classroom, the activity has perhaps empowered them in terms of feeling like they want to express something.

Enabling students to photograph, film and record themselves allowed them to take on other identities in concrete ways. This has the potential to foster the immersive elements that reader-response theories (Langer 2011; Rosenblatt 1995) suggest are important in literary understanding. It also has potential for enabling students to experiment with different identities as students and responders to text. If becoming more critical involves being able to adopt a broader range of stances in relation to texts, speaking from different positions may be beneficial.

Two students for whom the immersive activity of filmed performance appeared to be particularly valuable were Harvey and Will. Will rarely spoke in lessons and tended to answer most questions the teacher asked with 'I don't know.' Both Will and Harvey found written work challenging, struggling to form the coherent paragraphs of textual analysis expected of them. From class discussion and written work in their books, it was difficult to know what these students were making of the play.

In contrast, their performance of the confrontation between Tybalt and Romeo stood out because they used gestures and positioning, rather than remaining static and focusing on reading the script. Will, as Tybalt, delivers the line 'Turn thee Benvolio and look up thy death' with a (rather understated) opening of his jacket. It subtly echoes Baz Luhrmann's 1996 film adaptation, which the group had partially watched in an earlier lesson. This gesture, as he reveals his gun in its holster, makes sense of the line and menace. Will appears to have internalised this subtle move and, although the camera angle from the class video recording (Fig. 2) does not emphasize it as it does in the film, incorporates it into his interpretation. Harvey's representation of a pointed gun with his finger, their positioning opposite each other, separated by open space, and the ensuing gun battle in which they run around the room and shelter behind tables and chairs, suggests a strong mental image of the scene and how it should look.

Fig. 2 'Showing the gun thing': Envisioning *Romeo and Juliet*, Act 1, Scene 4

Visual elements of their experiences have influenced them strongly, echoing Bryer et al.'s (2014, p. 235) findings that tablet film-making offers 'a visual frame of reference...that seemed to be key to the students' engagement and learning.' Importantly, the visuals seemed to have helped them make sense of the language that they so often struggle with. Their line delivery was significantly more fluent than those of other groups, evidencing perhaps 'synaesthesia' (Kress 1996, p. 31) whereby they drew on various modes to construct the meaning for themselves as well as to create their own retelling.

Similarly, Ben and James' filmed performance of the conflict appears to draw on visuals of the film. They start with a comical conflict, slapping each other's hands as they stepped energetically but rather primly around the yard in what seemed to be a humorous imitation of a playground fight between two young boys. On first viewing, it seemed they had not produced a performance that merited much scrutiny but were just messing around, finding ways to make the task fun. After several viewings, I started to discern valuable aspects. My initial thoughts centred on gender: Did these boys feel that drama work was less valuable, or feminised? Or did they feel uncomfortable enacting 'high-culture' texts and seek to subvert their authority through parody? Arguably however, the foolishness of the scrapping citizens has its roots in Shakespeare's script. Benvolio's interjection, 'Part, fools! ... You know not what you do!' certainly positions the conflict as immature and unthinking. The Luhrmann film adaptation portrays the Montague servants as inept and fearful. The repetitive bashing of Sampson's head with a handbag, accompanied by the exaggerated sound of a woman screaming may well have influenced the performance as the violence has a comical and 'wimpish' edge. In performance terms, they were the only group who portrayed the conflict that Benvolio seeks to break up. Other groups portrayed only the speaking characters and did not make any visual sense of Benvolio's command to 'part!'

As I had not showed the students the film in recent lessons, and we had not done any work analysing the meaning of the lines together before asking the students to make their short films for that lesson, I was not entirely sure that the jacket gesture was deliberate or whether he was just adjusting his clothing. If it was a conscious and deliberate gesture it would evidence Will's understanding of the meaning of that line, of Tybalts' intentions and behaviour: something his other class work did not demonstrate. Playing it back to discuss with them later, I froze Will's subtle gesture on screen and said I'd found that moment interesting. His response was 'I was showing the gun thing.' He could not talk about why he did it or what he was intending, but Rob, another student who worked in a different group, immediately recognised the semiotic similarity with Luhrmann's film. Their multimodal text revealed they could make sense of the language with gesture and movement, but the discussion underscored their difficulty in talking about this analytically.

As I tried to discuss with them how they made their text and what they were aiming for, they mostly responded by nodding, shaking their heads or saying 'I dunno.' When asked about how they did the work, Harvey responded 'we just done it.' Their multimodal creative response certainly revealed an understanding and qualities that never emerged in written classwork (unsurprisingly, as this was always analytical). It also bypassed the difficulties these students experienced in expressing themselves in words, possibly enabling learning or at least engagement, despite these difficulties. Gesture, expressions and gaze can all convey information. Agreements can be reached without words. Of course, this does not help them in terms of developing their language skills in their own right, but it may give them experiences they are more interested in or more comfortable discussing. As they experience people recognising or misrecognising what they were intending and people discussing this, it may help them develop an awareness of their own thought processes and find ways, and language, to start to discuss them.

While Will and Harvey rarely engaged verbally in the business of the classroom, physically, they engaged readily and got to work without prompting. For other students that was not the case. Having to physically adopt postures and stances and photograph and film themselves had an impact on other students' learning experiences quite significantly and not always in positive ways. The first sign of this came during task one when Carly refused point blank to record her voice. All of the students were reluctant, but Carly was very vocal about it. Her discomfort centred on her accent and sounding 'like a proper farmer'. When we discussed this reluctance in the focus groups, I asked students how they would have felt had their enactments and performances been shared with the class. Abigail ventured 'we'd probably be embarrassed.' Holly added that it was because of 'hearing our own voices'. Roxy explained her feelings on hearing oneself played back: 'it's like, do I really sound like that? And you're like, oh no, I don't want to, cos in your head, you sound different to what you do on a recorder.'

The self-spectatorship (Bryer et al. 2014) involved in this cultural production with iPads resulted from the fact that they were not just showing or telling in their texts, but 'being' in them. Carly's fear of sounding 'like a proper farmer' could be interpreted as an awareness that she does not sound 'right'. She has perhaps internalised expectations around the use of Standard English and neutral accents in academic learning environments, something that does not match with who she is and how she sounds. The interviews saw them confronted with their identity in uncomfortable ways and many of them covered their eyes and showed some embarrassment to see themselves. If they are not keen on or used to being seen as an engaged student, then recording and watching themselves in this way could be very disconcerting.

Bourdieu's concept of *habitus* (1986, p. 170) suggests that ways of being in particular contexts are constructed in response to cultural influences long before schooling starts, but shape individual's responses and concepts of themselves and their relationships to contexts in complex ways. Feeling self-conscious is not unusual for teenagers, but it may be that putting themselves in the frame, opening themselves to scrutiny and visibly engaging with school work in the way this work demanded may conflict with a students' habitus in powerful but also uncomfortable ways.

While some students highlight positive aspects resulting from technology, such as enabling students to feel more like themselves as they work in their English literature class (Wissman et al. 2012), this study perhaps suggests some of the complexities involved when other aspects of their identity are brought into play. In Wissman et al.'s study, the students used the software Comic Life, creating a more impersonal text in that the students did not physically feature in it. Recording and watching themselves is fundamentally different and confronts students with representations of themselves that obviously unsettle them at times. In Bourdieu's (1986) work, a *field* is a 'system of social difference, differential deviations' which works to enable 'social differences to be expressed' (1986, p. 226). It is a social setting with its own rules, expectations and tastes: in this instance, the English literature classroom.

Bourdieu theorises that social agents (students) can experience a change in field (English classroom) when there is a disjunction between 'their habitus and the current conditions within the field' (Thomson 2008, p. 79). By experimenting with cultural production and the iPad, this study explored the potential to change the field so that students felt an improvement. Their discomfort suggests that they may be experiencing change; however, it is not a straightforward sense of liberation and enjoyment. At the very least, this underscores the fact that the process of developing a critical voice requires one to participate and expose oneself to critique and that this entails struggle and difficulty and is not a straightforward process.

The development of a critical voice is of course about more than self-expression, self-awareness and agency. It also requires students to adopt academic ways of communicating and grasping disciplinary conventions. The conventional way to assess students' critical voice development is through the essay, or possibly through class discussion. The recent focus on 'correct language' usage, however, risks masking the complexities of how students go about developing critical voices. Multimodal responses to literature using mobile technologies seem to have the potential to encourage the personal engagement, response and self-awareness necessary for critical voice development. Students will still need to be taught how to write essays, but this data suggests that teaching about the processes of interpretation and the conventions of articulation may need different approaches working alongside each other.

4 Critical Voice Strand 2: Participation and Engaging with Voices of Others: 'It Was Like Between Abigail and Holly's Idea'

The iPad work on *Romeo and Juliet* seemed to encourage participation in a way that the group's usual classroom tasks did not. Though the room was more chaotic, leaving me feeling uncertain about what the students were doing and whether they were doing anything worthwhile, each group returned having done what was asked of them. This felt different from other lessons I had observed, where students were generally reluctant to participate during whole-class discussion and practice paragraph writing. It may be that the iPads made different forms of participation possible. Students could do tasks based around the literary text that involved things other than writing or talking. They could be photographing, searching the web, downloading and combining items, or acting.

Students' comments suggest an appreciation of the active and creative aspects of the work. Rob suggested it was 'more enjoyable than sitting in class', echoing Roxy's comment that 'it's more fun than writing in a book.' They definitely equated English with writing and sitting still and saw the iPad work as a welcome contrast. Roxy alluded to this when she said, 'it's just like more fun so you actually want to do it, but then if someone's like "you have to go and write an essay", you're like, "oh, I don't want to do that", but then if someone's like "go and film this part of the play", then you actually wanna do that.'

The importance of doing and moving came up frequently in our conversations. Carly liked it because 'you're not just like sat around, you're actually getting up and actually doing something rather than just sitting down and like, not doing anything.' Rob felt similarly: 'it's more interactive and it's not as if you're just sat there writing in a book.' Not only do they strongly equate English with writing, but writing was seen as a solitary, still activity, qualified by both students with the word 'just', implying a sense that it is neither valuable nor significant to them, a sort of non-activity.

Rob's choice of the word 'interactive' is interesting. It is a word often associated with computer-based work, where the interaction is with the screen. However, I suspect he was rather referring to the social nature of the tasks. In each case the students worked in small groups on the iPads, something that contrasted with the largely individualised work normally undertaken in their English class.

There are interesting parallels with recent theorising that out-of-school students enjoy a 'participatory culture' that is growing up around new technologies (Jenkins et al. 2009). Here students expect to produce and make content themselves, work collaboratively to produce, create and share. Gee (2004) calls online environments where this kind of collaboration occurs *affinity spaces*: informal spaces where people gather to share their expertise around a common interest—a gaming advice site, for instance. For him, the fact that different people can contribute and participate in different ways makes these spaces motivating. There is not one expert but a network of individuals each with their own bits of expertise. Unlike formal education, which is static and conservative, these spaces are informal, driven by hobbies or interests that could be fleeting or changing. While formal education in a classroom cannot replicate these informal online spaces, the students' responses to the iPad work suggest that this appetite for participation may carry over into the classroom and there may be scope to harness it.

Jenkins et al. (2009) argue that 'the social production of meaning is more than individual interpretation multiplied'. For them 'it represents a qualitative difference in the ways we make sense of cultural experience' and 'represents a profound change in how we understand literacy' (p. 32). The social, active and interactive aspects of engaging with others' voices and the creativity this generates seemed to be something the students enjoyed in the classroom. Describing to me how they came up with the Jamaican slide (Fig. 1), Julianne said 'it was like between Abigail and Holly's idea.' This description implies it cannot be attributed to an individual and describes a negotiated creativity. Julianne added 'and like, I said I could try and do a voice of it and then I thought of the app that I had on my iPad.' These girls seem to be experiencing what can happen when students engage with other's voices and how new things can emerge that are surprising.

Data from the second research project also suggests that visual elements can play an important part in how students engage with other voices. Here, students were studying *The Curious Incident of the Dog in the Night Time*. The teacher was keen for them to focus on a character who they had not explored much: Christopher's mother, Judy. They were asked to select an image from a bank of images to represent Christopher's mother at a particular moment in the narrative.

The image this group chose was a photograph of a woman in a black suit and green shirt that had been edited so that she had 6 arms. In one arm she is holding a baby and in another arm she clutches a supermarket basket full of shopping. Another hand is holding two kitchen implements, a spatula and spoon while another hand holds a notepad to her side. The final two arms are extended above her head, palms pressed together. When explaining their choice to the class, one student commented during his group presentation that at first they thought she was 'irresponsible' but seeing the image 'makes me realise more, I wasn't thinking about it more.' Because the character walks out of the family home, leaving her husband to care for their autistic son, the class largely saw her as a villain, an irresponsible woman who let her family down. When they presented this image, they talked about the 'multitasking gestures' and discussed how it had made them rethink their judgement of her. They expressed some sympathy for how hard things must have been for her. The image here has been used as an interpretation of the character and its connotations have started new lines of thought for the students.

In later discussion, a student from a different group commented on the role the pictures and the visual whole-class presentations were playing in his thinking. He felt that the approach helped him to 'see how other people are thinking so that it can give you more ideas'. While the verb 'see' is often used to mean 'understand', here it may suggest that the visual mode has played a particularly important part in supporting his ability to engage with this other way of thinking. As teachers we often use images, moving or still, in order to try to get messages across effectively or evocatively to our students. For students, being able to use more modes in conveying their ideas may enrich their interactions with others' interpretations as well as giving them quick access to a range of different possible interpretations.

Both students' comments suggest that the visual mode may enhance empathetic engagement: on the one hand, empathetic identification with characters or situations, on the other, empathetic engagement with others' interpretations. Further evidence that suggests this emerged from filmed footage of students presenting their multimodal texts to the class, images from which are reproduced in Figs. 3 and 4 below.

In this particular task, students were aiming to represent the relationship between Antonio and Shylock in a particular scene of A Merchant of Venice. They had selected an image from a bank, added a quotation, a keyword and an emoji to represent the audience's reaction. This group was sharing a slide and ideas with the rest of the class (see Fig. 3) and hence engaged in translating ideas from the visual to the verbal: what Kress terms transduction. During the original activity, making the text, reasons did not have to be made explicit. Choices could be made and the presentation created without necessarily verbally articulating why it has been done that way. In the presentation however, students talk to the class to explain and discuss their presentation—why they selected particular images, emojis, quotations, colours, positions and so on. They had to publicly account for and explain their interpretations verbally with the support of the projection.

Fig. 3 Feeling the meaning: Student gestures while explaining the significance of Shylock's hat in their slide

Fig. 4 Feeling the meaning: Student gestures while explaining an interpretation of Shylock's gesture in their slide

Ben's use of gesture while talking (Fig. 4) suggests he is almost 'feeling the meaning' as he talks. He is discussing Shylock's gesture, the significance of this, what it reveals about his attitude to Antonio and how that relates to the quotation. Though the gesture is on the board for everyone to see, Ben re-enacts it, then uses his hands to show its subtle difference to other gestures. It seems as if his body is helping him to reflect on how they made this meaning from the image, as well as explaining to the class what they are trying to say. He seems to conflate his body with Shylock's body. He gestures to his own head when talking about the hat they have sketched onto the image of Shylock. He reaches out his own hand as if holding the walking stick that Shylock is holding in the image.

The choice of keyword they have chosen for this slide is interesting. They had been asked to select a keyword to summarise the relationship between the characters. Their choice was 'REALLY?!?!' The word itself here sums up Shylock's incredulity at Antonio's cheek at asking to borrow money despite being vocal in his hatred for him. The capital letters and excessive punctuation seem to draw on the conventions of text messaging where capitals suggest shouting or anger. The keyword comes in Shylock's voice rather than their voices. It is not so much their objective overview of the relationship as a moment of empathy with a character.

From the point of view of Langer's model, he seems to be re-entering his envisionment, feeling Shylock's emotions at this moment and exploring them. He does not seem to have fully 'stepped out' of this envisionment yet. There appears to be something valuably immersive about the creative process of making the multimodal texts. It seems to allow participation even where students are not really able to engage with the task in the way that the teacher had anticipated or hoped. The students can focus on making meaning from the text, engaging with the ideas, situations, emotions and relationships in the texts without necessarily being aware of how they did it. The presentation of those texts to the class may then offer a window into their meaning-making for the students themselves, their peers and the teacher. It can also give the teacher an opportunity to ask questions encouraging reflection and metacognitive development.

These presentations, or the ways that these student creations are dealt with in the classroom, seem to be central to their utility in helping students develop a critical voice. Visibly engaging with the business of the classroom, on screen in films and photographs of themselves, or physically sharing and pointing to aspects of their work at the front of the room, students start to take on the role of critical speaker in a concrete way. Gallas (2004) defines full literacy as being achieved

> when an individual lives in the body of a subject, identifying with it in a visceral way and translating that identification into action in the world. It requires both mastery of the subject itself, and a public presentation of self as expert. One must believe and know, and one must also convince others. (p. 124)

Engaging with others' voices and participating in classroom discussion of texts involves more than just adopting and using language. It involves social learning about how to get others to see things the way you do, how to manage disagreement and contradiction and how to physically adopt the expert position in a way which will not get you shot down in flames by your peers.

Gallas's (2004) notion of 'authoring' is useful here in theorising the importance of the presentations. Authoring, she argues is 'the process of metaphorically "writing" the world in a way that gives an interpretation of the world weight, voice, and agency, a way that has the ability to influence the thinking, feelings, and actions of others'. She distinguishes this from 'the pure exercise of imagination', which is 'introverted' because authoring is 'an event in which an individual creates a new text and intentionally attempts to influence an audience' (p. 136). Asking students to share and critique each other's multimodal texts exposes them to the sense of an audience of real people whose opinions matter to them a—feature of participatory cultures.

Widening the opportunities for representation means more students may be in with a chance of contributing to an 'influential text' and may therefore have a greater stake in participating. Not only students with confident presentation skills or well-developed literary analysis and vocabulary can impress. Students with technological knowledge who can come up with clever ways to edit or alter an image; those who have extensive knowledge of emojis, of an app or of popular culture can use this knowledge to contribute to a text that will influence an audience and have an impact on them.

5   Critical Voice Strand 3: Awareness of Disciplinary Conventions

Research into participatory cultures focuses on literacy practices in out-of-school spaces where there is a shared purpose. While we may be able to nurture features of these spaces and ways of operating in classrooms, they are fundamentally different in that the shared purpose is enforced, not chosen, and there is an authority figure in the teacher. While English literature teachers want to nurture personal response and original interpretations, they are also focused on helping students acquire a particular form of literacy. In order for their voice to be heard in that domain, students need to develop an awareness of expected manners of thinking and communicating.

In English, the conventions of essay writing and of Standard English are examples of this, and many English departments spend quite a significant amount of energy on trying to help students master the components of analytical writing in order to try to help them pass tests and hit assessment criteria. Teaching students to 'PEE', that is, to include a point, some evidence and some explanation of that evidence in every paragraph, has been one recent and widespread strategy. 'Star paragraphs', which contain each of five ingredients or points, are a more recent strategy adopted in the school at which the research was conducted. Through these means teachers try to scaffold students' progress by providing them with a tick list of components, which is supposed to help them to develop the complex range of skills they are expected to demonstrate. Likewise, recent changes to SAT examinations requiring students to show in-depth knowledge of SPaG (spelling, punctuation and grammar) is another focus on critical voices—this time focusing on the mastery of conventional grammar as a sign of a well-developed voice.

Fish's (1980) observation that 'meanings are the property neither of fixed and stable texts nor of free and independent readers but of interpretive communities' (p. 322) is very relevant here. He highlights the fact that in literary interpretation meanings are both objective and subjective: 'subjective because they inhere in a particular point of view and therefore are not universal; and they are objective because the point of view that delivers them is public and conventional rather than individual and unique' (p. 335). The awareness of conventions then is perhaps the most obvious aspect of the development of students' critical voices. It drives teachers' efforts as much as their desire to encourage personal response.

However, the challenge multimodality poses to this aspect of critical voice development is possibly the most keenly felt. Kress (2014) suggests that 'critique' is no longer an appropriate aim educationally. He suggests that critique is appropriate when there are fixed and stable genres. Technological and social change have led to a change of perspective from 'just following tradition' and following conventions to seeing all (semiotic) work as evidence of *design*. 'This perspective "foregrounds" a move away from anchoring communication in convention as social regulation' and 'focuses on an individual's realization of their interest in the world' (p. 4). In terms of student work in an English literature classroom, it chimes well with a shift towards giving greater attention to personal response and freeing up students to respond in a broader range of ways. However, for the English classroom to work as an interpretive community, the teacher must draw on convention to decide what to teach. In the work we did with the iPads, conventions served as guiding principles, ways of thinking and interaction that motivated and informed the planning of the activities and the evaluation of them.

Fish (1980) states that it 'is right to insist that notions of correctness and acceptability are institution specific' and that 'knowledge of these 'shared points of departure' is a prerequisite of what he calls 'literary competence'. But, it is 'wrong to imply that literary competence is an unchanging set of rules or operations to which critics must submit in order to be recognised as players in the game' (p. 366). So though the multimodal texts students made look nothing like the typical print-based texts usually produced as part of doing English, there is still something recognizable or conventional about them.

The classwork we have done with the iPads suggests that careful attention to task design may mean this sort of multimodal production can be used to support students in developing their awareness of these disciplinary conventions. While much more research will be needed to develop our awareness as teachers of the affordances of different modes, the data I have collected to date suggests at least that students draw on some of these discipline-specific ways of thinking and interacting when they make their multimodal texts. There seems to be evidence of students drawing on their emergent understandings of what it means to 'do' English literature in modalities other than those they might normally use. There is also evidence of them drawing from other textual experiences in order to produce the digital texts required.

Below I explore two 'disciplinary' conventions, discussing how task design may have encouraged students to focus on this before discussing apparent evidence of this skill in different modalities in the students' texts.

5.1   Evidencing

Justifying your interpretation, pinpointing which features of the text provoked it and explaining why form a central part of the textual analysis work required of students in secondary-level English literature lessons. The development of this close attention to textual detail needs to be constantly balanced against the ongoing negotiation of shared and evolving interpretations, over several weeks as the class read long, complex literary texts. Pausing on this journey to probe students' personal interpretations and give them time to explore their 'envisionments' is a strategy teachers employ at critical moments in the text, moments where experience tells them students may miss something, or where they feel a key theme or character development is underway. In this way, unless the task is very open-ended, the students' interpretations are carefully framed by a question or by the selection of a passage. This is a fairly typical approach in English literature classrooms and informed the task design as we worked with the iPads.

By showing them where to look and what to think about, students are encouraged to practise close text work rather than whole text work. When asking students to make multimodal texts, we upheld this convention of requiring students to give textual evidence in the form of a quotation. Students were given a short extract from Act 1, Scene 3, and asked to create three slides exploring how Shakespeare presents the relationship between Antonio and Shylock. The task stipulated that each slide must contain a quotation, a keyword, an emoji and an image selected from an image bank.

In making these texts students were practicing the selection of apt evidence from a passage to make different points and support their interpretation. Discussing how the language led them to select an image and what it is about the image that seems to reflect the relationship as implied by the words requires students to both refer to detail of the word and of the image. Practising this skill in two modalities may have the potential to reinforce this skill that is so important in English.

While students were used to the convention of selecting quotations to support their interpretations, there is evidence that they also sometimes applied this awareness in the multimodal texts by drawing attention to details in the images, albeit in different ways. In one slide students had selected a performance still depicting two figures (Shylock and Antonio) standing face to face against a dark background. Shylock, wearing his red hat, stares into the eyes of Antonio, his hands clasped together behind his back. Antonio, chin jutting forward stares back, one arm drawn back behind him. Between the eyes of the two figures, in red font, the students had added the word 'Pariah'. In the space between the chests of the two figures they had added a devil emoji. They had then included a quotation from the play across the centre of the screen: '"You call me misbeliever, cut throat, dog and spit upon my Jewish gabardine", pg25 line 103/104.'

The positioning of the text draws attention to the parts of the image that were meaningful to them. Presenting this to the class, the group said that the slide shows 'what Antonio's view of Shylock is' and that 'in Antonio's eyes, the Jews are like the devil in a way.' The positioning of the word 'Pariah' between the eyes of the characters serves to highlight the confrontational staring and hostility. It works effectively to communicate to the audience the quite complicated idea of how they see each other.

Another group produced two slides and drew visual attention to parts of an image that relate to their interpretation. In slide one, a red circle was added to draw attention to the character's face. They also added the text 'DISGUST!?' in red with a red arrow pointing from the word to the circle. This functioned to clarify the relationship between the image and the key word 'disgust'. It was clear that the group had chosen the picture because of the figure's facial expression, which they interpreted as conveying disgust, an emotion they connected with Antonio's disgust for Shylock. They also included a quotation from the play, again in red: 'to spit on thee again, to spurn thee too'. The connection between this quote and the picture is implied by the use of red font to match the red circle and line drawing attention to the facial expression. In discussion they also verbally pinpointed the word 'spit' as suggesting this attitude. The task design did not specify that they should add other elements such as labels or show how the image prompted their interpretation, but their selection of these conventions of visual diagrams and explanations suggest they have understood this to be an important aspect of the task and found, from their experience of other visual texts, a way in which to indicate this.

Their second slide features a performance still of Shylock on stage. He stands with his side toward the camera, facing the camera but with his body and shoulders turned to the side as if in the process of looking back and walking away. To the left of him, the group added an emoji (Fig. 5) and to the right of him was the text

Fig. 5 'Unamused' or
'side-eye' emoji

'would—keyword' in purple type. Across the bottom of the slide they had included a quotation from the play: 'I would be friends with you and have your love.'

This represents another aspect of evidencing: the ability to pinpoint the most significant word within a longer quotation. In all other multimodal slides from the group, the key words were a summary word, representing the students' interpretation, rather than an important word from a quotation. Here, though, the group selected 'would', seizing on the modal verb form, showing their understanding of Shylock's mistrust of Antonio and the way this word gives a sense of possibility but lack of definite commitment. The fact that they used a dash and then wrote 'keyword' suggests they realised that this is a slightly unusual interpretation of keyword. They did not label their keyword in this way in slide one. This shows a creative application of another function of evidencing that the students demonstrated in their multimodal work.

5.2 Connotative Thinking

Another important convention in English literature is connotative thinking. Interpreting metaphor and figurative language relies on this ability. Again, the data gathered highlight ways in which the task design can encourage students to think in this way as well as showing evidence of students drawing on this way of thinking when they create their own meanings.

Students' discussion as they selected images to represent Judy (a character in *The Curious Incident of the Dog in the Night Time*) included this exchange.

Christopher	I say that one
Paul	Sorry I can't hear you [joking]
Christopher	Hah! Ha ha!
Paul	It's like a fish out of water
Clare	Wateeer!
Paul	Yeah
Christopher	Ok, Paul put...she might feel as if
Paul	She might feel as if she made the wrong choice and should have stayed with Christopher and Ed
Clare	Yeah, I think that's kind of like mine
Paul	Probably sad and lonely, her emotions are depressed, well that's quite dark...because she might be thinking why she left and consequences...as in that's confused

Christopher	I think that's the best one
Clare	Ha ha ha
Paul	Well that's like that's a bunch of question marks
Christopher	Yeah
Paul	That's a heart being torn apart
Christopher	I like that one cos she's kind of split the family up and broke it
Paul	Yep, are we all ok with that one?
Clare	Yeah
Christopher	Yep ha
Paul	Download

Later when they are discussing what they could write, the following exchange took place

Paul	Right, so what do we want to say?
Clare	Judy is lonely
Christopher	This represents Judy splitting up her family
Paul	Ooh…this represents…
Christopher	Yeah
Paul	How Judy has torn her family apart
Christopher	Yeah…yeah…I can also say big words and smart words
Paul	No wait we're not done, this represents how Judy has torn her family apart…and
Clare	Er this…er…something about consequences
Paul	And has broken Christopher's…fragile heart
Christopher	Fragile heart ha ha
Clare	Yeah, put that [laughing]
Christopher	Paul the poet [singing]

The images encourage the students to engage in connotative thinking and think creatively about how they could represent the character. In this exchange, this enables consideration of multiple perspectives on a character. Again, the task design is important here in that the teacher and I pre-selected these images to offer a range of ways of looking at the character. Simply getting students to find an image themselves to represent a character may well have an entirely different outcome, as students may not naturally think in this way and may choose to represent somebody who looks like her or not work so conceptually.

The students' dialogue as they engaged in the connotative thinking here seems to offer interesting insights into the social aspect of acquiring discipline-specific ways of thinking, or a critical voice. The students construct a sentence for their slide together, developing each other's language in line with what they think would be appropriate. When Megan suggests 'Judy is lonely', Connor makes an alternative suggestion with 'this represents Judy splitting up her family.' That this way of talking is somewhat out of the ordinary is suggested by Paul's teasing 'ooh…this represents.' The students seem to be trying out in a less public forum the adoption of more formal ways of talking. Christopher's comment 'I can also say big words and smart words' again seems to acknowledge a slight discomfort involved in adopting these new ways of talking, but the humour also seems to egg them on to try to craft an impressive sentence with which they are happy. Teasing 'Paul the poet' seems to be a playful way of dealing socially with the fact that they are all having to speak not quite like themselves and ease them into the public adoption of these new voices in the later presentation.

In other tasks, students seem to have used this connotative thinking in taking their own images and making their own slides. In a task representing the relationship between Scrooge and Marley's ghost in *A Christmas Carol*, several groups used positioning of the characters to convey something of the power relationship. Five out of eight groups used the connotation of height in order to try to communicate Marley's dominance over Scrooge, or Scrooge's fear of Marley. In Fig. 6 this is achieved by one student standing and the other crouching; in Fig. 7 it is achieved through the position of two photographs, one higher than the other; and in Fig. 8 both posture and camera angle together achieve a sense of Scrooge's vulnerability. They draw on their embodied understandings and perhaps understandings from film and image to create their representation using connotative thinking to try to have an impact on the viewer.

Fig. 6 Envisioning Marley and Scrooge: Students stand at different heights to convey power imbalance and emojis to convey emotion

Fig. 7 Envisioning Marley and Scrooge: Image position on page, framing of shots and expressions used to create power imbalance and sense of relationship

Fig. 8 Envisioning Marley and Scrooge: Students construct and frame shot, using height, gesture and posture to create a sense of power imbalance and emotions

6 Conclusion

The students in these two classes were developing as they responded to and created texts: a core aspect of English as a school subject. Looking at their work through these three key strands, evolving self-awareness, participation with the voice of others and grasp of disciplinary conventions, enables closer attention to the richness of this development and thus to important aspects of this development that may often be under-recognised in classrooms. By offering a broader sense of the developments students can make through the study of English, it potentially offers teachers and students greater scope to imagine productive, new ways of working in the English classroom. Most importantly, though, these examples underscore the need for us to look at notions of criticality in rather more critical ways than we do currently.

References

Annenberg Foundation. (2017). *Introduction the Envisionment-Building Classroom*, Making Meaning in Literature Grades 6–8. Accessed on 25 July 2017 at https://www.learner.org/libraries/makingmeaning/makingmeaning/introducing/

Bearne, E., & Styles, M. (2003). Ways of knowing: Ways of showing – towards an integrated theory of text. In E. Bearne & M. Styles (Eds.), *Art, narrative and childhood* (pp. ix–xxvi). Stoke-on-Trent: Trentham Books.

Beavis, C. (2013). Literary English and the challenge of multimodality. *Changing English, 20*(3), 241–252. https://doi.org/10.1080/1358684X.2013.816527.

Bourdieu, P. (1986). *Distinction: A social critique of the judgement of taste*. London: Routledge.

Bryer, T., Lindsay, M., & Wilson, R. (2014). A take on a gothic poem: Tablet film-making and literary texts. *Changing English, 21*(3), 235–251.

Crook, C. (2005). Addressing research at the intersection of academic literacies and new technology. *International Journal of Educational Research, 43*(7–8), 509–518. https://doi.org/10.1016/j.ijer.2006.07.006.

Early, M., & Marshall, S. (2008). Adolescent ESL students' interpretation and appreciation of literary texts: A case study of multimodality. *The Canadian Modern Language Review, 64*(3), 377–397.

Fish, S. (1980). *Is there a text in this class? The authority of interpretive communities*. Cambridge/London: Harvard University Press.

Francis, D. (2006). Critical incident analysis: A strategy for developing reflective practice. *Teachers and Teaching: Theory and Practice, 3*(2), 169–188.

Gallas, K. (2004). "Look, Karen, I'm running like Jello":Imagination as a question, a topic, a tool for literacy research and learning. In C. Ballenger (Ed.), *Regarding children's words* (pp. 119–147). New York/London: Teachers College Press.

Gee, J. P. (2004). Situated language and learning. *Ebl., 40*, 58–59. https://doi.org/10.1111/j.1467-9345.2006.02802_1.x.

Goodwyn, A. (2012). The status of literature: English teaching and the condition of literature teaching in schools. *English in Education, 46*(3), 212–227. https://doi.org/10.1111/j.1754-8845.2012.01121.x.

Harrison, J. K., & Lee, R. (2011). Exploring the use of critical incident analysis and the professional learning conversation in an initial teacher education programme. *Journal of Education for Teaching: International Research and Pedagogy, 37*(2), 199–217.

Jenkins, H., Ravi, P., Margaret, W., Katie, C., & Alice, R. (2009). *Confronting the challenges of participatory culture: Media education for the 21st century* (Vol. 21, pp. 2–3). Cambridge/Lonndon. https://doi.org/10.1108/eb046280.

Jocson, K. M. (2012). Youth media as narrative assemblage: Examining new literacies at an urban high school. *Pedagogies: An International Journal, 7*(4), 298–316. https://doi.org/10.1080/15 54480X.2012.715735.

Kress, G. (1996). Reimagining English: Curriculum, identity and productive futures. In B. Doecke, M. Howie, & W. Sawyer (Eds.), *Only connect:English teaching, schooling and community* (pp. 27–30). Adelaide: Wakefiled Press/AATE.

Kress, G. (2003). *Literacy in the New Media Age*. London/New York: Routledge.

Kress, G. (2014). Design: The rhetorical work of shaping the semiotic world. In *Multimodal approaches to research and pedagogy: Recognition, resources, and access* (pp. 1–20). https://doi.org/10.4324/9781315879475.

Langer, J. (2011). *Envisioning literature: Literary understanding and literature instruction* (2nd ed.). New York/London: Teachers College Press.

Luhrmann, B. (Director) (1996). *William Shakespeare's Romeo + Juliet* [Motion Picture on DVD.] Twentieth Century Fox.

McGuinn, N. (2005). A place for the personal voice? Gunther Kress and the English curriculum. *Changing English: Studies in Culture & Education, 12*(2), 205–217. https://doi.org/10.1080/13586840500164243.

Mercer, N., & Littleton, K. (2007). *Dialogue and the development of children's thinking: A sociocultural approach*. Oxford: Routledge.

Moore, T. J. (2013). Critical thinking: Seven definitions in search of a concept. *Studies in Higher Education, 38*(4), 1–17. https://doi.org/10.1080/03075079.2011.586995.

OFSTED. (2009). *English at the crossroads, (June)* (Vol. 51, pp. 4–19). https://doi.org/10.2307/810222.

Pandya, J. Z. (2012). Unpacking Pandora ' s box. *Journal of Adolescent & Adult Literacy, 56*(3), 181–185.

Rosenblatt, L. M. (1995). *Literature as exploration* (5th ed.). New York: MLA.

Thomson, P. (2008). Field. In M. Grenfell (Ed.), *Pierre Bourdieu: Key concepts*. Stocksfield: Acumen.

Wissman, K., Costello, S., & Hamilton, D. (2012). "You're like yourself": Multimodal literacies in a reading support class. *Changing English, 19*(3), 325–338. https://doi.org/10.1080/13586 84X.2012.704583.

Yandell, J. (2013). *The social construction of meaning: Reading literature in urban English classrooms*. London: Routledge.

Using Facebook as a Conduit to Communicate: Translanguaging Online

Rhonda Oliver and Helen CD McCarthy

Abstract This chapter describes the translanguaging practices of young Aboriginal adults when they use the social media site Facebook. It is apparent that their language use in this medium reflects the complex and diverse nature of their language backgrounds. Specifically, they use their range of linguistic resources, including traditional language words and Aboriginal English forms along with Standard Australian English, according to context and topic to successfully communicate with their audience about a variety of content and for a variety of purposes. In doing so they are also able to construct individual, multilingual, personal and cultural identities through deliberate linguistic choices, moving fluidly between the different forms within their language repertoires, demonstrating their ability to use and to benefit from their translanguaging practices.

Keywords Translanguaging · Facebook · Indigenous · Aboriginal English · SAE · Identity creation

1 Introduction

Australia's Indigenous population has been described as one of the world's most ancient continuous civilisations spanning 75,000 years. Australia's first peoples adapted themselves to a diverse range of geographical environments and socio-cultural conditions and as such are not a homogenous group. In this chapter we use the terms Indigenous and Aboriginal reluctantly, acknowledging the colonial legacy in the naming conventions and recognising Australia's first people's ambivalence towards the proper nouns Indigenous and Aboriginal. Instead, our preference is to use the term of the local 'Aboriginal' research participant's geographic homelands. For example, we refer to two of our participants as Noongar, the people who live in the territory which extends from 'the Geraldton district south along the coast to

R. Oliver (✉) · H. CD. McCarthy
School of Education, Curtin University, Perth, WA, Australia
e-mail: Rhonda.Oliver@curtin.edu.au; H.McCarthy@curtin.edu.au

© Springer Nature Switzerland AG 2019
T. Dobinson, K. Dunworth (eds.), *Literacy Unbound: Multiliterate, Multilingual, Multimodal*, Multilingual Education 30,
https://doi.org/10.1007/978-3-030-01255-7_10

Cape Leeuwin, continuing southeast almost to Esperance and then in line northwest to re-join the coast at Geraldton' (Green 1984, p. 1) on the west coast of Australia. In this case, both participants live and work in the southwest of Western Australia. Two other participants are described as Ngudju (for a Noongar/Ngudju man) coming from an area just below the central part of Western Australia and Yawuru (for a Yawuru/Nyul Nyul man) coming from the northwest region of Western Australia. However, one of the female participants, also from the northwest region, does not self-identify with a particular language group as 'only the old people speak language' and so we have used 'Aboriginal' to refer to her.

Aboriginal Australians have strong family and cultural connections sustained by their relationship of reciprocity to country, connected and beholden by intersecting spiritual links or song lines across the nation. These connections are passed on orally. Not surprisingly, therefore, they have a rich background based on oral language traditions, including using various styles of humour such as irony, parody and satire to embellish their conversation. They speak a wide range of languages including traditional languages, creoles, Aboriginal English (AE) and Standard Australian English (SAE). These are described briefly below.

1.1   Traditional Languages

At the time of white settlement in Australia in 1788, there were approximately 250 traditional languages and 600 distinct dialects spoken by Australia's original inhabitants (Eades 1988). As shown by their reference to themselves by their geographic language group (as illustrated above in our description of the participants), language represents a crucial cultural marker to identity. Sign language and gesturing are also significant aspects of traditional communication.

Whilst some traditional languages remain strong as a result of neo-assimilationist policies beginning at the time of colonialization where the intention was to absorb Aboriginal people into white society, many have been extinguished, with only approximately 120 traditional languages now being spoken (AIATSIS 2018).

1.2   Pidgin Languages

Beginning with the first contact between traditional language speakers and speakers of other languages, pidgins developed as a new variety of language. They were created as a lingua franca to enable communication between speakers from all the different language backgrounds, and were used particularly for functional purposes. For instance, contact with traders such as the Macassans from Sulawesi (formally Celebes) in Indonesia and other mariners necessitated the inclusion of various Indonesian words and the development of a Makassar pidgin. With European settlement came the development of various other Pidgins including Port Jackson Pidgin

English. Over time the different pidgins were used within families and were passed from one generation to the next, evolving into Australian creole languages.

1.3 Creole Languages

As described, creole languages evolved from pidgin languages, but became languages in their own right once they became the first or home language of a number of speakers. One example used in the Torres Strait in the north of Australia is a creole called Yumplatok. Another example of a creole is Kriol, which is spoken as a first language in the north of Australia, from Western Australia into the Northern Territory and into parts of Queensland. Whilst many of the words are English or have an English base, the structure, grammar, spelling and sounds are unique as they have emerged from or at least been influenced by traditional languages. Kriol is one of the languages spoken by the families of some of the participants in this study.

1.4 Aboriginal English

Aboriginal English (AE) is the name given to a dialect of English spoken widely by Australian Aboriginal people. Like all dialects, AE is complex and rule-governed, differing from other dialects of English, such as Standard Australian English (see below), in systematic ways that include the way it is structured grammatically, phonologically, lexically and pragmatically. These differences also reflect the variation in the underlying conceptual systems associated with each dialect (Eagleson et al. 1982). AE is the first or home language of many Aboriginal children throughout Australia. As such, AE is a powerful vehicle for the expression of Aboriginal identity. It is spoken by all our participants, although only those identifying as Noongar or Noongar/Ngudju had it as their primary home dialect.

1.5 Standard Australian English

Standard Australian English (SAE) is perhaps the most common dialect used in Australia and it is the closest oral form of Australian English to writing (which is why it is called the 'standard' not because, as some may think, it is the 'correct' form). SAE is required and used in public discourse within Australian institutions including for governmental, legal and educational discourse. It is the linguistic code used by schools not only to teach students, but through which most assessment is conducted—particularly high-stakes national testing (e.g., the *National Assessment Program – Literacy and Numeracy* [NAPLAN]). Fulfilling important roles such as these means that it is Australia's most prestigious variety; however, it is no more complex than other forms of English spoken in Australia, including AE (Eagleson et al. 1982).

2   The Status of Aboriginal Home Languages

Despite their cultural and linguistic richness and diversity, Aboriginal traditional languages, creoles and AE suffer from low status. This reflects the ongoing subjugation Australian Aboriginal people have suffered since colonisation (Oliver et al. 2016). This is further demonstrated by such things as a general lack of support for the teaching of traditional languages and assimilationist policies, including the most recently enacted English only policy in the Northern Territory (McKay 2011). This policy directs teachers to follow the 'first four hour' rule in which Aboriginal children learn only in English for that time. Furthermore, the policy recommends this should be enacted as part of a larger program, such as direct instruction (DI). DI is a program designed in the late 1960s by American and Canadian behavioural psychologists for special needs children. It is currently being used in a large number of schools, particularly in the northern parts of Australia as part of the literacy program. Keeping strictly to the DI script the teacher executes what is required in a dyadic manner, placing the student and teacher relationship in what some would call a hierarchical power differential. This teaching and learning approach is contrary to many Indigenous epistemological traditions (Nicholls 2005). The English only policy came 10 years after the Northern Territory Minister for Education directed the Northern Territory Department of Education to close down all bilingual programs. This resulted in bilingual education being abolished in the Northern Territory, despite the lack of hard evidence to prove that bilingual education was failing students. As Nicholls (2005) observed, 'the government's lack of endorsement of Indigenous languages programmes ultimately discredits the status of Indigenous languages by undermining their legitimacy in Australian classrooms, and by extension, in other social settings as well' (p. 161). Such monolingual teaching runs counter to local communities' desire for bi-literacy approaches, or in some cases, having the curriculum taught through the vernacular (Nicholls 2005). The impact of this abolition of bilingual education cannot be underestimated (Amagula and McCarthy 2015), not only from an educational perspective, but also from a human rights perspective. To deny someone's language is to nullify their right to learn from within their own lived experience and cultural schematic framework.

The policy measures of the Northern Territory also run counter to the empirical evidence showing the importance of maintaining and supporting the home languages of students. For instance, McKay (2011) indicates that language maintenance is vital for Aboriginal people's well-being as it supports their self-identity and sense of belonging. Further, as the authors of the Western Australian Aboriginal Child Health Survey suggested, there is a clear association between traditional Aboriginal languages and culture, and where a language is lost, so too is the culture (Zubrick et al. 2005). The authors also produce evidence that Indigenous people who maintain their language are less likely to abuse alcohol and to resort to violence.

2.1 Aboriginal Home Languages and Education

Educators have long been aware that language, culture and identity are central to learning. Yet Ah Chee et al. (1997) suggested that there continues to be deep-seated racism in the Australian education system and that it has been one of the most destructive weapons employed against Aboriginal people: 'Australia's non-Aboriginal education systems have been deeply implicated in the systematic efforts over more than two hundred years to take from us our languages, our cultures, and our children, and therefore our essential identities as Indigenous peoples' (Ah Chee et al. 1997).

As Partington et al. (2000) indicated, Australian educational programs are designed in such a way that students must adjust to fit them. A better way forward would be for the programs to be developed based on the backgrounds and specific needs of the students. Furthermore, amongst educators there is insufficient awareness and acknowledgment of the unique linguistic background that Aboriginal students bring to schools (Oliver et al. 2012). McKay (2011), in fact, describes a general ignorance about Aboriginal people's cultural and language backgrounds and the historical and ongoing push in education for the Aboriginal population to become English speakers. Together these factors have had ongoing and negative consequences for Aboriginal students' learning, and this has contributed to the continued and significant disparity between the educational achievements of Aboriginal and other students (Nguyen et al. 2015). For example, on high-stakes national testing, Aboriginal students consistently perform below the required benchmark and below many others, including recently arrived children of migrants, and this is of considerable concern for those writing and implementing educational policy (Wigglesworth et al. 2011).

2.2 Both-Ways Learning for Success

Many argue that to improve education outcomes for Aboriginal students there needs to be more relevant schooling for them. Concomitant with this is the need to understand Aboriginal cultural understandings, linguistic abilities and aspirations. Since the 1980s there has been a growing desire amongst Aboriginal and non-Aboriginal educators for a two-way—or as many Aboriginal people called it, 'both-ways'—learning model. This is where the, 'students' learning experiences count as much as the teachers' knowledge. This "two-way" learning is also reflected in sharing authority in which learners assist in formulating the curriculum' (Burns 1995, p. 233). It has been suggested that incorporating negotiated course content into both

SAE and the vernacular enables students to operate as effectively as they possibly can in both worlds.

To address this, and commencing in the 1990s, the Department of Education, Western Australia, has been running a program of two-way literacy for Aboriginal English speakers to support research and teaching related to speakers of Aboriginal English. This program helps teachers understand the conceptualisations that Aboriginal students bring to school and the way they make sense of literacy materials written in SAE. The aim of this bi-dialectal program is to help students to move comfortably and successfully between their two (or more) dialects to maximise communication and engagement in both Aboriginal and non-Aboriginal society.

Despite the considerable levels of funding and the effort of the two-way learning team, the support for Aboriginal students to develop their bi-dialectalism/bilingualism has not been consistently translated into improved educational practices nor has it produced better outcomes for Aboriginal students (Nguyen et al. 2015). It seems that additional means are needed to achieve these goals. How this might be achieved, and the support needed for Aboriginal students so that they can develop their ability to move between their various language varieties and higher levels of literacy in SAE, is the focus of the current study.

2.3   Translanguaging

In the past this movement between language varieties was termed codeswitching. However, more recently it has been recognised that a speaker's different language varieties do not exist as separate internal linguistic monoliths. Proficient speakers instead draw on all the language resources at their disposal and will move between them fluidly, as required, and for this reason the term translanguaging is now being adopted. According to García and Li (2012), translanguaging is a term used to describe how speakers of more than one language move between them to make meaning in a way that is both psycholinguistic and sociolinguistic. It is more than just translation, as it reflects a complex process that enables speakers to fully understand and convey information being discussed (Lewis et al. 2012).

This chapter is based on the premise that promoting translanguaging is a way for speakers of various Aboriginal languages to gain greater proficiency in SAE and to access the cultural nuances of that language. It also enables speakers to build upon their own languages and cultural understandings and, therefore, supports two-way learning and additive bilingualism. That is, rather than reinforcing a deficit view of non-standard language it promotes speakers' use of their different language varieties as a way of retaining their own identities.

While schools have struggled to find effective ways to promote translanguaging, some Aboriginal dialect/language speakers have discovered a way of doing this for themselves. They are now using online experiences, and specifically Facebook, as a place in which they can express themselves using their range of linguistic resources. How they achieve this is the main question addressed by the current research. That is, we seek to examine how translanguaging practices are developed by Aboriginal dialect/language speakers through the use of Facebook.

2.4   Developing Translanguaging Practices Online

There has been a dramatic increase in the use of mobile phones by Aboriginal peoples throughout Australia, but particularly in remote locations (Brady et al. 2008). Mobile phones are used for speaking to others and increasingly to text or message (i.e., to communicate in written form) and to engage with social media. In fact, as with most Australian youth, online communication is the preferred way for younger Aboriginals to communicate.

Although educators are generally reluctant to use online texts for teaching purposes, there is no doubt they offer a valuable resource to help students to learn about other places and other people: how they interact and their actions, values and culture. Online learning also provides a place to create written texts of various forms and to do so in such a way that the potential audience extends beyond the classroom into the wider community.

One online resource where there is evidence of dramatic and increasing use worldwide is Facebook. This is also true amongst Aboriginal peoples. Like others, they use it to communicate with family and friends; to share their thoughts, ideas and opinions; and to construct their online identities (Kral 2012; Oliver et al. 2014). It provides interactive spaces that encourage multimodal literacy engagement including with digital, audio, imagery, graphic and linguistic forms.

One of the advantages for Aboriginal people of producing online texts for formats such as Facebook is that the genre closely aligns with their oral language traditions. Although the text may be written, the often more informal way it is presented for this digital platform means that in many ways it resembles the way they talk (as opposed to formal written language). By being publicly available, this type of communication can work to foster closer connection between family members, even when they may be separated by considerable distances. This is particularly important for those with transient family members. Of particular pertinence to the current research, Facebook also appears to legitimise their choice of language, especially for when they want to express their personal and cultural identity. It also seems to provide opportunities for Aboriginal individuals to make linguistic choices that best suit their purpose, whether this is using a creole, traditional language, AE or even SAE.

Current research (Oliver and Nguyen 2017) has suggested that the use of Facebook may be a useful way to facilitate students' development of translanguaging practices because it affords them the opportunity to express online their personal and cultural identities—doing so by moving back and forth between AE and SAE. This dynamic process allows them to exert themselves beyond being simply monolingual—something that is often propounded in mainstream educational literacy practices. In this research we extend our exploration further, examining how different learners use Facebook and whether or not this Facebook usage serves to:

- enhance their ability to move proficiently between their linguistic codes,
- promote Aboriginal students' development of proficiency in Standard Australian English (SAE) and
- foster Aboriginal students' ability to see a relevance for learning and using SAE.

3   Method

3.1   Participants

Participants in the study ranged in age from 18 to 25 years old. Their reading age at the commencement of the study represented a range from 6.5 years old through to age appropriate. Specifically, school-based reading tests showed that the Aboriginal woman from the northwest began the study with the lowest literacy level (6.5 years), the Noongar/Ngudju man began with a literacy level of that of a 12 year old and the Yawuru/Nyul Nyul man had the level of a 14 year old. Reading test scores were not available for the two Noongar women, but both had successfully completed secondary education by the commencement of the study and on this basis their literacy level was deemed age appropriate.

3.2   Procedure

All the participants in the study were known to the first author and had requested her friendship on Facebook. She is acquainted with their background, experiences and, in all but one case, members of their extended family. Although this reduced the objectivity of the analysis, it did allow for this research to be undertaken from an introspective observational perspective (Newk-Fon Hey Tow et al. 2008).

As a first step, each participant was asked for and gave informed consent for their posts to be collected. The data was collected in a way that abided by the Guidelines for Ethical Research in Australian Indigenous Studies (AIATSIS 2017). In so doing, the diversity of Indigenous individuals and communities was recognised, stereotypes avoided, and respect shown for individual rights and freedom. Acknowledgement of Indigenous Australians as traditional owners of the land was made.

The data was collected longitudinally with the posts and replies of the five participants collected from the first author's Facebook page over a 24-month period. These online contributions were collected and stored for analysis in chronological order.

3.3   Data Analysis

The Facebook posts were the unit of analysis in this study. These texts were examined from a number of perspectives: First, and most importantly, they were examined to see if there was evidence of translanguaging. To do this we identified their linguistic choices, which in most cases were either AE or SAE. Determination of language was made according to how closely the forms abided to the definition of each as described by Malcolm (2001). Next, we examined the posts to determine their content and purpose, looking in particular at the socio-cultural context of the language use (Paltridge 2006). A comparison was then made to see the relationship, content and purpose of the message and the language used. To do this it was necessary to examine the ongoing posts appearing on each participant's page as they provided the clues to the context of each message.

The data was independently coded by two raters to examine the patterns of language use (i.e., in relation to content and purpose). Comparisons were then made until satisfactory agreement was reached. At times it was necessary to revisit the data and look again at the context in which the post was made, but this occurred infrequently as the language choice, content and purpose were mostly self-evident. The patterns that emerged were then matched to those previously identified (Oliver and Nguyen 2017), which showed considerable consistency across the determinations, despite different individuals participating in the studies. These patterns are described in the findings that follow next.

4   Findings

As with Oliver and Nguyen (2017), in this study we found that Facebook offered the Aboriginal participants opportunities to express themselves about a variety of content and for a variety of purposes. When doing so there was considerable evidence that the participants drew on a wide range of linguistic resources and moved between their different varieties in their language repertoires as appropriate; that is, they each displayed translanguaging practices. The data also seemed to suggest that by posting online for a wide audience, their proficiency and their perceptions about the relevance of SAE was enhanced.

As they engaged in translanguaging practices, it was also apparent that the participants were able to create an identity as multilingual individuals. At times these identities encapsulated their Aboriginality, but at other times they simply represented themselves as being a young person with a range of interests and needs. Facebook also appeared to offer them opportunities to experiment with language, both their home language and also SAE, for an audience beyond their family and friends. However, it was apparent that there were times when their use of language, particularly AE, was chosen to exclude or include particular people from their communication, which they did by making particular choices about how they expressed themselves. In fact, in many ways Facebook seemed to prompt the participants to be much more attentive to language. In turn, this heightened linguistic consciousness appeared to afford some participants the chance to further develop their SAE, which had the added benefit of providing them with a forum to share their creative personas, sometimes through language, be this in AE or SAE, but also visually through drawings and photographs and the associated captions. These themes emerging from the data are discussed in more detail below.

4.1 Creating an Identity as a Multilingual 'Aboriginal' Individual

The posts made on Facebook by the participants in the current study demonstrated that online texts allow individuals to experiment with how they construct themselves (Turkle 1995). We observed how, through their translanguaging practices, Aboriginal teenagers created identities that were at the same time individual and multilingual that included conveying to their audience that they were Aboriginal and, in most cases, proud to be so. For example, one of the young Noongar women posted a video of a kangaroo with the simple caption:

Out bush! ☺

It should be noted that 'going bush', meaning going away from urban and regional communities, is a cultural practice highly valued amongst many Aboriginal families and, in this instance, the participant shared not only her video account of one part of this excursion, but her positive feelings about the event with the use of a smiley face emoji.

Interestingly, some of the participants shared references to their Aboriginality using only SAE rather than AE, which was not what was expected. For instance, SAE was used when the Yawuru participant borrowed from (or in Facebook terms 'shared') the lyrics of the song 'Bran Nue Dae' and posted this to his wall:

There would nothing I would rather be than to be an Aborigine...

On another occasion SAE was also used by one of the Noongar participants to describe the spirituality of Aboriginal people and their close connection to the land:

We are all connected to the land
And land is connected to us

Once again this text was shared from another source, but was appropriated by this participant on her wall—publicly demonstrating her cultural alignment.

The other young Noongar woman also used SAE to demonstrate her heritage, but her posts were often more about political issues related to being an Aboriginal person. For example, she wrote the following text about the injustices Aboriginal people have suffered in Australia, specifically in relation to the Stolen Generations (where children were forcibly removed from their families):

My heart goes out to all members of the Stolen Generation today including my dad and his brothers and sisters and thinking of my Nanna X and pop X in heaven now rip. The pain and struggle and trauma they endured over them years breaks my heart. As a daughter of a stolen generation member, I will keep honouring this day for the rest of my life, I do not need the Government to have our own 'Lest We Forget' for our families who have been through this tragic time in this nation

Mostly, however, the participants used AE, rather than SAE to convey their Aboriginal self-identity. When doing so they would insert Aboriginal English, creole or traditional lexical items into their written constructions. It appeared that the purpose of such language was to clearly display their identity as an Aboriginal person and also to reach out to family and Aboriginal friends. For instance, when away from home, the young Yawuru man expressed his frustration about not being able to contact any members of his extended family by phone. Note how he uses both AE words (i.e., 'mob', meaning family, extended family and/or cultural community), AE markers ('em' for 'them') and written representations of AE pronunciation ('owad' for 'or what?') to express himself[1]:

*Christ you **mob** know how answer **em** phone **owad**?*

One of the young Noongar women used AE pronunciation in her first sentence ('growin' instead of 'growing') and in the second sentence grammatical structures (no pronoun, copula or article) to talk about a child in her family, sharing her delight about his growth:

*My baby **growin** up too fast! Proper boy!*

At other times she used only Noongar words to express her happiness:

Ngany Djerapiny!

In other instances the participants' translanguaging practices were less consistent and they simply inserted a lexical item or used an AE grammatical marker within a mostly SAE form. This most often occurred whilst they were engaged in describing an activity 'outside' their Aboriginal home and culture but when their intended audience still appeared to be other Aboriginal people (a premise supported by those who then responded). For example, one of the Noongar women posted:

***Nyorn.*[2]** *. . had 2 free tickets to YG*

Similarly, the young Ngudju man would also make contact with family and friends whilst he was at work, especially when he was working night shift:

Larda *it's gonna be a long night let u guys no how I go later.*
Peace out.

---

[1] Here and elsewhere AE and other Aboriginal linguistic forms are indicated in bold in the examples.

[2] 'Nyorn' means no, sad or bad and is generally negative.

At times when he was lonely, he would reach out to other Aboriginals, in the following instance somewhat cheekily to interested women ('yorgas'):

*Any **yorgas** want a phone call inbox ur number*

At other times he was observed being more serious, expressing sympathy to a family member after something sad (i.e., *nyorn*) had happened to that person, for example:

Nyorn *poor thing.*

In addition, and as is very typical within the communicative practices of Aboriginal people, the intended purpose of many of the participants' Facebook posts appeared to be to express humour. However, again when the intention was also to make contact with family or friends back home (especially when the writer was away), AE forms appeared to be used to signify the intended audience for the message, for example, from the young Yawuru man when describing his diet:

*Everyone back home **getting like** broomstick*

& here I am turning into a burrito

And to express agreement with another

True dat. Haha  [Noongar]

Note that again in both of these the articles and copulas are missing, which is typical of AE form, and also 'dat' is the written form of the word 'that' as it is pronounced by AE speakers.

4.2   Creating an Identity as a Young Person

In addition to using AE on Facebook to make and maintain personal connections with Aboriginal family and friends, the participants also appeared to experiment with using SAE for an audience beyond these people. Once more, the intent of such posts often seemed to be to make others laugh and included appropriated or 'shared' text such as the following posted by the young Ngudju man:

Men cooking cos the last generation of women taught their daughters shit

And the intention of sharing humorous things, including funny photographs and videos was made quite explicit with accompanying comments such as:

Try not to laugh

or others would share a post and use a series of emojis to signify their intention:

Like most young people, the purpose of participants' Facebook posts often seemed to be to make contact with others. For many, this was simply an act of reaching out when feeling bored or lonely. For example, the young Yawuru man would make pleas such as:

Someone message me I'm so bored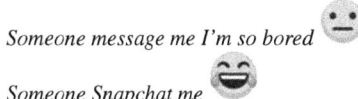

Someone Snapchat me

At other times their posts saw them representing themselves in ways all young people do, demonstrating a wide range of interests and needs and their engagement with various everyday activities, including their study and work:

Assignments up to my eyeballs [Noongar]

Graduation  *Tomorrow* [Yawuru]

Lovin night shift [Ngudju]

Fuck this I'm bored night shift is goin slow [Ngudju]

Like many young people, their Facebook posts also reflected their interests in music, sport, food, fashion and personal appearance. Interestingly when creating these young-person identities through their posts, they almost consistently did so using SAE not AE.
Music:

> *listening to hands across australia generation one.* [Noongar]
> *New fave song, thanks Bro for showing me* [Noongar]

Sport:

> *All Kevin Durant wanted was to win that's why he went to GSW, because he had no chance what so ever in Thunders to even reach the finals* [Yawuru]
> *I can't stand Kevin Durant and Stephen Curry* [Yawuru]
> *Hawthorn what the hack* [sic] *are they doing* [Aboriginal]
> *Hawthorn not worth watching* [Aboriginal]

Food:

> *Pancakes with pure Canadian maple syrup and a tall glass of chilled milk for breakfast for me and my baby this morning! Mm mm! Sooooo tasty!* [Noongar]

> *Restaurant + Food + Music = Life* [Yawuru]

Personal appearance:

Hairdressers  **SOON** [Yawuru]

When you get stuck in the rain at the beach [Noongar]

Like many young people, all the participants posted photos of themselves, especially when dressed up to go out, even at family funerals, and with special or interesting clothes or make-up. In fact, the Aboriginal woman participant from the northwest described herself as 'the selfie-queen', meaning that she is always taking photos of herself and posting them to her Facebook page.

One main difference from findings in the previous study was the way in which the relationship posts were created. Previously, the participants were more focussed on romantic relationships, and although there were a few posts of similar ilk in the current data, relationship posts were more generic, for example:

Stick with the man who stood by you when your hair wasn't done!

Also in the current data set the online texts relationship posts were most often about platonic (non-romantic) or family relationships. Most appeared to be written for the purpose of maintaining established relationships and included positive and happy comments, such as:

Happy birthday bro josh [Aboriginal participant]

Or in response to someone making contact and suggesting they meet up socially:

Aha that's good and for sure brus it'll be good to catch up [Ngudju]

However, there were other texts that reflected the writer's angst:

Wow! It's so crazy how you can be socially bullied at age 26...
    i guess some people can't escape their high school mindset. [Noongar]

And:

Deleting ignorant people who dont say 'boo' when they see me in person.
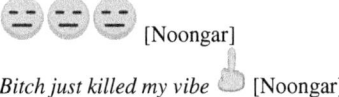 [Noongar]

Bitch just killed my vibe 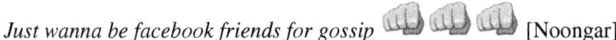 [Noongar]

It is interesting to note how once again the writers use emojis in a multimodal way to construct text to clearly express their feelings. Here is another example:

Just wanna be facebook friends for gossip 👊 👊 👊 [Noongar]

Therefore, just as other young people do, the participants in this study used these icons extensively to reflect their emotions, particularly about relationships. The participants also appeared to use language in very specific ways, particularly their choice of AE to exclude or include others in their communication. Strategies such as shaming, teasing, ridicule and humour play an important relational role in Aboriginal Australia. The type of joking that occurs, particularly between certain same-gender relatives, involves 'rowdy exchanges of sexually explicit epithets and mock abuse, with much body contact and sexual horseplay which amuses onlookers at least as much as the joking pair' (Tonkinson 1978, p. 47).

When directed at other Aboriginal people, these choices were often accompanied by swearing, with no words being off limits despite facebook being public, for example, when the Ngudju man was annoyed at another family member:

Larda one c*** gettin on my nerves tru, I'll tell him wer to go soon

And in response to a friend talking about the arrival of a new baby into his family, the young Yawuru man stated possessively:

Pff bitch Fuck off I'm The Godfather 👆

Even the young women also engaged in similar language use, as shown in a post that appeared on the pages of both the Noongar women:

WTF!

Another common phenomenon observed with all the participants was their association with being a young black person. For example, the young Aboriginal woman from the northwest wrote:

#BlackMagicGirl

These statements about colour were beyond being Aboriginal, with the participants appropriating photos and sayings that showed alignment with all black people, be they African Americans, African or other non-white populations, for instance:

Lookit her lovely skin [Noongar with a photo of a friend from Sri Lanka]

All the participants would also post photos of black sporting heroes, including American basketballers and Australian Aboriginal football players, accompanied by accolades about their prowess. However, posts about colour could also be quite political, as represented by the following, which was appropriated and posted by one of the Noongar participants:

Too white, too black, or not black enough:
    This is not a question for others to decide.

At times 'being black' saw the participants sharing political statements such as the following, posted by the same Noongar participant as above:

Share if you stand against racism in Australia.

4.3   Attention to Language and the Development of SAE

In following the participants longitudinally, it was evident that Facebook not only provided the participants with general writing practice—writing with purpose and for an audience—but that it seemed to heighten the participants' attention to language. This was most evident with the young Aboriginal woman from the northwest. When the first author met her in the late 2000s, her literacy was determined to be at a beginning year 1 level (i.e., at the level of a 6 year old). She would rarely write and would do so with considerable difficulty. Initially her Facebook posts were mostly photos; as indicated previously, these were often selfies and with barely more than simplest of captions, for example:

#Beautiful sunset
KFC for dinner

Now she creates texts such as:

L following the cat in the bushes!

So great to catch up with my beautiful R!!
Happy birthday M hope you have a wonderful time on your special day.

She was not alone. Although having slightly higher SAE literacy levels at the commencement of the study, the young Ngudju and Yawuru men also demonstrated increasing written SAE proficiency. Whilst their posts were initially quite brief, over time the length and complexity of their constructions developed, for instance:

Would like too say thank u too everyone for the birthday
wishes yesterday may god bless u all thanks [Ngudju]

Happy Birthday to this amazing young woman X.

May you have a beautiful day as beautiful as you xx
[Yawuru]

4.4   Creative Practices of Aboriginal Translinguals

In addition to creating texts as described above, it appeared from the data that Facebook afforded the participants a context in which to express their creativity. The two Noongar participants, both talented artists, frequently uploaded and shared their latest works online, sometimes commenting in AE.

This Noongar Yorga going good now!

And sometimes in SAE:

Getting ready for the Noongar Country Exhibition 2017

Late night sketching

Whilst previous research saw participants sharing text drawings (creating art work with letters and fonts), in the current data this did not occur. Apart from the posts by the Noongar participants, creativity was most often demonstrated through the sharing of photographs. These were mostly nature scenes of outstanding beauty taken by the participants—sometimes of places they see as 'their country', but other times from places they had visited or near their workplaces. Often these photos were labeled with their location (e.g., the beach, a sunset), but also with messages for friends, for example:

> *Good morning family and friends*
> *hope u all have a great day an god bless u all* [Ngudju]

In addition to photos, the participants also appropriated text from others in ways that demonstrated their appreciation for the arts. For example, the young Ngudju man posted the following song lyrics on his Facebook page:

> *My old man I know one day we'll Meet again as he's looking downMy old manI hope he's*
> *proud of who I am ...*
> *I'm tryin to fill the boots*
> *Of my old man*
> *My old man*
> (From "My Old Man" by the Zac Brown band)

And then commented: 'I love this song'.

This was a practice used to varying extents by all the participants, most often done in SAE, but at times also using AE when the text or songs had been written that way (such as some of the lyrics from 'Bran Nue Dae'). Therefore, such appropriation of text for creative purposes further served to heighten the participants' awareness of language form and use.

5   Conclusion

From the data it was clear that online writing on Facebook served to connect the participants with their family, enabled them to collaborate with friends and, overall, to be a part of their collective communities (often in their physical absence from home). Facebook provided a conduit to help them communicate and deal with problems such as homesickness, loneliness, extraneous living conditions, cross-cultural confusion and lack of financial support. The respondents also used Facebook to communicate humour and feelings (mostly platonically) and to share goodwill, but also to tease (e.g., *'Any yorgas want a phone call inbox ur number'*). By using Aboriginal words and expressions they were able to clearly signify their cultural alignment. Further, through their posts, the participants were able to celebrate their culture and language and demonstrate to others the importance these aspects have in their lives.

The participants' self-motivated engagement had them using this platform purposefully for a range of communications, moving proficiently between their various linguistic codes, applying on most occasions appropriate protocols analogous to the circumstances. Of particular interest, especially given its pedagogical importance, the participants' SAE proficiency appeared to increase over the time frame of the study. Their posts indicated that they developed a greater awareness of the transactional purpose of SAE, which in turn served to enable them to fully participate on Facebook not only informally with family and friends, but also formally with the wider community. In doing so they demonstrated a rationalised progressive attitude for learning and using SAE as they came to appreciate its applicability. Whilst initially wary of using SAE, over time they demonstrated an awareness of when to use it to enhance their communications. In this way Facebook clearly provides a platform to apply digital, socio-cultural and linguistic knowledge for proficiently translanguaging and in ways that enable those who post online to express themselves purposefully, comprehensively and creatively. This transformation towards pragmatic and imaginative utilization of language both in the vernacular and SAE has encouraging implications especially for the next generation of young Indigenous learners.

Overall, our findings suggest that it would be advantageous for educators to utilise similar translanguaging opportunities to encourage and motivate Aboriginal school students. We do need to note, however, that this research was undertaken with only a small number of participants, albeit longitudinally, and on this basis much further research is required. However, the findings are similar to previous work carried out by the current author (Oliver and Nguyen 2017), and this consistency shows considerable promise especially with regard to their potential contribution to pedagogy.

References

Ah Chee, D., Beetson, J., & Boughton, B. (1997). *Indigenous peoples' education rights in Australia*. Paper presented at the Indigenous Rights, Political theory and the reshaping of institutions conference. Canberra: Australian National University.

AIATSIS [Australian Institute of Aboriginal and Torres Strait Islander Studies]. (2017). *Guidelines for ethical research in Australian indigenous studies*. Retrieved from https://aiatsis.gov.au/research/ethical-research/guidelines-ethical-research-australian-indigenous-studies

AIATSIS [Australian Institute of Aboriginal and Torres Strait Islander Studies]. (2018). *Indigenous Australian languages*. Retrieved from https://aiatsis.gov.au/explore/articles/indigenous-australian-languages

Amagula J., & McCarthy H., (2015). Red Ochre Women: Sisters in the struggle for educational reform. In H. Huijser, R. Ober, S. O'Sullivan, E. McRae-Williams, & R. Elvin (Eds.), *Finding common ground: narratives, provocations and reflections from the 40 year celebration of Batchelor Institute* (pp. 59–64). Batchelor: Batchelor Press. Retrieved from https://www.batchelor.edu.au/biite/wp-content/uploads/Common-Ground-ebook.pdf

Brady, F., Dyson, L., & Asela, T. (2008). Indigenous adoption of mobile phones and oral culture. In F. Sudweeks, H. Hrachovec, & C. Ess (Eds.), *Proceedings: Cultural attitudes towards communication and technology* (pp. 384–398). Perth: Murdoch University.

Burns, R. (1995). *The adult learner at work*. Sydney: Business and Professional.

Eades, D. (1988). They don't speak an Aboriginal language, or do they? In I. Keen (Ed.), *Being black: Aboriginal culture in settled Australia*. Canberra: Aboriginal Studies.

Eagleson, R. D., Kaldor, S., & Malcolm, I. (1982). *English and the Aboriginal child*. Canberra: Curriculum Development Centre.

García, O., & Li, W. (2012). *Translanguaging: Language, bilingualism and education*. London: Palgrave.

Green, N. (1984). *Broken spears Aboriginals and Europeans in the Southwest of Australia*. Perth: Focus Education Services.

Kral, I. (2012). *Talk, text and technology: Literacy and social practice in a remote indigenous community.* Bristol: Multilingual Matters.

Lewis, G., Jones, B., & Baker, C. (2012). Translanguaging: Origins and development from school to street and beyond. *Educational Research and Evaluation, 18*(7), 641–654. https://doi.org/1 0.1080/13803611.2012.718488.

Malcolm, I. (2001). Aboriginal English: Adopted code of a surviving culture. In D. Blair & P. Collins (Eds.), *English in Australia* (pp. 201–222). Amsterdam: John Benjamins.

McKay, G. (2011). Policies and Indigenous languages in Australia. *Australian Review of Applied Linguistics, 34*(3), 297–319.

Newk-Fon Hey Tow, W., Dell, P., & Venable, J. (2008). Understanding information disclosure behaviour in Australian Facebook users. *19th Australasian conference on information systems,* 3–5 December, Christchurch.

Nguyen, B., Oliver, R., & Rochecouste, J. (2015). Embracing plurality through oral language. *Language and Education, 29*(2), 97–111. https://doi.org/10.1080/09500782.2014.977294.

Nicholls, C. (2005). Death by a thousand cuts: Indigenous Language Bilingual Education Programs in the Northern Territory of Australia 1972–1998. *The International Journal of Bilingual Education and Bilingualism, 8*(2 & 3), 160–177.

Oliver, & Nguyen. (2017). Translanguaging on Facebook: Exploring Australian Aboriginal multilingual competence in technology-enhanced environments and its pedagogical implications. *Canadian Modern Language Review/La Revue canadienne des langues vivantes, 73*(4), 463–487. https://doi.org/10.3138/cmlr.3890.

Oliver, R., Vanderford, S., & Grote, E. (2012). Evidence of English language proficiency and academic achievement of non-English speaking background students at an Australian university. *Higher Education Research & Development, iFirst,* 1–15.

Oliver, R., Grote, E., & Nguyen, B. (2014). Australian Indigenous students developing literacy and code-switching skills through online communication: A study of Facebook as an education tool. In A. C. Cree (Ed.), *Literacies: The power to change, Volume 2 – Literacy in a changing world* (pp. 88–104). Oxford: World Literacy Summit.

Oliver, R., Chen, H., & Moore, S. (2016). Review of applied linguistics in Australia 2008–2014. *Language Teaching, 49*(4), 1–37. https://doi.org/10.1017/S0261444816000148.

Paltridge, B. (2006). *Discourse analysis: An introduction.* London: Continuum.

Partington, G., Godfrey, J., Harslett, M., & Richer, K. (2000). *Can Non-Indigenous teachers succeed in teaching Indigenous students?* Paper presented at the Australian Indigenous Education Conference, Perth: Edith Cowan University.

The National Assessment Program Literacy and Numeracy (NAPLAN). https://www.nap.edu.au/naplan

Tonkinson, R. (1978). *The Mardudjara Aborigines: Living the dream in Australia's desert.* New York: Holt, Rinehart and Winston.

Turkle, S. (1995). *Life on the screen: Identity in the age of the internet.* New York: Simon and Schuster.

Wigglesworth, G., Simpson, J., & Loakes, D. (2011). NAPLAN language assessments for Indigenous children in remote communities: Issues and problems. *Australian Review of Applied Linguistics, 34*(3), 320–343.

Zubrick, S. R., Silburn, S. R., Lawrence, D. M., Mitrou, F. G., Dalby, R. B., & Blair, E. M., (2005). *The Western Australian aboriginal child health survey: The social and emotional wellbeing of aboriginal children and young people.* Perth.

Goldilocks and the Three Semiotic Bears: Young Children's Engagement with Early Literacy—A Vygotskian Approach

Paul Gardner

Abstract Premised on the notion of young children as natural semioticians, this chapter explores a case study in which an early educator works with a group of two-and-a-half to three-year-old children as they navigate early literacy development. The approach used fuses Vygotskian thinking with pedagogic processes that have emerged from Reggio Emilia. The educator scaffolds children's literacy development using story and symbolic representations of characters and objects in the story, before replacing them with alphabetic symbols. The case study challenges the dominant discourse that privileges synthetic phonics as the exclusive method of early reading, currently in vogue in several Anglophile countries. What emerges is a broad multileveled approach to literacy in which children demonstrate agency, engagement and creativity as they acquire letter-sound recognition alongside higher order levels of reading.

Keywords Semiotics · Synthetic phonics · Reggio Emilia · Storytelling · Multimodality

1 Introduction

Unlike many of the other chapters in this volume that deal with language at the tertiary level, this chapter introduces a study of an experimental approach to literacy acquisition implemented in a Western Australian school for early learning. The approach begins from the premise that children are natural semioticians and that their first encounters with meaning-making is through engagement with the signs and symbols that can be found in their textual environment. These semiotic encounters in which children begin to understand that symbols represent objects, actions and emotions in the real world are the precursor to being able to use the alphabetic code (Rubizzi and Bonilauri 2012, p. 213). This study runs counter to the current

P. Gardner (✉)
School of Education, Curtin University, Perth, WA, Australia
e-mail: paul.gardner@curtin.edu.au

© Springer Nature Switzerland AG 2019   203
T. Dobinson, K. Dunworth (eds.), *Literacy Unbound: Multiliterate,*
Multilingual, Multimodal, Multilingual Education 30,
https://doi.org/10.1007/978-3-030-01255-7_11

dominant discourse in early literacy acquisition prevalent in the education systems of the US, England and Australia in which it is postulated that the exclusive teaching of systematic synthetic phonics (SSP) should be the exclusive method of teaching early reading (Donnelly and Wiltshire 2014; Moats 2014; Rose 2006; Westwood 2009). Arguments about the most effective means of teaching early reading have persisted for decades (Snyder 2008), but in recent years, SSP has been privileged over a more holistic approach that integrates several strategies, such as children's implicit knowledge of syntax and semantics and implicit contextual understanding. The argument for the exclusive use of SSP is currently being won by political diktat and selective research evidence rather than comprehensive reviews of research, experiential knowledge or theories of language.

After briefly discussing these current arguments and reviewing recent findings on the subject from England, where the government is a strong advocate of SSP, the chapter explores a Vygotskian approach to early reading. The central questions underpinning the chapter are as follows: What can a study of young children's early literacy acquisition tell us about the nature of language? What might be an appropriate pedagogy for language learning more generally? As these questions are investigated, answers reveal insights into young children's capacities as semioticians, language as social practice and children's ability to use language as a multi-levelled and multi-faceted system of meaning making. What also emerges as influential components in these children's explorations of language are the important functions of the pedagogic context in which literacy is developed, the social relationships formed in the process of acquiring literacy and recognition of children as competent agents in their own learning. The lessons learned from the study of young children's early engagement with literacy have wider implications for our understanding of language learning more generally.

2   The Phonics Debate

Current approaches to literacy education in the school systems of the US, England and, increasingly, Australia, are dominated by a return to basics and the teaching of SSP as the sole method for teaching early reading. Snyder (2008, p. 8) charts the domino effect of the method's trajectory, starting in the US in 2001 with George Bush's No Child Left Behind Act; moving to England where the Blair Government commissioned the *Independent review of the teaching of early reading* (Rose 2006); and subsequently to Australia, where advocates of the approach allegedly used the Murdoch press to propagate their views (Snyder 2008, p. 5). The extent to which arguments around the teaching of early reading have been politicised is perhaps best exemplified in the introduction to the *Independent review of the teaching of early reading*. The review team, led by Sir Jim Rose, was 'guided' to report on the following aspects:

- What best practice should be expected in the teaching of early reading and synthetic phonics?
- What range of provision best supports children with significant literacy difficulties and enables them to catch up with their peers, and what is the relationship of such targeted intervention programmes with synthetic phonics teaching?

Making synthetic phonics the a priori finding of the review undermined the review team's propensity for impartiality, making the claim to independence questionable, if not redundant. In their analysis of the report, Wyse and Styles (2007) also raised questions about the report's impartiality, highlighting the wealth of research evidence that recognised the importance of phonics as one method of teaching reading integral to a range of other strategies.

The review recommendation that SSP be the exclusive method of teaching early reading subsequently became a statutory requirement in England in 2007. The statute only applies to England because Scotland and Northern Ireland have curriculum bodies that are independent of the UK parliament. As an ironic aside, it is worth noting that the Rose Report drew heavily on a study in the Scottish county of Clackmannashire. The findings of a seven-year longitudinal study advocated that the exclusive teaching of synthetic phonics was the best method of teaching early reading (Johnston and Watson 2005). Recently, reading was identified as a cause for serious concern in the county's schools because pupils on average were achieving reading scores below their chronological age (Stirling and Clackmannanshire Council 2015, p. 14). This finding adds to growing concerns about the continued advocacy of synthetic phonics as the exclusive method of teaching early reading. As the Clackmannanshire study was pivotal in Rose's justification for advocating synthetic phonics as the 'first and fast' method of teaching early reading, a closer critique of the study is made below.

3   'Ghoniks Roolz?', or 'Phonics Rules?'

There are two phonic approaches to the teaching of early reading: synthetic phonics and analytic phonics. The latter begins with the identification of whole words that are then deconstructed (analysed) into their constituent sounds. A key strategy involves analogy. Students are taught to analyse words using *onset* and *rime*. Onset refers to the word's initial phoneme, whilst the rime is the subsequent part of the word. For example, the onset of the word *hat* is *h*, whereas the rime is *at*. Once this phonological awareness has been acquired, students are then shown how to read similar words by means of analogy. Students who are able to read *hat* can then apply their knowledge to words such as *cat*, *mat* and *sat*. In contrast, the teaching of reading by means of synthetic phonics begins with recognition of individual letter sounds, or phonemes. It is estimated there are 44 phonemes in English that correspond to approximately 185 graphemes, the written form of a phoneme. The title of this section provides an example of how in English a single letter sound can be formed using several different graphemes. For example, the sound produced by the letter *f* can be represented in three ways: *f*, *ph* and *gh*, as demonstrated in the words *fun*, *philosophy* and *enough*. In the early stages of teaching synthetic phonics, students are familiarised with simple letter-sound connections, or to use the appropriate metalanguage, letter-sound correspondences. To return to our example of the word *hat*, students would therefore be taught the letter-sound correspondences for each of the letters *h*, *a* and *t* and would then be shown how to blend, or synthesise, them to read the word *hat*. Synthetic phonics is said to become systematic when letter-sound correspondences are taught progressively, starting with individual graphemes and then progressing to digraphs (e.g., *ch*, *sh*, *ck*, *th*) and trigraphs (e.g., *igh*, *air*, *ure*, *tch*) and when taught daily. In support of a systematic approach, the UK Department for Education and Science (DfES) produced a programme for teaching synthetic phonics, called Letters and Sounds (DfES 2007), but following the election of a Conservative-led coalition government in 2010 funds were also made available to schools to purchase commercial programmes.

4 A Critique of Synthetic Phonics

Whilst synthetic phonics may be an effective way to decode regular CVC words, English, unlike languages that have a one-to-one correspondence between the letters of the alphabet and phonemes, has an opaque writing system (McGuinness 2004, p. 3). The multiple ways of writing some phonemes and diverse ways of decoding letters and letter strings makes English less transparent than most languages (Ziegler and Goswami 2005). Thirty percent of the 100 most commonly used words published in Letters and Sounds (DfES 2007) are not readily decodable using phonics, and Kear and Gladhart (1983) estimate that the same applies to 75% of words in early reading materials. Advocates of synthetic phonics refer to such words variously as 'common exception words' or 'tricky words', which include words such as *was*, *one* and *the*. Some advocates of synthetic phonics concede that common exception words need to be learned by means of visual recognition; however, in England, teachers are mandated to use synthetic phonics as the initial means of decoding such words (DfE 2013). This is despite contrary evidence from neuroscience that suggests that because English is orthographically complex readers need to be able to process multiple knowledge systems as they read. These knowledge systems include morphemic knowledge, semantic knowledge, syntactic knowledge, phonological knowledge and contextual knowledge (Davis 2005).

This method of teaching early reading is prescribed by statute and is also a requirement enshrined in the Teachers' Standards (DfE 2011). Furthermore, students' ability to decode individual words is tested by means of the 'phonics screening check', which was implemented for all six year olds in 2012 (DfE 2010). Since its implementation, the then Australian Minister for Education, Simon Birmingham, also expressed his interest in implementing the check in Australian schools (The

Australian 2017). The 'check', which has been erroneously conflated with an assessment of students' reading ability by the UK Government, consists of 40 discrete words, half of which are pseudo-words. Pseudo-words are letter combinations that appear to construct words and that can be decoded using phonic knowledge but have no meaning (e.g., 'trape', 'bluck'). Following the first 'check' in 2012, when only 58% of children passed the test, a United Kingdom Literacy Association (UKLA) survey of approximately 500 schools reported a trend in which more able readers were failing the test (UKLA 2012). Whilst these students were able to identify the separate letter-sound correspondences in the pseudo-words, they tended to translate them as real words when synthesising sounds (e.g., 'st-r-o-m' might have been read as 'storm'). The logical explanation for assuming the pseudo-words to be real words was that students who were already able to read understood that words have meaning (UKLA 2012). Apart from the confusion caused by mixing real words with pseudo-words, Gibson and England (2015) identified further problems with the phonics check, including: the issue of the pronunciation of pseudo-words caused by regional variations; failure to provide teachers with useful information about students' reading ability; encouraging teachers to 'teach to the test'; the process of decoding individual letters leading to slow reading and the difficulty of keeping letter sounds of polysyllabic words in the students' working memory (Landerl 2000 cited in Gibson and England 2015, p. 503). Teaching students pseudo-words raises the philosophical question about the definition of what we mean when we refer to the term *word*. Semiotics draws attention to the links between signs (in this case, words) and their meanings. Humans are able to communicate with each other because there is common agreement about the definition of specific words and implicit acceptance that words carry meaning. Consequently, teaching students to read discrete nonsense words appears absurd because the practice runs contrary to the very purpose and nature of language.

Even if pseudo-words were excluded from the check, there is no comprehensive evidence that synthetic phonics, as an exclusive method of teaching early reading, is better than any other method (Marshall 2012, p. 124). McGuinness (2004) has attempted to prove otherwise by means of what she considered a review of the literature, but her findings were premised on positivist research to the exclusion of longitudinal studies of other approaches, leading to criticism from reviewers of her work (Harvey 2005; Kaufman 2005; Ellis 2007a, b).

Although a systematic approach to phonics is advisable, research evidence discerns no significant difference between synthetic and analytic phonics (Ellis and Moss 2014, p. 243). The drive towards synthetic phonics has largely come from research undertaken by cognitive psychologists, causing Ellis (2007a, b) to argue that findings derived from the lens of a single paradigm do not provide a full view of the complexity of research into reading and that this complexity can be more fully viewed using multi-disciplinary approaches. Indeed Ellis and Moss (2014) identify several lenses that bring the teaching of reading into sharper focus. These include ethnographic studies such as those of Heath (1983) and Street (1985), which situate literacy in social practice, including students' perceptions of the purposes and uses of literacy (Moss 2009). Gender and socioeconomic status influence how well children read (Mullis et al. 2007, cited in Ellis and Moss 2014) as does breadth and depth of reading (OECD 2010, cited in Ellis and Moss 2014). In summary, Ellis and Moss (2014, p. 243) posit that students' engagement as readers is best facilitated when pedagogy integrates cognitive, social, cultural and affective domains combined with tasks that stimulate students' interests and offer choice, coherence and collaboration. These are the domains in which language derives and conveys meaning. If we begin from the premise that language is a semiotic system, to reduce early reading to the acquisition of single sounds devoid of semiotic connotation makes the process so abstract as to constitute something akin to anti-language. The argument that teaching synthetic phonics improves reading is not supported by the research evidence. A systematic review of research on the teaching of early reading by Torgerson et al. (2006, p. 10) found that although synthetic phonics teaching had a positive impact on reading accuracy, it had little effect on reading comprehension.

Despite the wealth of evidence for a multi-levelled approach to reading acquisition, the question remains as to why the UK Government has prescribed the statutory teaching of synthetic phonics on schools in England. As discussed above, the rationale for doing so was largely premised upon a single study conducted in Clackmannashire. One might expect that for a government to enact educational policy on the basis of a single study, the research design would be exemplary. However, the study has attracted widespread criticism from literacy experts with substantial knowledge and experience of educational research. Glazzard (2017) has collated findings of interrogations of the study undertaken by other academic teams. He notes Wyse and Goswami's (2008) conclusion that the study was far from being rigorous. The study claimed to have found that the exclusive teaching of synthetic phonics had resulted in students having better reading, spelling and comprehension than groups taught by other means (Johnston and Watson 2005). On closer inspection of the research design, Wyse and Style (2007) identified serious flaws in the conduct of the investigation: students in the analytic phonics group were taught fewer letters than those in the synthetic phonics group, and the groups received different allocations of teaching time. Ellis and Moss (2014) also found the study had ignored other possible contributory factors such as teacher effectiveness, parents' educational attainment, quality of home literacy, and other literacy interventions and activities undertaken in the school and in the home and the time spent on these activities.

It would seem from the above discussion that debate around synthetic phonics and the most effective means of teaching early reading is one in which, on one side, advocates prescribe a tightly 'bound' view of literacy premised on an atomised view of language and, on the other, a view of literacy that is 'unbound' in the sense that reading acquisition is located in a more holistic multi-method approach.

The approach to early reading explored in this chapter is very much located in this unbound view of literacy.

5   Children as Semioticians?

From an early age children experience a world in which signs and print are an integral part of their cultural environment that, for many, form their first reading material (McMahon-Giles and Wellhousen-Tunks 2010, p. 23). Signs consist of two aspects; the sign itself (signifier) and its meaning (signified). The relationship of the signifier and signified is culturally constructed, giving sign systems coherence and permanence (Kalantzis et al. 2016, p. 215). Drawing on the work of Peirce (1998), Kalantzis et al. identified the following three forms of sign: icons, indicators or indexes, and symbols. Children's picture books, advertisements and posters utilise iconic signs, that is, visual representations of real things. Dark clouds signify impending rain, a smile implies happiness, a red light signals stop—these are all forms of signs as indicators in that they point to something specific. Symbols, however, are more abstract than the other two forms of sign in that they have an arbitrary relationship to the referent, or thing they represent. In explaining the function of signs, we might identify three elements: the signifier, the signified and the referent. If we take the word *dog*, for example, the signifier is the letter-sound representation, the word itself, whether written or spoken; the signifier is the meaning of what a dog is; and the referent is the dog itself. However, the letters used to construct the signifier are arbitrary and change from language to language. Therefore, the signifier changes but the referent remains constant. Most words can be classified as symbols, although some words are iconic. Onomatopoeic words can be classified as iconic because they resemble physical sounds. Pronouns and some adverbials are examples of words that are indexical because they specify particular people (e.g., he, she, I or they) or specific places (e.g., here or there). At the heart of language then is the communication and interpretation of meanings through complex, socially constructed semiotic systems. Anstey and Bull (2009, p. 28) identify five such semiotic systems as follows:

- Linguistic: oral and written form, including lexis, syntax, punctuation, format and genre
- Visual: static and moving images, including colour, vectors, line, perspective and viewpoint
- Gestural: facial expressions and body language, including movement, pace, stillness and body position
- Aural: music and sound effects, including volume, pitch, rhythm and silence
- Spatial: layout and juxtaposition of objects and space, including proximity, direction and position in space.

The process of enculturation in a literate environment involves children developing an expanding repertoire of meaning-making as they are exposed to signs of differing complexity across these semiotic systems. Prior to the turn of the twenty-first century, the New London Group (1996) recognised the interconnectedness of these semiotic systems and advocated a reconceptualization of literacy from the singular to the plural and promoted the term multiliteracies. The group drew our attention to the fact that these sign systems are not exclusive entities but often interact with one another through the construction of forms of multimodal expression (Cope and Kalantzis 2000; Lankshear and Knobel 2011). A casual everyday conversation between two speakers may involve each of them simultaneously processing three semiotic systems, i.e., the linguistic, aural and gestural. Not only are the speakers attending to the meanings of the individual words being used and their relationship to one another syntactically, they are also decoding meanings embedded in their interlocutor's tone of voice and intonation, as well as their facial expressions, hand gestures and general body language. Hence, the understanding of spoken language is supported by two other cuing systems. Written language, however, is much more self-contained in the sense that the reader processes a single semiotic system, devoid of other cues, unless the text is accompanied by illustrations. The word is a highly abstract form because it lacks the contextual references of other signs. For the young child, the written word, however, is a configuration of marks that have no immediate, explicit significance. For this reason, enculturating young children into a literate society requires conscious effort on the part of literate 'experts' to teach the young how to encode and decode written language. It is questions around how best this might systematically be achieved in mass education systems that are at the heart of the ongoing and often heated debate in literacy education.

In this chapter, I begin from the premise that children are natural semioticians who begin to decode signs in their semiotic environments from an early age. They understand that the real world can be represented by pictures, photographs, televisual images in motion and sounds and that facial expressions and gestures can signify a person's emotions, convey approval or disapproval, imply commands etc. They understand the meanings of many iconic and indexical signs before they are able to comprehend the symbolic form of the word. However, the word consists of one or more morphemes and therefore has signification, unlike the individual letters that comprise the word. Letters and combinations of letters represent sounds rather than meanings and belong to a language's phonological system rather than its morphological system. The letters *a*, *c* and *t* have no intrinsic meaning but become a meaningful sign when amalgamated as the conventional sign, *cat*. Yet children must learn the relationship between a language's phonological system and the corresponding 'marks', or graphemes, in the process of learning to read. It is questionable, however, if this is best achieved by reducing language to discrete letter sound connections (graph-phonic correspondence) devoid of morphological context.

In the Vygotskian approach to early reading discussed later in this chapter, an attempt was made to recognise children's semiotic competence. A scaffolded process was implemented to support their acquisition of literacy in the linguistic system by building on their pre-existing knowledge of how signs work to convey meanings. Before explaining how this was done, it is important to establish an understanding of the pedagogic context in which the scaffolded process was implemented.

6   The Educational Context

Educational settings are places in which learning is, to a greater or lesser extent, formalised as transacted meanings that occur between educators and students and between students and students. Learning involves not only the accommodation and assimilation of new data on the part of the learner (Piaget 2002) but engagement between learners and 'more expert others' who are cognisant of the learner's present level of understanding and future needs (Vygotsky 1986). Hence, learning and teaching constitute a symbiotic social process that occurs within a social context in which the behaviour of teaching and learning is informed by pedagogic practices, educational paradigms and beliefs about the nature of knowledge and how knowledge is constructed. Once an educational setting is conceptualised in this way, it is possible to think of learning as a complex process of social participation in which participants belong to a community designed for the purpose of jointly acting to make sense of their world (Wenger 2005). So, what was the nature of the community of practice (Lave and Wenger 1991) for the young students in this study?

6.1   Physical Space

In terms of its physical context, the educational setting in this study consisted of an internal space with a carpeted area; several tables at the periphery of the room; students' lockers at one end; several doors, one leading to shared toilets; and a second opening on to the dining area and a sliding door providing access to an outdoor area. The outdoor area included a sizable sand play space, a climbing frame, and a raised deck area and miscellaneous play equipment. Students also had access to a well-equipped artist's studio where they worked in small groups with a skilled resident artist. Although initially sparse, the environment reflected children's learning and therefore evolved with their emerging interests to include artefacts and outcomes of the processes of learning.

6.2   The Classroom Context

The actors in this context consisted of children in the age range 2 years and 9 months to 3 years and 6 months who were selected by means of purposive sampling. As part of the ethical clearance for the study, parental permission was granted and data collected was anonymised. Approximately 16–20 young students per day attended the class. A few of these attended every day, but most did so for a minimum of two days per week. The composition of learners changed periodically throughout the year as older children moved out of the class and younger ones entered. The class had a lead educator and two supporting assistant educators. Assistant educators had a

Certificate III qualification in Early Childhood Education and Care, which is a first-tier qualification, and the lead educator had a Diploma in Early Childhood Education and Care, which is a second-tier qualification. The Diploma is required before an educator can lead a room of children. In addition to these qualifications, all educators attended monthly professional training delivered by senior educators, many of whom had graduate or post-graduate qualifications. It was one of the assistant educators who was the person leading the literacy project in this study.

6.3 The Local Community

The social community that this setting served was urban, largely socio-economically affluent and multicultural. It was, therefore, a community in which families shared similar levels of wealth and occupational status but had different cultural and ethnic identities. Approximately 15% of children were in the early stages of acquiring English as an additional language. Most of the children had two working parents, although one of them was often in part-time work, and were brought to school by car between 7:30 and 9:00 a.m. Children were collected from school between 4:30 and 6:00 p.m. The majority of children lived in nuclear families and their only contact with children of their own age would have been on the days they attended school. Most children attended either two or three days but a minority attended full-time. Investigation of the literacy practices of the home was not systematically undertaken in this study, but anecdotal evidence acquired from everyday discussion with parents suggests a variety of approaches were adopted. A few parents were explicitly teaching their children alphabetic script at home. However, for the majority this was not a central feature of their literacy practice. It was a common practice for parents to read to their children, but it was not universal. Some parents considered their children too young to be concerned about developing literacy by means of direct instruction.

6.4 Pedagogy

Pedagogy is more than teaching technique; it encompasses ideas and actions about teaching and learning that emanate from a society's value system and its history (Alexander 2008, p. 92). In this sense, educational practice might be viewed as the enactment of a particular educational paradigm, the 'viewpoint that shapes ideas and actions within a particular field' (McArthur 1992, p. 747).

Pedagogic practice in the school was informed by a clear paradigm of education, which was influenced both by the Early Years Learning Framework produced by the Australian Government's Department of Education, Employment and Workplace Relations (DEEWR 2009) and the philosophy and practice of Reggio Emilia. The framework explicitly refers to children engaging with and gaining meaning from a range of texts (p. 41), as well as beginning to understand how symbols and pattern systems work (p. 43). The approach discussed below was conducive to both these requirements of the framework. Reggio Emilia is a municipality in Northern Italy where, in the post-war period, under the guidance of an inspirational educator named Loris Malaguzzi, a radical approach to early learning was developed to the extent that it is now a world-renowned educational philosophy and practice. It is necessary to briefly explore this philosophy and practice in order to capture the essence of the pedagogy adopted in this community of learners.

6.5   The Philosophy and Practice of Reggio Emilia

The 'Reggio approach' to education is closely aligned to constructivist and socio-historical psychology, post-war Italian left wing reform politics and postmodern philosophy (Edwards et al. 2012b, p. 8). The agency of the child, as a sentient meaning maker, is central to the pedagogy of Reggio Emilia, and great importance is placed on educators taking time to listen to children and give them opportunities to exercise initiative whilst also constructively guiding them. It is an educational approach that encourages an epistemological paradigm devoid of dichotomies, favouring holistic views of knowledge rather than neatly packaged compartmentalised subject content. In the Reggio approach, a curriculum emerges out of children's interests, and learning is premised upon inquiry and research. Other key features of the Reggio Emilia educational philosophy and pedagogy include:

- collaboration premised on the notion of intersubjectivity, i.e., mutual understanding of the thinking of others and problem solving;
- collegiality and open, democratic styles of learning;
- learning as a progressive recursive process;
- the environment as a source of cognitive and affective stimulation as well as a stimulus for inquiry;
- acceptance of the concept of multiple intelligences (Gardner 1993);
- recognition of children's multiple expressive modes, e.g., symbolic, metaphorical, imaginative and relational;
- encouragement of self-reflective practice in learning;
- emphasis on deep meanings and affective relationships to subject matter rather than the acquisition of skills for their own sake;
- inclusiveness and respect for diversity;
- integration of content and method;
- affirmation of the learner's identity, sense of belonging and self-confidence;
- creativity embedded in everyday experience;
- meaning-making as a generative process influenced by and influencing other meanings; and
- a 'curriculum' that evolves based on the interest of learners and the questions they ask (Edwards et al. 2012a, b).

The role of the teacher is perceived as complex and multi-functional and includes:

- the interpretation of educational phenomena;
- flexibility to meet the needs of children, families and society;
- the co-construction of knowledge and negotiation of meanings;
- the creation of aesthetic environments designed to stimulate children's interests, questions and inquiries;
- facilitating the exchange of ideas and understandings; and
- observation and documentation as a researcher (Edwards 2012, p. 149).

In addition, the Reggio approach strongly advocates a perspective of language use in which children are encouraged to make meanings by inventing symbols in a variety of media rather than focussing on the translation of print (Edwards et al. 2012b, p. 5). It was in the context of this philosophy and practice that the project was undertaken.

7 Designing the Study

Given that the educational approach at the school emphasised inquiry-based learning initiated by children's interests, the investigative design of the study was influenced by qualitative methodology. This allowed the direction of the research to match the fluidity of the pedagogic approach. The primary means of data collection were participant observation (assistant educator), field notes (researcher), video and still image capture, documentary evidence and naturalistic discussion with parents. The researcher made regular visits to the school to observe literacy events and to record the progress of the research and direction the investigation was taking, in line with the changing interests of the children. In this way, the study was minimally intrusive, allowing both educators and children to engage in teaching and learning unencumbered by outside influence.

7.1 Documentation

Documenting the learning journey and the development of students is a central feature of educational activity in settings following a Reggio Emelia approach. Ways of documenting the work in this project and its outcomes replicated methods of data collection in more general forms of interpretivist research. It is the norm for educators in this setting to regularly note children's significant achievements and to produce daily written and photographic feedback to parents through a daily journal, which was displayed at the entrance to the room. These documents were used as one means of data collection.

7.2   Emergence of the Research Question

As with many projects in educational settings influenced by the philosophy and practice of Reggio Emilia, our investigation began with a question: What can I do in literacy with my children? At face value it was a simple question, but it was a question that emerged out of the encroaching shadows of synthetic phonics. Some of the parents of the children in the study were becoming more insistent that educators teach their children to read. The drive towards synthetic phonics that had begun in England almost a decade earlier was gaining ground in Australia, driven by several politicians and academics, including Jennifer Buckingham, a Senior Research Fellow at The Centre for Independent Studies, a neoliberal think tank based in Sydney. Buckingham (2016), along with the Minister for Education in the Liberal-led coalition government, Simon Birmingham (2017), reiterated arguments used to promote synthetic phonics in England. Hence, the search for an innovative approach to early literacy was driven by the need to satisfy parental pressure without compromising the school's educational philosophy by resorting to a synthetic phonics approach premised upon didactic teaching and direct instruction.

8   Implementation of the Project

In keeping with curriculum development following a Reggio approach, the project evolved as the assistant educator 'read' the interests of the students. In retrospect, however, it is possible to discern three interrelated elements to the project: educator-initiated activity, educator-facilitated activity and child-initiated activity. The first of these elements relates to the storytelling process itself, beginning with the use of symbols to represent characters and objects. Over several days, the assistant educator told three stories using symbols drawn on a whiteboard. The stories were: 'Goldilocks and the Three Bears', 'The Three Little Pigs' and *The Very Hungry Caterpillar* (Carle 2011). The first of these three appealed most to the students, so for a period of approximately three months, 'Goldilocks and the Three Bears' was told and retold numerous times. Cognisant of the fact this story is from the European tradition of fairy tales, and for the benefit of readers who may be unfamiliar with it, a synopsis follows:

> Goldilocks was walking in the woods one morning when she came across a house. The house belonged to three bears (daddy bear, mummy bear and baby bear) who had gone for a walk, leaving their breakfast of porridge (a mixture of oats and water or milk) to cool down. Goldilocks entered the house and on seeing the three bowls of porridge, a big bowl, a middle sized bowl and a little bowl, she instantly felt hungry. So she tasted the porridge in the big bowl and found it too hot. She did the same with the middle sized one and fond it too cold but baby bear's porridge in the small bowl was 'just right'. So, she ate it.

Venturing into the sitting room she found three chairs. The biggest, daddy bear's chair, was too hard; mummy bear's chair, the middle sized one, was too soft, but baby bear's chair, which was the smallest, was 'just right'. So, she sat on it and broke it.

Goldilocks then felt quite tired so she climbed the stairs to the bedroom where she lay on daddy bear's bed but it was too hard. She tried mummy bear's bed, but that was too soft. So she lay on baby bear's bed and that was 'just right'. She fell asleep straight away.

As she slept, the three bears returned and saw that baby bear's porridge had been eaten and that his chair had been broken. When they entered the bedroom, they saw a little girl asleep in baby bear's bed. Already distraught about his broken chair, baby bear cried out and woke Goldilocks. Seeing the three bears she screamed, jumped out of the window and ran all the way home.

This is normally how the story ends but the assistant educator experimented with endings to the story. On one occasion, she ended it with Goldilocks being put in gaol by the police. The students were inquisitive about the reason and were told that Goldilocks had not only trespassed in the house of the bears, she had also stolen their porridge and broken a chair. This version of the story became the students' preference at each telling. The second element of the project took two forms. The first involved minor changes to the students' learning environment designed to encourage spontaneous literacy activities related to the storytelling. The second brought students into contact with students from other rooms. The older children acted out the story for the younger ones. This enabled them to use their own language to 'reinvent' and internalise the story through the embodied actions of the characters. The third element might be described as activities undertaken by the students through which the story 'seeped' into the imaginative and cultural life of the class. Further details of the three elements are depicted in Fig. 1 below.

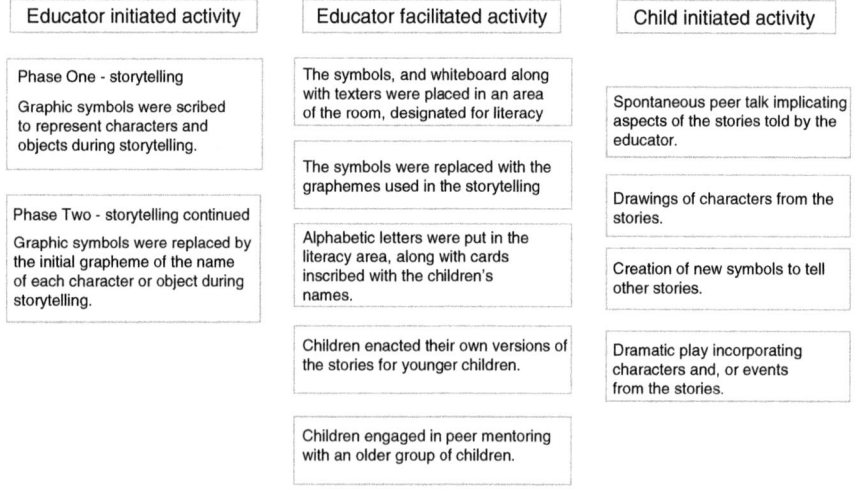

Fig. 1 The three elements of literacy development in the project

8.1 Element One: The Storytelling

The storytelling element involved two phases. In the first phase, the stories were told through symbols. Figure 2 includes most of the symbols used to tell the story of 'Goldilocks and the Three Bears'. In the second phase of development, the symbols used in the first phase morphed into the initial graphemes of the words they represented, as follows:

- The three straight, vertical lines representing the three bears were replaced with three lower case *b*'s of different sizes.
- The three 'circles' of porridge became three lower case *p*'s of different sizes.
- The triangles that had been chairs were translated into *ch*'s, again of three different sizes.
- The symbol for Goldilocks in the original story was represented by a spiral shape. This was replaced by a lower case *g* in the cursive script.
- In the initial phase, the stairs in the story, taken to reach the upper part of the house, were replaced with *st*. It was decided to replace the rectangles representing the beds with the whole word bed because the visual appearance of the word resembled the shape of a bed.

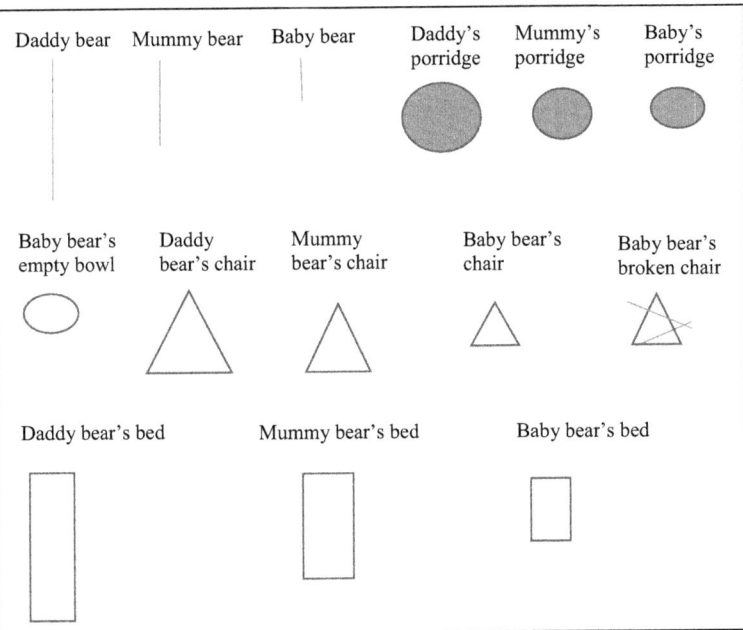

Fig. 2 Examples of symbols used in the first phase of the early literacy project

8.2   Element Two: Educator-Facilitated Activity

The symbols shown in Fig. 2 were drawn on a card, mounted on magnetic strips and placed in the literacy area where students were free to spontaneously engage with them. Individuals and groups were observed using the symbols to either tell the story in its entirety or to tell parts of the story. Some students also appeared to classify elements of the story. For example, several children placed the symbols representing items belonging to each of the bears in separate places on the magnetic board. Other students focussed on retelling part of the story, such as Goldilocks being put in gaol. A few students invented their own symbols and used a whiteboard pen on the whiteboard to tell the story of 'The Three Little Pigs'.

Students appeared to have no difficulty manipulating symbols to represent their imagined world. However, this will come as no surprise to early years practitioners or parents who have observed children's propensity to improvise with objects, using them as metaphors for elements of the physical world. Cereal packets can be cars and heavy vehicles and large cardboard boxes can be morphed into space rockets or cubby houses. As the symbols in the storytelling element were changed, so letter symbols were introduced into the literacy area. Letter symbols were referred to both by their respective names and sounds. There were opportunities for students to 'construct' letters using clay, cutters in playdough, paint and whiteboard pens. Transcripts of students' conversations during these activities show how they made heuristic connections between narrative and real life. For example, whilst investigating the shape of letters, one student observed a round pot on the table where she was working and commented: 'That's like Goldilocks' porridge'.

They also scaffolded the learning of peers as they observed one another. As a student wrote the letter *b*, another informed her she had missed a bit, pointing to the gap in the loop at the foot of the vertical line. A second student explained to the boy next to him how he had written the letter *p*, saying, 'I just did the straight line and then did the round bit.' On another occasion whilst working on the upper-case initial of their first names in clay, children began to identify how each letter was constructed:

'I have three lines', said Harvey.
'I have two said', said Tim.
'I need to cross it', said Anna, referring to the horizontal line in the letter *A*.

In other learning activities students were observed applying their phonemic awareness:

Educator, holding the grapheme *ch*: 'What is this one?'
Jay: 'Goldilocks.'
Educator: 'Yes, but what from Goldilocks?'
Jay: 'Chair.'

In this example, it appears that the student mentally located the grapheme in its textual context before identifying it as an initial phoneme. This was a common occurrence when letter symbols were first used. For example, the letter *g* was only seen to signify Goldilocks. It was not until the assistant educator initiated a mentoring arrangement with older children from another class that students began to make generalisations about letter-sound correspondences. The older children pointed out to their younger counterparts that both the letter *g* and other letter symbols from the Goldilocks story were the initial letters for other words too. It seems that this naturalistic collaborative talk around letter symbols was sufficient to initiate the younger children's development across their zone of proximal development (ZPD; Vygotsky 1986). Subsequently, students began to make connections between letter sounds, shapes and names in the story and words outside the story. The assistant educator reinforced this emerging awareness by expanding the repertoire of stories. As letter symbols were introduced in the story of 'The Three Little Pigs', students were encouraged to make parallel connections with the story of Goldilocks:

> Damien: It's *p* for pigs.
> Sam: Goldilocks …. Because it is *p* for porridge.
> Paul: It's a *b* [bricks]
> Educator: What is it in Goldilocks?
> Tony: For bear.
> Educator: Why have I used *bbw* for the wolf?
> Zac: 'Cause the big bad wolf starts with *b*.

The realisations that had occurred during storytelling became a form of spontaneous learning as students saw similarities in the names of their peers. Initially, connections were made in relation to initial phonemes when names were called:

> Ethan: *E* is in my name and in Emile's.

The same applied to letter-sound/name knowledge when names were written, e.g., Chad and Chloe.

Then more general connections were observed:

> Olivia: I have two *i*'s in my name and Sonia has one.
> Annie: We end the same [pointing to Ronnie's name].

Gradually, students became more interested in exploring letters in words than the stories in which they had been first embedded. It was the students themselves that had re-contextualised their learning. In commercial synthetic phonic programmes, the emphasis is on teaching and assessing: it is a process that is done to children. In the approach described here, students were the agents of change and learning processes were devised in response to students' readiness to take the next step across their ZPD. Other differences will be discussed below, but after six months students were able to write their names and the names of other peers. It might be argued that the more intense and systematic approach of synthetic phonics could have achieved the same result more quickly, but it would have been at the expense of the children's agency. In addition, a focused phonics approach might not have included the range and depth of exposure to and experience of language that was evident in this study.

8.3   Element Three: Child Initiated Activity

Observations of students during 'free play' revealed, through impromptu play and spontaneous talk, the extent to which the story of 'Goldilocks and the Three Bears' was woven into the narratives of their daily lives. For example, on hearing the siren of a passing emergency vehicle, one student speculated that it was the police looking for Goldilocks. The comment incited other students to contribute comments about what Goldilocks might have done, where she might be and where the police would take her once they had caught her. The circular climbing frame became a gaol and a bench the police car as students improvised the scene. One student justified putting another in the climbing frame on the grounds that he had 'been naughty and ate all the porridge'. These 'moments', along with developments more generally, were reported to parents, who reciprocated by sharing instances of how the story-telling and mark-making had been extended by the children in the home environment. Hence, divisions between home and school became porous as the children exported literacy learning. These impromptu scenarios are also indicative of children's exploration of text-to-life relationships through dramatic play and, as such, lay the grounds for understanding the function of literature in the socio-cultural landscape. A few students expressed concern that Goldilocks was at large and that people needed to be informed about her 'crimes'. The astute assistant educator responded by suggesting that maybe they should create a warning poster. Figure 3 is the outcome of the shared writing activity initiated by the students' concerns. The assistant educator elicited the students' language as she scribed and assisted them to collaboratively edit the text. Several copies of the poster were reproduced and displayed around the school, thereby contributing to the school's textual environment.

Fig. 3 Warning poster

WARNING !

There is a girl called Goldilocks who is breaking into houses, eating bowls of porridge, breaking chairs and sleeping in little beds.

If you are thinking about going for a walk, you should put a cover over your porridge and write your name on it.

From the children of XXXXXXXX room.

This scaffolded process, in which students and their educator collaborated to construct the text, gave children their first experience in school as authors, using conventional print. This is an empowering position for students and one they will never receive from a purely phonics-driven approach. Implicit to this process are the use of writing as a means of recording extended thought, rather than scribing single letters or words; an introduction to how language is syntactically constructed to create meaning; the format of a poster; the lexis and syntax of a form of persuasive writing; and the function of literacy as a social mechanism for communication and 'getting things done'.

In addition to the child-initiated learning activities in school, parents reported on their children's increased activity in the home environment around mark-making, storytelling, dramatic play and interest in books.

9 Outcomes of the Project

One significant difference between the approach to literacy acquisition in this project and the systematic approach using synthetic phonics advocated by proponents of that method is the breadth and depth of learning that occurred. In a synthetic phonics approach, students learn discrete letter-sound correspondences that are abstractions from language and the broader phonological system of English. Furthermore, these letter-sound abstractions are divorced from not only the semantic of individual words, but also language more generally. In contrast, this study shows that as students acquired increasing alphabetic and letter-sound knowledge, they understood its relevance by making connections between letters and sounds in different words. Although this knowledge was initially located in the stories, students were able to expand on these contexts and translate their knowledge into the graphophonia of the names of their peer group. The knowledge became generalisable as they recognised letter patterns and sounds across different words.

Although this was a relatively short, small-scale project, it serves as a useful prototype for those wishing to reclaim a place for more holistic approaches to early literacy development than is offered by synthetic phonic programmes and the repetition of decodable books. Instead of the rote learning of letter-sound correspondences, worksheets and a diet of made-up words, that often characterises synthetic phonic teaching, this project drew on children's implicit knowledge of signs and how they convey meaning. It contextualised small signifiers in stories that children appropriated into the narratives of their imagined and actual lives. The educator responded to their emerging interests and realisations rather than steering them though a battery of letters and sounds mandated by a manual.

What this project with very young children suggests is that literacy acquisition can be effective when small units of language are embedded in texts that engage students and where language is seen as multi-levelled, holistic and fluid. Furthermore, the project took place in an environment in which inquiry-based learning and the agency of the learner was central to the educational philosophy and pedagogic practice of the school.

References

Alexander, R. (2008). *Essays on Pedagogy*. Abingdon: Routledge.

Anstey, M., & Bull, G. (2009). Developing new literacies: Responding to picturebooks in multi-literate ways. In J. Evans (Ed.), *Talking beyond the page: Reading and responding to picture books*. Abingdon: Routledge.

Birmingham, S. (2017). Literacy and numeracy tests for Australian Year 1 students. The Australian. Retrieved from http://www.theaustralian.com.au/national-affairs/education/literacy-and-numeracy-tests-for-australian-year-1-students/news-story/fa826a1ae116a9a954abb1ff303b37c2

Buckingham, J. (2016). *Research report 22 focus on phonics: Why Australia should adopt the year 1 phonics screening check*. Sydney: Centre for Independent Studies.

Carle, E. (2011). *The very hungry caterpillar*. London: Puffin.

Cope, B., & Kalantzis, M. (2000). *Multiliteracies: Literacy learning and the design of social futures*. London: Psychology Press.

Davis, C. (2005). *A report of the OECD-CERI learning sciences and brain research. Shallow vs Non-shallow orthographies and learning to read workshop*. Centre for Neuroscience in Education, St. John's College, Cambridge University, 28–29 September 2005.

DEEWR [Department of Education, Employment and Workplace Relations]. (2009). *Belonging, being, becoming: The early year's framework for Australia*. Barton: Commonwealth of Australia.

DfE [Department for Education]. (2010). Reading at an early age the key to success. Retrieved from https://www.gov.uk/government/news/reading-at-an-early-age-the-key-to-success

DfE [Department for Education]. (2011). *Teachers standards in England*, Department for Education. Retrieved from https://www.gov.uk/government/uploads/system/uploads/attachment_data/file/283566/Teachers_standard_information.pdf

DfE [Department for Education]. (2013). *The national curriculum in England: Key Stages 1 and 2*. Retrieved from http://www.gov.uk/dfe/nationalcurriculum

DfES. (2007). Letter and sounds: Principles and practice of high quality phonics. Primary national strategy. Department for Education and Skills. Retrieved from https://www.gov.uk/government/uploads/system/uploads/attachment_data/file/190599/Letters_and_Sounds_-_DFES-00281-2007.pdf

Donnelly, K., & Wiltshire, K. (2014). *Review of the Australian curriculum: Final report*. Canberra: Australian Government Department of Education and Training.

Edwards, C. (2012). Teacher and learner, partner and guide: The role of the teacher. In C. Edwards, L. Gandini, & G. Foreman (Eds.), *The hundred languages of children: The Reggio Emilia experience in transformation*. Santa Barabara: Praeger.

Edwards, C., Gandini, L., & Foreman, G. (Eds.). (2012a). *The hundred languages of children: The Reggio Emilia experience in transformation*. Santa Barabara: Praeger.

Edwards, C., Gandini, L., & Forman, G. (2012b). Introduction: Background and starting points. In C. Edwards, L. Gandini, & G. Foreman (Eds.), *The hundred languages of children: The Reggio Emilia experience in transformation*. Santa Barbara: Praeger.

Ellis, S. (2007a). Review: early reading instruction: What science really tells us about how to teach reading. *Educational Review, 59*(4), 522–523.

Ellis, S. (2007b). Policy and research: Lessons from the Clackmannanshire Synthetic Phonics Initiative. *Journal of Early Childhood Literacy, 7*(3), 281–297.

Ellis, S., & Moss, G. (2014). Ethics, education policy and research: The phonics question reconsidered. *British Education Research Journal, 40*(2), 241–260.

Gardner, H. (1993). *Frames of the mind: The theory of multiple intelligences 10th anniversary edition*. New York: Basic Books.

Gibson, H., & England, J. (2016). The inclusion of pseudowords within the year one phonics "Screening Chec" in English primary schools. *Cambridge Journal of Education, 46*(4), 491–507.

Glazzard, J. (2017). Assessing reading development through synthetic phonics. *English in Education, 51*(1), 44–57.

Gove, M. (2013, September 5). Speech on improving the quality of teaching and leadership, at Policy Exchange, London. Retrieved from www.gov.uk/government/speeches/michael-gove-speaks-about-theimportance-of-teaching (3/11/13).

Harvey, P. (2005). Review: Early reading instruction: What science really tells us about how to teach reading. *Reading in a Foreign language, 17*(1), 78–82.

Heath, S. B. (1983). *Ways with words: Language, life and work in communities and classrooms.* New York: Oxford University Press.

Johnston, R., & Watson, J. (2005) *The effects of synthetic phonics teaching on reading and spelling attainment: A seven year longitudinal study.* Retrieved from http://www.gov.scot/Resource/Doc/36496/0023582.pdf

Kalantzis, M., Cope, B., Chan, E., & Dalley-Trim, L. (2016). *Literacies* (2nd ed.). Port Melbourne: Cambridge University Press.

Kaufman, D. K. (2005). Review: Early reading instruction: What science really tells us about how to teach reading. *Social and Behavioural Sciences, 43*(10), 1872.

Kear, D. J., & Gladhart, M. A. (1983). Comparative study to identify high-frequency words in printed materials. *Perceptual and Motor Skills, 57*(3), 807.

Landerl, K. (2000). Influences of orthographic consistency and reading instruction on the development of nonword reading skills. *European Journal of Psychology of Education, XV,* 239–257.

Lankshear, C., & Knobel, M. (2011). *New literacies.* Maidenhead: McGraw-Hill Education.

Lave, J., & Wenger, E. (1991). *Situated Learning: Legitimate Peripheral Participation.* Cambridge: Cambridge University Press.

Marshall, B. (2012). Synthetic phonics: The route to reading? In P. Adey & J. Dillon (Eds.), *Bad Education: Debunking myths in education.* Maidenhead: McGraw Hill/Open University Press.

McArthur, T. (Ed.). (1992). *The Oxford companion to the English language.* Oxford: Oxford University Press.

McGuinness, D. (2004). *Early reading instruction. What science really tells us about how to teach reading.* Cambridge, MA: MIT Press.

McMahon-Giles, R., & Wellhousen-Tunks, K. (2010). Children write their world: Environmental print as a teaching tool. *Dimensions of Early Childhood, 38*(3), 23–29.

Moats, L. (2014). Systematic, not 'balanced', instruction. *Learning Difficulties Australia Bulletin, 46*(3), 9–12.

Moss, G. (2009). The politics of literacy in the context of large-scale education reform. *Research Papers in Education, 24*(2), 155–174.

Mullis, I. V. S., Martin, M., Kennedy, A. M., & Foy, P. (2007). *PIRLS 2006 international report: IEA's progress in international reading literacy study in primary schools in 40 countries.* Chestnut Hill: Boston College.

OECD. (2010). *PISA 2009 results: Learning to learn – Student engagement: Strategies and practices* Vol III. Paris: OECD

Peirce, C. S. (1998). What is sign? In The Pierce Edition Project (ed). *Selected philospohical writings,* Volume 2 (1893–1913) (pp. 5–10). Bloomington: Indiana University Press.

Piaget, J. (2002). *Language and thought of the child.* London: Routledge.

Rose, J. (2006). *Independent review of the teaching of early reading.* London: DfES.

Rubizzi, L., & Bonilauri, S. (2012). From messages to writing: Experiences in literacy. In C. Edwards, L. Gandini, & G. Forman (Eds.), *The hundred languages of children: The Reggio Emilia experience in transformation* (3rd ed.). Santa Barbara: Praeger.

Snyder, I. (2008). *The literacy wars: Why teaching children to read and write is a battleground in Australia.* Crows Nest: Allen & Unwin.

Stirling and Clackmannanshire Education Service. (2015). *Scottish attainment challenge in Clackmannanshire 2015: Improving life through learning.* Sterling: Stirling and Clackmannanshire Education Service.

Street, B. (1985). *Literacy in theory and practice.* Cambridge: Cambridge University Press.

The Australian. (2017). *Literacy and numeracy tests for Australian Y1 students* – 29th January 2017. Retrieved from http://www.theaustralian.com.au/national-affairs/education/literacy-and-numeracy-tests-for-australian-year-1-students/news-story/fa826a1ae116a9a954abb1ff303b37c2

The New London Group. (1996). A pedagogy of multiliteracies: Designing social futures. *Harvard Educational Review, 66*(1), 60–93.

Torgerson, C. J., Brooks, G., & Hall, J. (2006). *A systematic review of the research literature on the use of phonic in the teaching of reading and spelling.* London: Department for Education and Skills.

UKLA. (2012). UKLA analysis of schools' response to the year 1phonics screening check Retrieved from https://www.teachers.org.uk/files/y1psc-survey-october-2012.pdf

Vygotsky, L. S. (1986). *Thought and language.* Cambridge: MIT Press.

Wenger, E. (2005). *Communities of practice: Learning, meaning and identity.* Cambridge: Cambridge University Press.

Westwood, P. (2009). A sound beginning for literacy: Three cheers for New South Wales. *Learning Difficulties Australia Bulletin, 41*(3), 10–12.

Wyse, D., & Goswami, U. (2008). Synthetic phonics and the teaching of reading. *British Educational Research Journal, 34*(6), 691–710.

Wyse, D., & Styles, M. (2007). Synthetic phonics and the teaching of reading: The debate surrounding England's 'Rose Report'. *Literacy, 41*(1), 35–42.

Ziegler, J. C., & Goswami, U. (2005). Reading acquisition, developmental dyslexia, and skilled reading across languages: A psycholinguistic grain size theory. *Psychological Bulletin, 131*, 3–29.

'To Blog, Not to Block': Examining EFL Learners' Language Development and Intercultural Competence in the Blogosphere Through the Sociocultural Lens

Julian Chen

Abstract The popularity of using blogs as online dialogue journals to share day-to-day activities with virtual audiences has grown substantially in the twenty-first century. As learners in English as a foreign language (EFL) contexts are growing in number, research on the extent to which blogging can bolster EFL learners' L2 development and intercultural competence is needed in order to contribute to the field of second-language acquisition (SLA). Specifically, studies situated within EFL contexts and framed by sociocultural theory (SCT) can provide dynamic and nuanced insights into how blogs as a digital platform can mediate and scaffold learners' knowledge construction, acquisition of language skills and cross-cultural awareness shaped by a wider blogging community. The purpose of this chapter, hence, is to examine EFL learners' language practices in the blogosphere as a social milieu. It is intended to enrich the discussion on the interplay between EFL learners' cultural and linguistic repertoires and their co-construction of new knowledge with authentic audiences. Empirical studies are critically reviewed through the SCT lens as an SLA framework to further explain how blogging can break the in- and outside-class boundaries and empower EFL learners. Research and pedagogical implications are also synthesized and highlighted by a selection of commonly used blog platforms for language teaching and research.

Keywords Blogging · Sociocultural theory · English as a foreign language · Learner autonomy · Authentic audience · Knowledge co-construction · Intercultural competence · Virtual community building

J. Chen (✉)
School of Education, Curtin University, Perth, WA, Australia
e-mail: julian.chen@curtin.edu.au

© Springer Nature Switzerland AG 2019
T. Dobinson, K. Dunworth (eds.), *Literacy Unbound: Multiliterate, Multilingual, Multimodal*, Multilingual Education 30,
https://doi.org/10.1007/978-3-030-01255-7_12

1   A Brief Overview of the Blogging Phenomenon in Language Education

Since their debut in the digital age two decades ago, blogs (derived from 'weblogs') continue to be favoured by Internet users worldwide in addition to other popular social networking tools (e.g., Facebook, Twitter and Instagram). Bloggers update posts regularly to share their thoughts, pictures, music and even videos with family, friends and other bloggers who also share similar beliefs, values and interests in this virtual community. According to a statistical report conducted by Statista (2017), the number of blog sites increased globally from 35.8 million in 2006 to 173 million in 2011, and 65% of active blog users are aged between 18 and 44 (Technorati 2010). Blogging mania has also attracted language teachers, educators and researchers, who are exploring how this vibrant blogosphere, 'the "intellectual cyberspace" that [bloggers] occupy' (Ferdig and Trammell 2004, p. 12), can offer pedagogically feasible and theoretically sound applications for language learners in and outside the classroom (Bloch 2007; Campbell 2003; Lee 2015; Miceli et al. 2010; Mynard 2008).

As far as online learning tools are concerned, the network-based environment has been distinguished into two sequential spheres: the first-generation web and the second-generation web (Godwin-Jones 2003). The former is composed of two different online tools: asynchronous and synchronous tools. Asynchronous tools, such as emails and discussion boards typically embedded in a learning management system, encourage peer-to-peer networking and collaborative learning at students' own pace and enhance student engagement beyond the class walls. Synchronous tools, such as chat rooms and instant messengers, promote spontaneous communication with peers or others in real time. The second-generation web manifests itself in blogs and wikis that facilitate peer collaboration and knowledge co-construction in an online environment. Blogs, also another form of asynchronous tool, have piqued the widespread interest of teacher educators to create a collaborative online environment for language teaching and learning. The personalised design and user-friendliness of blogs also make them more socially appealing and conducive to stimulating interaction between blog authors and an authentic audience, who could be blog readers in real life outside a class (Kennedy 2003; Oravec 2002). The editing interface in Blogger, a website for creating blogs, for example, is as intuitive and simple as writing in a Microsoft Word environment. Blog authors can track the most updated pageviews of each blog entry and the number of followers coming from all over the world (see Fig. 1). The ease of self-publishing and control of 'my own blog' fosters a sense of ownership that encourages students to take responsibility for their learning as independent thinkers and creators (Pinkman 2005; Thorne and Payne 2005). These affordances also heighten students' motivation and willingness to invest more self-directed linguistic effort into language learning than do academic discussion boards configured in learning management systems (e.g., Blackboard or Moodle) with a more "serious" feel (Miceli et al. 2010; Sun 2009, 2012).

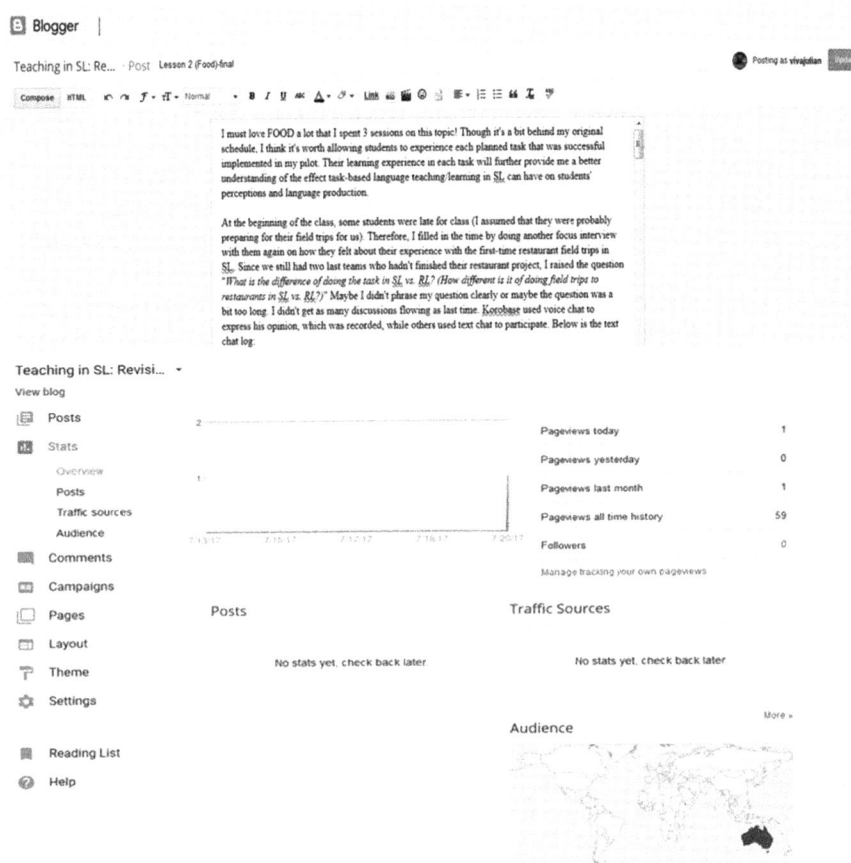

Fig. 1   The editing features and pageviews tracking system in Blogger

Blood (2002) further identifies two different types of blogs based on their distinct styles and functions: (a) traditional weblogs (filter style), which provide a filtering service and tools for carefully controlling information available on the web, and (b) free-style blogs (journal style), which lend themselves to freedom of self-expression. She argues that blogging can mediate peoples' thinking processes, promote new web genre literacy, and transform both writers and readers from 'audience' to 'public' and from 'consumer' to 'creator'. This view is echoed by Thorne and his colleagues' longitudinal study following Spanish language learners in high school for an academic year and examining their attitudes toward keeping regular blog entries as online diaries (Thorne and Payne 2005). They found that students favoured blogging over traditional journals: the open, sharing online atmosphere and the fact that they could keep track of their own and peers' posts and respond to peer comments on their posts heightened the level of their interest and motivation. Students also perceived positive language gains in relation to the writing fluency and attention they paid to the quality of the writing in their posts because they were writing for an audience.

The potential of blending language play into blogging is also vividly evidenced in Sauro and Sundmark's (2016) study. In order to bridge the 'language and literature divide in English language teaching' (p. 415), the authors set up a task-based fan-fiction project for 55 student teachers enrolled in a literature course at a Swedish university. J. R. R. Tolkien's *The Hobbit* was selected for this project due to its popularity with the online fan fiction communities and students' familiarity with this fantasy novel. The students, in groups of three to six, were responsible for taking on characters from *The Hobbit* and recreated missing moments in the storyline from their chosen characters' perspectives through collaborative role-play blogging. Student reflection papers and oral presentations illustrated how a collaborative fan-fiction task project could foster Swedish EFL students' linguistic competence in vocabulary expansion and grammar knowledge and their literacy competence in building rhetoric and audience awareness for creative writing. More specifically, 'reading the sourced text sufficiently' (p. 421) enabled them to create a more logical and sound storyline following the fan-fiction genre. This blog project further nurtured their vocabulary repertoire and reading fluency, capitalizing on the collaborative writing that shaped and was shaped by all the contributors in a spontaneous and authentic way.

The recent advancement of mobile technology, configured in smartphones and tablet devices, has also changed the way we teach and learn in the twenty-first century. These digital devices allow language teachers to visually and textually synergize input enhancement and output stimulation through multimodal blogging (Hauck and Youngs 2008). A case in point is asynchronous voice blogs (or audio blogs) that go beyond standard text-based posting and enable learners to use multimodal representations (e.g., text, pictures, audios and videos) to reinforce voice-based blog posts and elicit oral comments from peers (Huang 2015). VoiceThread, for example, is an educational platform where users can use a built-in microphone and camera in a computer or texting function in a smartphone to make voice or textual comments on peers' threads in multimodal representations (see Fig. 2). Learners can produce and monitor their language output at their own pace (Sun 2009), which in turn provides rich oral samples for teachers to assess student speaking performance as measured by complexity, accuracy and fluency (Hsu 2016; Sun 2012).

Finally, compared with other popular social media (e.g., Facebook, Twitter and Instagram) that herald rapid communication and brief texting, blog posts can be used for social networking purposes that tend to be informal and shorter or for educational purposes that are typically lengthier and academically demanding. As such, their versatility, user-friendliness, interactivity and personalized layout (Tan et al. 2005) have made blogs a digital platform that is appealing to language teachers and researchers who are keen on exploring its impact on language pedagogy and research.

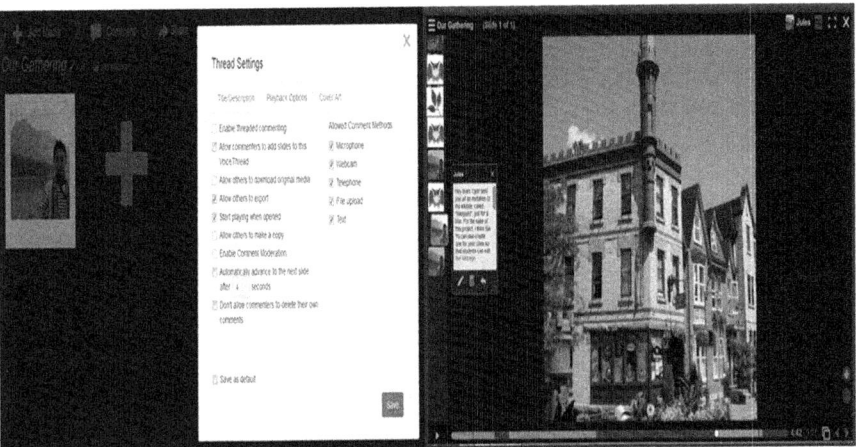

Fig. 2 Multimodal commenting features in VoiceThread and a snapshot of text commenting demonstration

2 Why Blogging in EFL Teaching and Research?

While blogs are deemed a promising digital tool for language pedagogy, we also need to critically evaluate those positive claims in terms of relevant SLA theories and instructional settings before wholeheartedly pursuing this blogging approach. Research on blogging in EFL contexts is specifically worth exploring. A common trend in classroom-based observation in EFL contexts (e.g., China, Japan and Korea) is that students lack opportunities to use English for meaningful communicative purposes. Students' exposure to and practice of the target language are unfortunately limited to the language class, ranging from two to four contact hours weekly, and the curriculum is typically textbook driven, with greater weight placed on scripted oral practices, vocabulary and grammar drilling (Huang 2015). Since English is not a language commonly used in EFL contexts on a daily basis, students often switch back to their native language outside the class. The lack of using English for meaningful and real-life purposes also demotivates and challenges them when it comes to productive skills in speaking and writing (Azari 2017; Chen 2012). Furthermore, because of budget concerns, large class sizes are not uncommon. For example, there may be 30–50 students in a college freshman English class or 100 students in a reading/writing class offered at a medical university in Taiwan. Large class sizes, therefore, make classroom management for communicative practices even harder and time sufficiently given to each student even more challenging (Hsu 2016). Another case in point is Seargeant's (2009) critical review of the English teaching/learning phenomenon in Japan. Despite the "communicative approach" promoted by the Ministry of Education, he concluded that Japanese EFL students still find English learning a daunting task even after years of English instruction. Complex socio-political and ideological factors, such as examination-driven educational systems and teacher-led and pattern-drilled instruction, unfortunately still predominate in how English is taught and learned not only in Japan but also in some other EFL countries. As such, it would give us some insight to examine whether incorporating blogs in EFL contexts could offer an innovative alternative to classroom-based language instruction, benefit EFL learners' language development, foster intercultural competence and promote a sense of autonomy and audience awareness through blogging (Sun 2012).

Drawing on Vygotsky's social learning theory, it has been argued that learners use the target language to mediate knowledge construction through the process of meaning making and interaction with others. In this sense, 'knowledge construction is discursive, relational and conversational in nature' (Ferdig and Trammell 2004, p. 13), and blogs provide a space for students to transform and publish their knowledge construction and for teachers to get a sense of their meaning making while providing feedback using the commenting feature. Student learning experiences are hence scaffolded and enriched during the interactive process of knowledge sharing and feedback exchange. Additionally, blogs provide a sociocultural playground for language acquisition to take place and knowledge to be socially constructed in a collaborative virtual community. Miceli et al. (2010) also argue that the personalisation, authentic communication and communal support available through peer collaboration in the blogosphere provide a less threatening platform for students who tend to be shy or anxious to have their say more freely with less inhibition than in face-to-face classrooms. This view is also shared by Ducate and Lomicka's (2008) finding, in that their students in blogging appeared to be 'comfortable expressing themselves more openly than in class' (p. 18). In this sense, another research lens could zoom in on how blogging can raise EFL learners' metalinguistic awareness, mediate their use of language for cognitive development, strengthen their construction of new language knowledge and foster their intercultural competence through interaction with peers, teachers and other English speakers. Also worth noting is that studies on the effects of blogging on foreign language teaching and learning from the sociocultural approach are relatively scarce, despite the fact that research on educational blogging is not in its infancy, since it first occurred in the late 1990s (Huang 2015; Sun 2009). Hence, taking a sociocultural lens to examine the interplay between EFL learners' language development and intercultural awareness and competence that are co-constructed in and shaped by the blogging community deserves more research attention in the field of SLA.

In light of the pedagogical and research concerns raised above, this chapter will go on to examine the blogging phenomenon in EFL contexts by first reviewing sociocultural theory as an SLA framework and discuss the underpinning principles in relation to studies on the effects of using blogs for language teaching and learning. The conceptual discussion will pave the way for arguing why sociocultural theory could provide a more dynamic and holistic framework for situating blogging research, particularly in EFL contexts. Empirical studies on blogging will then be critically examined in terms of their conceptual frameworks, research contexts and gaps that still need to be bridged. The chapter will then conclude with implications for future research and practice in blogging with attention paid to EFL learners' SLA, intercultural awareness and competence, and sense of ownership and authentic audience that are usually lacking in a conventional EFL class.

3 Sociocultural Theory as a Conceptual Stance

> Language instruction was viewed not just in terms of providing comprehensible input, but rather as helping students enter into the kinds of authentic social discourse situations and discourse communities that they would later encounter outside the classroom. (Kern and Warschauer 2000, p. 5)

Kern and Warschauer (2000) indicate that EFL learners and teachers are now standing at the crossroads of a traditional classroom and an interactive network-based environment. Given the fact that students are connected to various social networking platforms on a daily basis, disconnecting English learning from their real-life practices using these online tools is doing them a pedagogical disservice. The commenting feature of blogs promotes the interactional process of realizing the language acquisition of EFL learners, breaking the in- and outside-class boundaries in EFL settings. Blogs can infuse real-life interactivity into language learning if effectively implemented into practice. This notion further indicates that the nuanced social aspects of the dynamic blogging phenomenon in which language acquisition is socioculturally co-constructed, justifying the adequacy of using a sociocultural lens to examine learners' language practices mediated by blogs. The key word *social* comes into play to foreground the aspects of sociocultural and intercultural competence that 'emphasize linguistic and personal benefits to be gained through stretching competence with a partner or within a community of learners' (Chapelle 2005, p. 60). This opens up a new research avenue for exploring how EFL learners acquire new knowledge, develop language skills, establish learner identity and boost positive motivation through social interaction with other blogging members (Lee 2015).

4 Sociocultural Theory (SCT)

> We also use symbolic tools, or signs, to mediate and regulate our relationships with others and with ourselves ... , in Vygotsky's view, ... to understand how human social and mental activity is organized through culturally constructed artefacts and social relationships. (Lantolf 2000, p. 1)

In this section, SCT related to blogging research will be reviewed. Taking the Vygotskian approach, I will justify why SCT (Lantolf 2000, 2006; Warschauer 2005; Wells 1999) provides a viable framework for research on the interplay of blogging and EFL learners. Warschauer (2005, p. 41) suggests that 'examining

Vygotsky's contributions helps us to understand how sociocultural theory can be applied to computer-assisted language learning'. With *mediation*, the key notion of Vygotskian SCT, it can be conceptualized that the higher forms of human mental processing are mediated (Lantolf 2000). What we can deduce from this Vygotskian view in terms of CALL is that modern technological artefacts—such as computers, digital tools (e.g., blogs, IMs and Skype) and language itself—mediate our thoughts in the course of interactive activities in which we are participating. The concept of mediation also sheds pedagogical light on how language is acquired through complex socio-cognitive processes, since language is also one of the key symbolic tools mediating our day-to-day practices. If we venture to realize this SCT notion in the blogosphere from the standpoint of activity theory under the Vygotskian framework (see Leontiev 1981, in Mitchell et al. 2013), online blogging interactivity (*activity*) is undertaken by learners (*subject*) who are motivated toward improving their literacy competence (*goal* or *object*) and is mediated by the blogging tool (*artefact*) through collaboration with the other members in blogosphere (*community*). By the same token, the learners' cognition and behaviours are intertwined within and across themselves, the symbolic tool used and the activities jointly constructed with other members, who are also mediated by the same tool. In other words, the learner initiates blog posts as an active agent who explores, processes and synthesizes content information to improve language proficiency (e.g., reading) outside the class, while refining and sharing written blog posts with the audience (Miceli et al. 2010). This concept illustrates how online communication tools can socially mediate language learners' acquisition of a target language and construction of new knowledge.

Social learning, the second pivotal Vygotskian concept, centres on the notion that children's cognitive development levels are twofold: their cognitive development in problem solving independently and the 'higher level' of cognitive development in problem solving through collaboration with capable peers or guidance received from adults (see Vygotsky 1978). This view of *apprenticeship learning*, also known as *zone of proximal development* (ZPD), has been an integral part of Vygotskian SCT: 'the domain of knowledge or skill where the learner is not yet capable of independent functioning, but can achieve the desired outcome given relevant assistance' (Mitchell et al. 2013, p. 223). Within this ZPD scope, learning is viewed as a social inter-mental activity, and appropriation of new knowledge (e.g., language) is jointly constructed with peers or experts in the sociocultural context in which learners are involved. But how can this concept be valuable for conducting research on computer-based communication (CMC)? Warschauer (2005) answers the question by illustrating that 'it [social learning] can help us understand, for example, both how learners incorporate others' linguistic chunks (phrases, collocations, etc.) in CMC … and also how they refine their writing for, and with input from, an authentic audience' (p. 43). Blogs, a CMC tool, enable language learners to stretch their ZPD in their current target-language repertoire by reflecting, co-constructing and internalizing newly learned linguistic knowledge through interaction with peers. Feedback received from their peers can further scaffold their language acquisition when they are blogging in or outside the classroom, thereby operationalizing ZPD in the blogosphere (Huang 2015). That is, less competent learners have the chance to emulate their language use and style and improve the writing quality of blog posts to reach their full potential. As Wells (1999) vividly illustrates, 'To learn in the ZPD does not require that there be a designated teacher; whenever people collaborate in an activity, each can assist the others, and each can learn from the contributions of the others' (p. 333).

Conceptualized in Vygotskian SCT theory, language is viewed as a symbolic tool that mediates not only our mental functioning but also social communication. Lantolf (2006) extends the notion by debunking the dichotomous view that 'language serves only to transmit thought,' asserting rather that, 'language and culture should be seen as a whole' and grounded in 'languaculture' (p. 73). Since languaculture 'shapes consciousness, shapes ways of seeing and acting, shapes ways of thinking and feeling' (Agar 1994, p. 71; for further discussion on languaculture [or linguaculture], see Risager 2012), it mirrors Vygotskian theory that learning is first social and then individual. Our mental functioning, mediated by symbolic tools (e.g., language, technology), also depends on how these tools are used. In this sense, learners' mental processing may develop over time as they 'appropriate the semiotic systems of their languaculture' (Lantolf 2006, p. 78). Since the nature of blogging transcends the boundaries of in- and outside-class activities, it serves as a mediating device to regulate learners' development, not of language per se, but languaculture as a whole in the dynamic blogosphere. Blogging also extends and stretches the learning potential to appropriate new knowledge through interacting with or receiving scaffolds from members in the collaborative virtual community. Hence, the social, collaborative blogging phenomenon is 'consistent with the Vygotskian sociocultural perspective in which knowledge is defined as social in nature and is constructed through a process of collaboration, interaction and communication among learners in social settings and as the result of interaction within the ZPD' (Nassaji and Swain 2000, p. 49).

Through the SCT lens, I will now examine studies on the application of blogs for SLA and scrutinize the strengths and weaknesses of their research and their pedagogical implications for EFL teaching and learning.

5   A Critical Analysis of Empirical Studies on Blogs

Studies related to blogging were analysed against two key parameters: the SLA theoretical frameworks on which they are based and the contexts in which they are conducted. In general, most studies have been framed by interactionist theory and suggest that the commenting feature of blogs creates an interactive dialogue between the student blogger and the audience. One of their key findings resonates with the cornerstone of interactionist theory, negotiation for meaning, and is that collaborative blogging can promote the development of L2 learners' linguistic competence and literacy skills in reading and writing (Bloch 2007; Huffaker 2005; Oravec 2002; Pinkman 2005). The whole blogging process also demonstrates that learners' linguistic awareness is heightened by the feedback received from their authentic audience through negotiation for meaning, which makes their blog posts more refined and 'presentable' to their audience (Lee 2015). In other words, the negotiation process can promote linguistic modifications due to the received comprehensible input, which will draw their conscious attention to those trouble spots in linguistic forms, leading to their language development.

As Canale and Swain (1980) assert, grammatical competence is only one of the elements of communicative competence, which also comprises sociocultural, discourse and strategic aspects. Despite the positive claims reported above, research on blogging from the interactionist approach has only addressed the linguistic benefits of blogging at the expense of the nuanced personal, social and cultural aspects that subtly shape and are shaped by learners' interactivity with members in the blogging community.

Studies grounded in Vygotskian SCT illustrate that blogs enable students to take ownership of their learning via the self-publishing feature (Arslan and Şahin-Kızıl 2010; Azari 2017; Sun 2009). Utilising multimodal artefacts (e.g., pictures and audio and video files) further mediates their thoughts and processing of the target language (Ferdig and Trammell 2004; Hauck and Youngs 2008; Thorne and Payne 2005). In voice blogs, for example, feedback can be exchanged with peers, and learning from peer blog posts that establish a role model in language use can foster the use of metacognitive strategies to monitor, reformulate and evaluate the quality of language production (Sun 2009, 2012). The socially co-constructed blogging process, in this case, leads to metalinguistic awareness of both form and meaning in the target-language output. As such, blogs can serve as an optimal vehicle to mediate the ongoing social learning of EFL learners' language development in knowledge construction and meaning-making processes (Ducate and Lomicka 2005).

Through the Vygotskian ZPD lens, the findings discussed above also illustrate that less proficient learners benefit from the scaffolds provided by their capable peers who share resources and offer constructive comments and learning strategies in the blogging community (Chen 2016). The collaborative virtual community in the blogosphere promotes peer scaffolding, which, in turn, reinforces learners' development of metacognitive skills and quest for knowledge construction guided by capable members within their ZPD. The more technologically proficient students, for example, can help their less competent counterparts in order to finish a problem-solving task through collaborative blogging (Tan et al. 2005, 2006). Above all, this 'dialogic mediation' fosters a sense of ownership as EFL learners move from the role of possibly passive and reticent students in class to content contributors and knowledge providers in the blogging community (Lee 2015).

When it comes to the interplay of language and culture, Thorne and Payne (2005) argue that using internet-mediated technologies such as blogs can promote intercultural communication that builds on learners' development in L2 pragmatics and awareness of languaculture. The advancement of smartphones nowadays also facilitates intercultural communication. The affordances of mobile blogging enable students to use built-in multimodal features (e.g., video/audio recording, image capturing and texting) to enrich blog posts in cross-cultural projects that are linguistically, culturally and affectively stimulating (e.g., interviewing native speakers of the target culture or project partners from different cultures by sharing their intercultural awareness and understanding; see Hauck and Youngs 2008). When studying abroad or conducting telecollaborative tasks, students can not only use mobile phones to initiate blog posts at any time and anywhere, but also reply to comments from cohorts with different cultural backgrounds—a 'liberating experience, allowing students both to explore cultural insights and experiment with the target language' (Godwin-Jones 2013, p. 5).

Finally, regarding research contexts of studies on blogging, most studies focus on how the blogging phenomenon has an impact on language learning and teaching in ESL classrooms (Bloch 2007; Campbell 2003; Huffaker 2004, 2005; Kennedy 2003) or foreign language settings, such as German, French or Chinese (see Ducate and Lomicka 2005, 2008; Tan et al. 2005, 2006). The findings of these studies indicate that blogs can be beneficial for language learners' cultural and communicative competences, critical thinking skills, improvement of literacy proficiency and construction of new knowledge through meaningful interaction (Lee 2015). However, some studies only draw on personal or anecdotal teaching experience in adopting blogs in class without theorizing their research (Campbell 2003; Tan et al. 2005) or grounding them in any relevant SLA theories to justify why blogs can contribute to SLA research and pedagogy (Huffaker 2004, 2005; Kennedy 2003). As far as EFL contexts are concerned, some studies address the advantages of incorporating blogs in EFL classrooms. For example, blogs can optimize the development of EFL learners' writing proficiency (Johnson 2004), promote a sense of autonomy and use of learning strategies (Mynard 2008), lower learning anxiety (Sun 2012), boost engagement and motivation (Pinkman 2005), and facilitate EFL teaching and learning (Wu 2006). This opens up a potential avenue for future research in this area.

6   Implications from Incorporating Blogs in EFL Contexts: Teaching and Research

As evidenced in the reviewed studies, ease of use without complex technical skills, low cost, personalized design and flexible access make blogs suitable for implementation in EFL classrooms (Oravec 2002; Pinkman 2005; Thorne and Payne 2005; Sun 2012). Given that no HTML or FTP knowledge is required in blogging and it is convenient to publish blog entries instantly (Blood 2002; Godwin-Jones 2003; Huffaker 2004), EFL teachers can easily set up a *tutor blog* that provides updated resources to extend student learning. Teachers can also introduce a personal *learner blog* for students to get more writing practice, or create a *class blog* that facilitates peer-to-peer and student-to-teacher interaction, streamlines content delivery and assignment submission, and enables cross-cultural language-exchange projects (Campbell 2003; Johnson 2004). Blogs offer free personal spaces and the 'easy archival' feature of 'reverse chronological arrangement' (Tan et al. 2005, p. 4) for student bloggers to easily organize and systematically search entries, write blog posts and receive constructive feedback from peer and teacher readers during the drafting and revision stages (Thorne and Payne 2005). This mechanism facilitates the process approach to writing in an EFL writing class (Azari 2017) and 'fosters development of metacognitive strategies for monitoring the progress of learning on the blog' (Sun 2009, p. 89).

Due to their multimodal features that allow for textual, audio and video postings, EFL teachers can capitalize on the multimodality of blog functions and incorporate blog activities seamlessly into assessment across language skills. Take voice-based blogs, for example. Sun (2012) demonstrated that EFL teachers can provide extensive speaking practice by having students post voice blog entries in response to their chosen topics as well as make voice responses to peers' blogs in order to overcome the insufficient time for speaking practice in most EFL classrooms. Teachers as researchers can then examine student speaking performance and their perceived language gains on the levels of accuracy, complexity, fluency and pronunciation. A voice-based blogging project can further develop learning strategies in planning and gathering ideas for an appropriate topic (conceptualizing stage), organizing ideas and writing down a script (brainstorming stage), rehearsing and recording voice blog entries (articulation stage), monitoring the quality of the speaking performance before publishing (monitoring stage) and evaluating the content and language delivery before redoing the recording (evaluating stage; Sun 2009). This robust versatility affords EFL teachers the opportunity to take advantage of each publishing mode in conjunction with other synchronous tools (e.g., real-time text/voice chat) and tailor language tasks to the needs and interests of their students, ranging from reflecting on assigned readings or keeping personal journals (textual mode: reading/writing), posting reactions to radio news clips or English podcasts (audio mode: listening) and to making a five-minute show-and-tell presentation on a specific topic (video mode: speaking; Hauck and Youngs 2008). As such, 'blogs have emerged in many educational contexts as a promising tool to facilitate learning' (Sun 2012, p. 495).

In the following, eight research and pedagogical implications have been identified and highlighted by the educational affordances of blogging inside and beyond EFL classrooms: sense of ownership and autonomy; virtual community building; awareness of authentic audience; motivation and knowledge construction; language skills development and metalinguistic awareness; project-based, task-supported learning; intercultural competence and empowerment. A selection of commonly used blog platforms for research and educational purposes are also annotated and presented in the Appendix. Each of these implications is explored in further detail below.

6.1 Sense of Ownership and Autonomy

The nature of blogging for online diaries stimulates bloggers to regularly post blog entries to freely express personal thoughts and reflections about their worldviews in order to engage in ongoing conversations with like-minded bloggers who also share similar interests or find their posts interesting. From the educational standpoint, blogs promote a sense of ownership, encouraging students to make informed decisions about what to display and to take responsibility for their learning (Mynard 2008; Pinkman 2005; Tan et al. 2005; Zorko 2007). Blog features, such as self-publishing, personalised customisation, personal blog space, control of archival structure and alerting of reader comments, afford language students a sense of ownership as blog authors (Thorne and Payne 2005; Sun 2012). Therefore, blogging develops their own identity as 'real authors' (Godwin-Jones 2003) and '[transforms] both writers and readers from "audience" to "public" and from "consumer" to "creator"' (Blood 2002, p. 16). In a process-oriented writing class supported by blogging, Azari (2017) found that gaining multiple perspectives on their writing as authors, and comparing their written products with those 'role models' written by peers, stimulated EFL students to write more and refine their work. As such, blogging motivates them to take ownership for their own learning as 'subject-matter experts' who are responsible for and take pride in the content and information they contribute (Ferdig and Trammell 2004, p. 14).

6.2 Virtual Community Building

The commenting feature of blogs promotes interaction where students can freely comment and respond with teachers, peers or even an authentic audience (e.g., invited guests) to form a virtual community outside the class (Blood 2002; Farmer 2004; Ferdig and Trammell 2004; Godwin-Jones 2003; Huffaker 2004, 2005). From the Vygotskian perspective, EFL teachers can extend the use of personal blogging to a class blog, in that student bloggers can exchange ideas and share resources by publishing entries, posting comments and responding to feedback received from peer bloggers or the teacher (Huffaker 2004). This social network building can also go beyond the class walls and reach out to another blogging community, be it language exchange partners or cross-cultural project counterparts. Kennedy (2003), for example, highlighted one of the case studies on using blogs in an English class. A high school English teacher created a class blog for his students in American literature to post responses to the assigned reading, *The Secret Life of Bees* by Sue Monk Kidd. The teacher not only asked students to use different angles, such as artistic interpretations, to critique the selected images and chapters from the novel, but further invited the author to respond to the comments and questions posted by the students in the blog. He also noticed the impact this class blog had on his students' writing by raising their awareness of the writing quality with a potential audience in mind. Miceli et al. (2010) also argued that the affordances of authentic communication, mutual contributions via posting and commenting, peer collaboration and connectedness can nurture a sense of belonging and heighten the communal bonding outside the class. Reticent EFL students, in particular, benefit more from this community building extended to a class blog, a shared third space for them to be more proactive as blog contributors.

6.3 Awareness of Authentic Audience

Self-publishing blog entries online and receiving feedback from different readers gives students a purpose in that they are writing for a real audience. EFL teachers, hence, can '[reach] out into virtual and professional communities for collaborative opportunities' by involving subject experts, real authors and even parents to serve as a virtual audience and editors of student blogs (Kennedy 2003). Authentic interaction with a 'global audience' (e.g., native English speakers) other than a de facto teacher/classmate audience will also heighten learner motivation and independence (Pinkman 2005). The sense of audience awareness (Chen 2012; Chen and Brown 2012; Lee 2015) also leads to learners' attention being paid to the quality of language output (e.g., content and organization in writing; see Arsian and Şahin-Kizil 2010; Azari 2017), allowing them to internalize comprehensible input received during feedback exchange with the authentic audience (Ducate and Lomicka 2005, 2008; Ferdig and Trammell 2004; Oravec 2002). Miceli et al. (2010) suggested that writing through authentic interaction with the teacher and peer readers in blogs lends itself to the awareness of 'a real audience' and a stimulus for ongoing commitment and refinement of the written products during different stages of recursive writing (Chen and Brown 2012). This approach of incorporating blogging into writing also sets it apart from a traditional writing class where the teacher is usually the sole reader. EFL teachers can also make the blogs public to invite a real audience to comment on students' published posts, as opposed to solely the teacher and classmates. This communal channel allows learners to receive multiple perspectives from a wider authentic readership, thereby fostering knowledge co-construction and stimulating them to invest more time and effort in publishing their blog entries (Ferdig and Trammell 2004).

6.4 Motivation and Knowledge Construction

The interactive two-way communication of posting exchanges boosts students' self-motivation and engagement (Pinkman 2005; Zorko 2007). That is, being able to exchange ideas with different readers and responding to their comments serves as a motivator for student authors to look forward to spontaneous and authentic reader comments while developing critical thinking skills to address constructive feedback (Mynard 2008; Oravec 2002). From the Vygotskian SCT perspective, a case study conducted by Lee (2015) illustrates how blogging as a digital platform to mediate extensive reading can scaffold literacy development in the depth of reading (measured by the number of idea units) and writing fluency (measured by the number of words). During a year-long extensive reading program, intermediate-level EFL college students demonstrated progress in an experimental literacy club project where they were required to reflect on self-selected readings (e.g., *Holes* by Louis Sachar or *Harry Potter* by J. K. Rowling), exchange feedback and offer support on reading materials through blogging. They were able to express more content-specific ideas, get motivated to read and write for communicative and meaningful purposes, gain control of their own learning and develop critical thinking skills, and co-construct knowledge with the club members. Similarly, Huang's (2015) study also indicates the benefits of using voice blogs as scaffolding to help EFL learners not only develop oral communication skills but also construct new knowledge through synthesizing content information and getting inspired by those shared and exchanged ideas for authentic and meaningful purposes.

6.5 Language Skills Development and Metalinguistic Awareness

Blogging enhances EFL learners' language skills development, such as reading authentic materials about topics and incorporating blogging into a process approach to writing (Azari 2017; Blood 2002; Ducate and Lomicka 2008; Huffaker 2004, 2005; Johnson 2004) or improving listening and speaking skills via voice blogging (Huang 2015; Hsu 2016; Sun 2012). Given the fact that blogs are similar in nature to online journal or diary keeping, this feature promotes the exploration of creativity and self-expression, which in turn facilitates the task of digital storytelling and fosters literacy development in an EFL reading/writing class (Huffaker 2004, 2005). Additionally, storytelling through blogging is not only limited to the fictional genre, but can be multidisciplinary across academic subjects in ways such as exchanging ideas and reflecting on lessons learned from a scientific project or vicariously transporting oneself and reacting to a historical event (Huffaker 2004). Metalinguistic awareness can also be raised during the process of interactive blogging, as evidenced in Chen's (2016) study. Twenty-six Taiwanese EFL students in a university English writing class were randomly assigned to a control group that completed writing assignments in paper format (i.e., essay writing, learning journal and peer essay review) and an experimental group that used a class blog and student blogs for the same assignments. A statistically significant result was found in the metalinguistic awareness demonstrated by the blog-integrated group. Blogs enabled the students to learn from peers' writings and access the exchanged feedback in an archival fashion at any time and anywhere. As such, the dynamic interaction through blogging provided greater exposure to the rich input from online feedback and more opportunities to notice the linguistic areas that still needed refinement than did the in-class setting of the control group.

6.6 Project-Based, Task-Supported Learning

Blogs are conducive to peer collaboration in project-based learning (Tan et al. 2005; Zorko 2007) to support task-based language teaching that brings the real world into language classes and helps students transfer their L1 repertoire to meaningful L2 tasks (Sauro and Sundmark 2016). For example, Pinkman's (2005) study demonstrates how blogs can promote outside-class learning in EFL contexts. In her blogging project, Japanese tertiary students were required to write about their chosen topics and read and comment on their peers' blog posts outside their English class. Results suggest that reading peers' blog posts and receiving comments from classmate readers motivated them to write better and more regularly, leading to the improvement of their writing skills. In Chen's (2012) case study, he also found that EFL learners' cross-cultural awareness can be developed through jointly collaborating on a blog project to promote home culture tourism to foreign visitors. Tan et al. (2005) argued that the archival reflection-sharing and feedback-exchanging functions, such as e-portfolio, afforded by blogs facilitate project-based learning. They suggested that EFL teachers can follow a five-stage portfolio-building process through blogging:

1. Inception: Students are introduced to the rationale of using blogs as the e-portfolio platform; expected learning outcomes and guided tutorials and practices are on the blogging interface.
2. Orientation: Students familiarize themselves with the blogosphere, customize their own blogs, post a self-introduction, visit peers' blogs and even assist less proficient counterparts (i.e., 'peer coaching') throughout the process (p. 8).
3. Independent reflection: Students start building the portfolio by posting the summaries and reflections of a wide variety of reading pieces within a time frame based on their language proficiency.
4. Interactive reflection: Students are tasked to visit peers' blogs and read and comment on their reflections in order to gain multiple perspectives and broaden their knowledge.
5. Self-directed portfolio building: Students develop a sense of ownership by reflecting on both selected readings and individual chosen readings while, from the standpoint of ZPD, the teacher scaffold is gradually removed.

Regarding self-regulated portfolio assessment that gives voice back to the students, Kennedy (2003) proposed that students can present their writing examples that they deem the strongest and the weakest and provide their self-evaluations. They can also follow a rubric that lays out the criteria of evaluating not only linguistic elements, such as grammar, but the content, organization and discourse of their writing.

6.7 Intercultural Competence

Blogging can foster intercultural competence through problem-solving negotiated cultural blogging tasks between telecollaborative institutions (Garcia-Sanchez and Rojas-Lizana 2012; Godwin-Jones 2013; Fuchs 2016; Melo-Pfeifer 2015). Blogs can also link the cultural and linguistic experiences of learners studying abroad to the vicarious experience shared by their counterparts who still reside in the home country (Blood 2002; Ducate and Lomicka 2005; Elola and Oskoz 2008). For instance, Thorne and Payne (2005) used several compelling study abroad projects from StudyAbroad.com, a blog-based website that offers comprehensive information about different types of study-abroad programs highlighted by student experiences through blogging, to make a case for this aspect. Students in three programs (Chile, Italy and Senegal) kept their own blogs documenting their own study-abroad experiences, and their updated entries were read by around 500-1,000 fellow students weekly who were also keen on pursuing this experience. They concluded that study-abroad blogs serve as a robust vehicle for vicarious cultural exposure and resourceful orientation materials for students located at their home university and a way of solidifying the intercultural experiences of those students currently studying abroad into narrative learning evidence (Thorne and Payne 2005, p. 383).

6.8 Empowerment

The self-publishing feature and personalized design afforded by blogs can give 'voice' back to the students, 'convey a portrait of individuals' accomplishments and perspectives,' and 'empower students to become more analytical and critical' (Oravec 2002, p. 618; Zorko 2007). Even though the positive effects of blogging on learning have generally been reported, drawbacks can also be seen in learner disengagement when peer comments are not taken seriously due to the lack of depth and variety (Lee 2011) and when more knowledgeable learners are empowered while others, who are more concerned about publicizing their less refined work, feel disadvantaged (Chen 2015; Lee 2015). Despite well-intended task designs, teacher educators therefore need to take into consideration factors that might inhibit learners' willingness to participate and invest time and effort in blogging activities.

7 Final Remarks

Blogging in EFL contexts entails a rich, vibrant and complex virtual arena. It is socially situated in EFL learners' day-to-day practices in a network-based environment, featuring their dynamic interaction with peers, teachers, and authentic audiences. Blogs as a scaffolding platform provide a fertile ground for language acquisition to take place through blogging interactivity. Owing to the nature of blogging that blurs the in- and outside-class boundaries, EFL learners are able to extend their cultural and linguistic repertoires outside the class walls, thereby socially co-constructing knowledge and negotiating their intercultural awareness and competence with other members in the virtual community. This allows them to utilize and internalize the target language for meaningful, communicative and authentic purposes.

Blogging further promotes a sense of autonomy and authorship, empowering learners to be active contributors who take ownership for their own learning and raising awareness of an authentic audience. The latter also has a positive impact on the quality of learners' writing and the time and effort invested on the breadth and depth of the content ideas for posting. Taking the lens of Vygotskian SCT to examine the effects of blogging on EFL teaching and learning opens up a theoretically sound and pedagogically feasible research avenue.

Appendix

Features of commonly used blogs for educational and research purposes

Blog	Weblink	Comments
Blogger	http://www.blogger.com	Blogger is a free tool hosted by Google that allows users to easily create their own blog sites featuring themes, layouts, multimodal formatting (text, image and video), comments, stats (pageviews), campaigns (increasing blog visibility on Google) and multiple contributors. The Blogger app is also available for quick and easy publishing on a mobile phone.
WordPress	https://wordpress.com	A WordPress Blog is one of the free options provided by WordPress.com. The flexibility to choose a personal blog, portfolio or website makes it popular with users worldwide. In addition to common blog features, such as customizable themes, user-friendly blog editor and multimodal plugins, it is also mobile friendly.
Edublogs	https://edublogs.org/	As its name suggests, Edublogs is a blog tool widely used for various educational purposes, such as for teachers and students in K-12 classrooms or a whole school and university. Depending on demand, Edublogs can be offered for free with general features for creating and publishing blog posts like Blogger or for a fee as Pro and CampusPress memberships that provide more robust features, such as embedding videos and other multimodal tools in posts and integrating blogs into learning management systems (e.g., Blackboard). Mobile apps are also available to publish posts on the go.
LiveJournal	http://www.livejournal.com/	LiveJournal is a free social networking site that allows users to blog in journal or diary form. Users can choose a free membership that provides common blog functions in customizing, embedding videos and publishing one's blog entries, or a paid membership that enables mobile blogging and texting. Its social networking vibe also features a 'friends list' to receive blog updates from the user's friends. It also allows users to create a 'LiveJournal Community' to collectively post blog entries with multiple contributors who share similar interests of a subject matter.

(continued)

Blog	Weblink	Comments
SpeakPipe	https://www.speakpipe.com/	SpeakPipe is a user-friendly voice message tool that allows users to record, send and receive audio messages on one's personal site or blog. It can be easily installed (embedded) in a personal or class blog where the audience can easily leave a voice comment using the built-in microphone on a computer or mobile device. The blog author can also reply to the received 'voicemails' on the go.
VoiceThread	http://voicethread.com/	As one of the most popular digital platforms for education, VoiceThread allows students and teachers to create, share and discuss threads in a collaborative virtual community. Students can upload an image or audio/video clip for their threads and reflect on their thoughts. Their audience (the teacher, peers and visitors) can also choose voice, text or webcam when leaving the comments. It is also mobile friendly and can be seamlessly integrated into a learning management system.

References

Agar, M. (1994). *Language shock: Understanding the culture of conversation.* New York: Morrow.

Arslan, R. Ş., & Şahin-Kızıl, A. (2010). How can the use of blog software facilitate the writing process of English language learners? *Computer Assisted Language Learning, 23*(3), 183–197.

Azari, M. H. (2017). Effect of weblog-based process approach on EFL learners' writing performance and autonomy. *Computer Assisted Language Learning,* 1–23.

Bloch, J. (2007). Abdullah's blogging: A generation 1.5 student enters the blogosphere. *Language Learning & Technology, 11*(2), 128–141.

Blood, R. (2002). Weblogs: A history and perspective. In J. Rodzvilla (Ed.), *We've got blog: How weblogs are changing our culture* (pp. 7–16). Cambridge, MA: Perseus Publishing.

Campbell, A. (2003). Weblogs for use with ESL classes. *The Internet TESL Journal, 9*(2), 33–35.

Canale, M., & Swain, M. (1980). Theoretical bases of communicative approaches to second language teaching and testing. *Applied Linguistics, 1*, 1–47.

Chapelle, C. A. (2005). Interactionist SLA theory in CALL research. In J. Egbert & G. M. Petrie (Eds.), *CALL research perspectives* (pp. 53–64). Mahwah: Erlbaum.

Chen, J. C. (2012). Designing a computer-mediated, task-based syllabus: A case study in a Taiwanese EFL tertiary class. *Asian EFL Journal, 14*(3), 62–97.

Chen, R. T.-H. (2015). L2 blogging: Who thrives and who does not? *Language Learning & Technology, 19*(2), 177–196.

Chen, P.-J. (2016). Learners' metalinguistic and affective performance in blogging to write. *Computer Assisted Language Learning, 29*(4), 790–814.

Chen, J. C., & Brown, K. L. (2012). The effects of authentic audience on English as a second language (ESL) writers: A task-based, computer-mediated approach. *Computer Assisted Language Learning, 25*(5), 435–454.

Ducate, L. C., & Lomicka, L. L. (2005). Exploring the blogosphere: Use of web logs in the foreign language classroom. *Foreign Language Annals, 38*(3), 410–421.

Ducate, L. C., & Lomicka, L. L. (2008). Adventures in the blogosphere: from blog readers to blog writers. *Computer Assisted Language Learning, 21*(1), 9–28.

Elola, I., & Oskoz, A. (2008). Blogging: Fostering intercultural competence development in foreign language and study abroad contexts. *Foreign Language Annals, 41*(3), 454–477.

Farmer, J. (2004). Communication dynamics: Discussion boards, weblogs and the development of communities of inquiry in online learning environments. In R. Atkinson, C. McBeath, D. Jonas-Dwyer, & R. Phillips (Eds.), *Beyond the comfort zone: Proceedings of the 21st ascilite conference* (pp. 274–283). Perth, Western Australia.

Ferdig, R. E., & Trammell, K. D. (2004). Content delivery in the 'Blogosphere'. *T.H.E. Journal, 31*(7), 12–16. Retrieved from https://thejournal.com/Articles/2004/02/01/Content-Delivery-in-the-Blogosphere.aspx

Fuchs, C. (2016). Are you able to access this website at all? – team negotiations and macro-level challenges in telecollaboration. *Computer Assisted Language Learning, 29*(7), 1152–1168.

Garcia-Sanchez, S., & Rojas-Lizana, S. (2012). Bridging the language and cultural gaps: The use of blogs. *Technology, Pedagogy and Education, 21*(3), 361–381.

Godwin-Jones, B. (2003). Blogs and wikis: Environments for on-line collaboration. *Language Learning & Technology, 7*(2), 12–16.

Godwin-Jones, R. (2013). Integrating intercultural competence into language learning through technology. *Language Learning & Technology, 17*(2), 1–11.

Hauck, M., & Youngs, B. L. (2008). Telecollaboration in multimodal environments: The impact on task design and learner interaction. *Computer Assisted Language Learning, 21*(2), 87–124.

Hsu, H.-C. (2016). Voice blogging and L2 speaking performance. *Computer Assisted Language Learning, 29*(5), 968–983.

Huang, H. (2015). From web-based readers to voice bloggers: EFL learners' perspectives. *Computer Assisted Language Learning, 28*(2), 145–170.

Huffaker, D. (2004). The educated blogger: Using weblogs to promote literacy in the classroom. *First Monday, 9*(6). Retrieved from http://www.firstmonday.org/issues/issue9_6/huffaker/

Huffaker, D. (2005). Let them blog: Using weblogs to promote literacy in K-12 education. In L. T. W. Hin & R. Subramaniam (Eds.), *Handbook of research on literacy in technology at the K-12 level* (pp. 337–356). Hershey: Idea Group.

Johnson, A. (2004). Creating a writing course utilizing class and student blogs. *The Internet TESL Journal, 10*(8). Retrieved from http://iteslj.org/Techniques/Johnson-Blogs/.

Kennedy, K. (2003). Writing with weblogs. *Tech Learning.* Retrieved from http://www.techlearning.com/db_area/archives/TL/2003/02/blogs.php

Kern, R., & Warschauer, M. (2000). Introduction: Theory and practice of network-based language teaching. In R. Kern & M. Warschauer (Eds.), *Network-based language teaching: Concepts and practice* (pp. 1–19). New York: Cambridge University Press.

Lantolf, J. P. (2000). Introducing sociocultural theory. In *Sociocultural theory and second language learning* (pp. 1–26). Oxford: Oxford University Press.

Lantolf, J. P. (2006). Re(de)fining language proficiency in light of the concept "Languaculture". In H. Byrnes (Ed.), *Advanced language learning: The contributions of Halliday and Vygotsky* (pp. 72–91). London: Continuum.

Lee, L. (2011). Blogging: promoting learner autonomy and intercultural competence through study abroad. *Language Learning & Technology, 15*(3), 87–109.

Lee, S.-Y. (2015). Joining the 'literacy club': When reading meets blogging. *ELT Journal, 69*(4), 373–382.

Melo-Pfeifer, S. (2015). Blogs and the development of plurilingual and intercultural competence: Report of a co-actional approach in Portuguese foreign language classroom. *Computer Assisted Language Learning, 28*(3), 220–240.

Miceli, T., Murray, S. V., & Kennedy, C. (2010). Using an L2 blog to enhance learners' participation and sense of community. *Computer Assisted Language Learning, 23*(4), 321–341.

Mitchell, R., Marsden, E., & Myles, F. (2013). Sociocultural perspectives on second language learning. In *Second language learning theories* (3rd ed., pp. 193–222). Oxon: Routledge.

Mynard, J. (2008). A blog as a tool for reflection for English language learners. *The Philippine ESL Journal, 1*(1), 77–90.

Nassaji, H., & Swain, M. (2000). A Vygotskian perspective on corrective feedback in L2: The effect of random versus negotiated help on the learning of English articles. *Language Awareness, 9*(1), 34–51.

Oravec, J. A. (2002). Bookmarking the world: Weblog applications in education. *Journal of Adolescent & Adult Literacy, 45*(7), 616–621.

Pinkman, K. (2005). Using blogs in the foreign classroom: Encouraging learner independence. *JALT CALL Journal, 1*(1), 12–24.

Risager, K. (2012). Culture and context: Overview. In C. A. Chapelle (Ed.), *The encyclopedia of applied linguistics*. Bognor Regis: Wiley-Blackwell.

Sauro, S., & Sundmark, B. (2016). Report from Middle-Earth: Fan fiction tasks in the EFL classroom. *ELT Journal, 70*(4), 414–423.

Seargeant, P. (2009). *The idea of English in Japan: Ideology and evolution of a global language.* Clevedon: Multilingual Matters Ltd.

Statista. (2017). *Number of blogs worldwide from 2006 to 2011 (in millions).* Retrieved from https://www.statista.com/statistics/278527/number-of-blogs-worldwide

Sun, Y.-C. (2009). Voice blog: An exploratory study of language learning. *Language Learning & Technology, 13*(2), 88–103.

Sun, Y.-C. (2012). Examining the effectiveness of extensive speaking practice via voice blogs in a foreign language learning context. *CALICO Journal, 29*(3), 494–506.

Tan, Y. H., Teo, E. H., Aw, W. L., & Lim, W. Y. (2005). Portfolio building in Chinese language learning using blogs. In *Proceedings BlogTalk Downunder 2005 Conference*, Sydney, Australia, 19–22 May. Retrieved from https://edulab.moe.edu.sg/edulab/slot/u110/pubs/blogtalk.pdf

Tan, Y. H., Ow, E. G. J., & Tan, S. C. (2006). Audioblogging: Supporting the learning of oral communication skills in Chinese language. Paper presented at the *AECT Research Symposia*, Indiana University, Bloomington, Indiana. Retrieved from https://pdfs.semanticscholar.org/1296/e3acd743707a64e58d2496be8fc2ca36960d.pdf.

Technorati. (2010). *State of the blogosphere 2010 report.* Retrieved from http://technorati.com/state-of-the-blogosphere-2010

Thorne, S. L., & Payne, J. S. (2005). Evolutionary trajectories, internet-mediated expression, and language education. *CALICO Journal, 22*(3), 371–397.

Vygotsky, L. S. (1978). Interaction between learning and development. In M. Cole, V. John-Steiner, S. Scribner, & E. Souberman (Eds.), *Mind in society: The development of higher psychological processes* (pp. 79–91). Cambridge, MA: Harvard University Press.

Warschauer, M. (2005). Sociocultural perspectives on CALL. In J. Egbert & G. M. Petrie (Eds.), *CALL research perspectives* (pp. 41–51). Mahwah: Erlbaum.

Wells, G. (1999). The zone of proximal development and its implications for learning and teaching. In *Dialogic inquiry: Towards a sociocultural practice and theory of education* (pp. 313–334). Cambridge: Cambridge University Press.

Wu, C. (2006). Blogs in TEFL: A new promising vehicle. *Online Submission US-China Education Review, 3*(5), 69–73.

Zorko, V. (2007). A rationale for introducing a wiki and a blog in a blended-learning context. *CALL-EJ Online, 8*(2). Retrieved from http://callej.org/journal/8-2/zorko.html

Printed by Printforce, the Netherlands